Collins

Collins Revision

GCSE Foundation Science

Revision Guide

FOR OCR GATEWAY B

Contents

Fit for life

Respiration

- During exercise, muscle cells use oxygen to release **energy** from **glucose**. This process is called **respiration**. As muscles do more work, they need more oxygen and glucose.

- **Breathing** is simply getting air into and out of the body. **Breathing rate** and **pulse rate** increase during exercise. This also helps to get rid of the waste carbon dioxide produced by the cells as quickly as possible. Carbon dioxide is breathed out of the lungs.

- Respiration that uses oxygen is called **aerobic respiration**.

  glucose + oxygen $\longrightarrow$ carbon dioxide + water + energy

- During hard exercise not enough oxygen gets to the muscle cells. The cells also have to carry out **anaerobic respiration**. Less energy is released from anaerobic respiration.

  glucose $\longrightarrow$ **lactic acid** + energy

- When lactic acid collects in muscles it causes pain and fatigue.

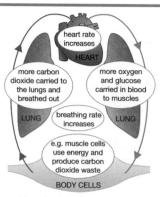

How the body removes carbon dioxide.

Top Tip!

Read the question carefully. It's easy to get confused between aerobic respiration and anaerobic respiration.

G–E

D–C

Fitness

- After exercise, heart rate and breathing rate take time to return to normal. The fitter someone is, the faster they return to normal.

- However, fit people still become ill. Being fit does not stop infection by bacteria.

D–C

Blood pressure

- **Heart muscles** contract to make your heart beat. This squeezes blood through blood vessels called **arteries**. The blood in arteries is under pressure.

- Blood can reach all parts of the body because it's under pressure.

- Blood pressure is measured in millimetres of mercury. This is written as **mmHg**.

- Blood pressure has two measurements:
  - **systolic pressure** is the maximum pressure the heart produces
  - **diastolic pressure** is the blood pressure between heart beats.

- Blood pressure changes with age. As people get older their blood pressure increases.

- Diet and exercise can also affect blood pressure.

- People with high blood pressure are often asked to fill in a questionnaire about their lifestyle.

Top Tip!

Blood vessels going away from the heart are called arteries. Blood vessels returning to the heart are called veins.

G–E

D–C

Blood pressure questionnaire

Questions	Notes	Answers Yes	No
1 Do you take regular exercise?	Strong heart muscles will lower blood pressure		✓
2 Do you eat a healthy balanced diet?	Reducing salt intake will lower blood pressure		✓
3 Are you overweight?	Being overweight by 5 kg raises blood pressure by 5 units	✓	
4 Do you regularly drink alcohol?	A high alcohol intake will damage liver and kidneys	✓	
5 Are you under stress?	Relaxation will lower blood pressure	✓	

What changes should this person make?

Questions

Grades G-E

1 Name the process used to release energy from food.

Grades D-C

2 Write down the word equation for anaerobic respiration.

Grades G-E

3 Name the type of blood vessels that take blood away from the heart.

Grades D-C

4 Describe the effect a high salt diet has on blood pressure.

What's for lunch?

Food

G–E

- Animals need an **energy source** called food. The food you eat is called your **diet**.

- A **balanced diet** contains:
  - **protein** for growth and repair
  - **carbohydrates**, **fat** and sometimes **protein** for energy
  - **vitamins** such as vitamin C which prevents scurvy
  - **minerals** such as iron to make haemoglobin
  - **fibre** to prevent constipation and **water** to prevent dehydration.

- Some people are overweight (**obese**). They have a higher risk of suffering from arthritis, heart disease, breast cancer and diabetes.

- Teenagers need a high protein diet because they are growing rapidly. In some countries in the world there is a shortage of protein.

> **Top Tip!**
>
> It's often easier to remember lists rather than pages of information. For example, make a list of the chemicals in our diet and what they're used for.

D–C

- Proteins from meat and fish are called **first class proteins**. They contain amino acids which can't be made by your body.

- In developing countries children often suffer from protein deficiency (**kwashiorkor**).

- To calculate the recommended daily amount (**RDA**) of protein use the formula:
  RDA (in grams, g) = 0.75 x body mass (in kilograms, kg)

- A balanced diet depends on age, gender and activity.

- To calculate Body Mass Index (**BMI**) use the formula:
  $$BMI = \frac{mass\ (in\ kilograms,\ kg)}{height\ (in\ metres,\ m^2)}$$

- A BMI chart is used to see if you are the correct weight.

Look up your height and weight on the BMI bands to see where you come.

Digestion

G–E

- When you eat, teeth cut and grind food into smaller pieces. The food can then easily pass down your **digestive system**. This is an example of **physical digestion**.

- Physical digestion also happens when the stomach wall squeezes the food to keep it moving.

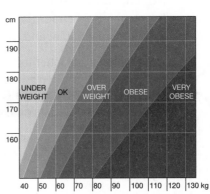

Examples of different enzymes.

carbohydrase in mouth

starch (a complex carbohydrate) → glucose (a simple sugar)

protease in stomach

protein → amino acids

lipase in small intestine

fat → glycerol + fatty acids

D–C

- Parts of the digestive system produce digestive **enzymes**. Different enzymes break down carbohydrates, proteins and fats into smaller and soluble molecules. These molecules **diffuse** through the walls of the small intestine and into the blood plasma (carbohydrates and proteins) or lymph (fats) and are carried to the cells.

- The stomach makes **hydrochloric acid** to help the enzyme called pepsin work.

Questions

(Grades G-E)
1 Name one type of food eaten to provide energy.

(Grades D-C)
2 Calculate the RDA for someone with a body mass of 80 kg.

(Grades G-E)
3 Describe one type of physical digestion.

(Grades D-C)
4 What do digestive enzymes do?

Keeping healthy

Microorganisms and disease

- **Microorganisms** that spread disease are called **pathogens**.

- There are different types of pathogens:
  - **fungi** that can cause athlete's foot
  - **bacteria** that can cause cholera
  - **viruses** that can cause influenza (flu)
  - **protozoa** that can cause dysentery.

- These pathogens cause **infectious diseases**, which means the diseases spread to other people. Diseases such as cancer aren't caused by pathogens. You can't catch cancer from another person; it's **non-infectious**.

- Mosquitoes are called **vectors** and carry microorganisms that cause malaria. Malaria is caused by a protozoan that is a **parasite** as it gets its food from its living **host**, humans. Mosquitoes pass malaria on when they bite humans.

> **Top Tip!**
>
> Mosquitoes carry pathogens that cause diseases; they don't carry diseases.

- Lifestyle and diet can cause different disorders.
  - A diet high in sugar often causes **diabetes**.
  - Not enough vitamin C causes **scurvy**.
  - People develop **anaemia** if they don't eat enough iron.
  - Eating a healthy diet and not smoking can reduce the risk of developing some cancers.

- Some disorders are inherited. For example, genes cause red-green colour deficiency.

Protection against microorganisms

- The body uses the skin, clotting blood, mucous membranes and hydrochloric acid as protection from pathogens. White blood cells are part of the body's **immune system**. They engulf pathogens and make antibodies.

- People can be **immunised** against certain diseases such as measles and mumps.

- More and more new drugs are needed as new diseases appear around the world. A new drug must be thoroughly tested before it can be used.

- Symptoms of a disease are caused by the pathogen damaging cells or making **toxins**.

- Pathogens have **antigens** on their surface. When a pathogen invades the body, white blood cells make **antibodies**, which lock on to the antigens and destroy the pathogen.

- **Active immunity** happens when a pathogen invades the body a second time. The white blood cells recognise it and make antibodies, quickly destroying the pathogen before the symptoms occur. Active immunity can last a lifetime.

- **Passive immunity** only lasts a short time and you're given antibodies in a **vaccine**.

- **Antibiotics** are drugs that attack bacteria and fungi but *not* viruses.

- New drugs have to be tested in different ways: on animals, specially grown human tissue or computer models. Some people object to animal testing.

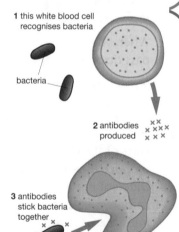

1 this white blood cell recognises bacteria

bacteria

2 antibodies produced

3 antibodies stick bacteria together

4 a different type of white blood cell eats bacteria

How white blood cells work.

Questions

Grades G-E
1 Name the four types of pathogens.

Grades D-C
2 Explain why mosquitoes are called vectors.

Grades G-E
3 Name the body system that protects against pathogens.

Grades D-C
4 Describe the role of antibodies.

Keeping in touch

Sense organs

G–E

- Sense organs (**receptors**) keep us informed of what is happening:
  - eyes for vision
  - ears for sound and balance
  - nose for smell
  - tongue for taste
  - skin reacts to pressure, temperature and touch.

Top Tip!

Use diagrams to help your revision. Exam questions on eyes often ask you to label a diagram.

Eyes

G–E

- Humans have **binocular** vision. Our two eyes work together to help us judge distance.

- Some animals such as rabbits have **monocular** vision. Each eye sees a different view.

- Problems with the eyes include **long sight**, **short sight** and **colour deficiency** like red-green colour blindness.

ciliary muscles control suspensory ligaments
convex lens refracts light rays
retina a focused image forms on the retina, which is sensitive to light
outer cornea refracts light rays
cornea
iris
lens
pupil (gap in the iris)
optic nerve carries nerve impulses to the brain
optic nerve
pupil allows light rays to enter the eye
blind spot
suspensory ligaments alter the shape of the lens in focusing
coloured iris controls the amount of light entering the eye

The parts of the eye.

D–C

- Binocular vision helps us to judge distances because the range of vision from two eyes overlaps. However, it only gives a small range of vision compared to monocular vision.

- People are short- or long-sighted because their eyeballs or lenses are the wrong shape.

- A lack of specialised cells in the retina causes red-green colour deficiency, which is inherited.

Reflexes

G–E

- **Reflexes** are actions we take without thinking. They are fast and automatic. For example, changing the size of our pupils, knee jerk (tapping below the knee) and snatching a hand away from a hot plate.

- Actions we think about first are **voluntary** actions.

- Information is carried round the body mainly by electrical impulses carried in nerve cells called **neurones**. These form our **nervous system**.
  - The **central nervous system** (CNS) is made up of the brain and spinal cord.
  - The **peripheral nervous system** is made up of nerves to and from the brain and spinal cord.

stimulus
receptor
sensory neurone
relay neurone in spinal cord
motor neurone
response

A reflex arc.

D–C

- A **reflex arc** shows the direction in which an impulse travels.
- Touching a hot plate is an example of a **spinal reflex arc**.

Neurones

D–C

- **Motor neurones** carry impulses to the **muscle**.
- The nerve impulse is carried in the **axon** of the neurone.

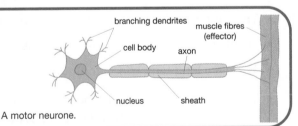

branching dendrites
muscle fibres (effector)
cell body
axon
nucleus
sheath

A motor neurone.

Questions

Grades G-E

1 Name the five sense organs.

Grades D-C

2 Name the part of the eye that controls the amount of light entering it.

Grades G-E

3 Explain the difference between a voluntary and reflex action.

Grades D-C

4 Write the following in the correct order so that they describe a reflex arc.

**effector   CNS   motor neurone   response
sensory neurone   receptor   stimulus**

Drugs and you

Drugs

- Useful drugs help the body. You need a doctor's prescription to get useful drugs.

- Harmful drugs damage your health. Alcohol and cannabis are examples of harmful drugs.

- Drugs affect our nervous system. **Depressants** slow down brain activity. **Hallucinogens** change what you see and hear. **Painkillers** stop nerve impulses. **Performance enhancers** develop muscles. **Stimulants** speed up brain activity.

- A person can become **addicted** to a drug, which means that it's hard to give it up.

- **Tolerance** is when someone needs to take bigger doses of a drug to get the same effect.

- **Rehabilitation** groups try to help people to give up taking drugs.
  The person suffers **withdrawal symptoms** if they try to give up the drug.

- Drugs are classified by law based on how dangerous they are and the penalties for possession.

	class A	class B	class C
maximum prison sentence	7 years and fine for possession	5 years and fine for possession	2 years and fine for possession
types of drugs	heroin, methadone, cocaine, ecstasy, LSD	amphetamines, barbiturates	anabolic steroids, Valium®, cannabis

- Here are some examples of different drugs:
  - depressants: alcohol, solvents and temazepam
  - hallucinogens: cannabis and LSD
  - painkillers: aspirin and heroin
  - performance enhancers: anabolic steroids
  - stimulants: ecstasy and caffeine.

G–E

D–C

Tobacco

- Emphysema; bronchitis; heart disease; mouth, throat and lung cancer are all linked to smoking.

The main chemicals in tobacco smoke.

stops red blood cells getting oxygen

carbon monoxide

nicotine is addictive

irritates, causes cancer

tar

particulates

collect in lungs and block them

- Cells that line the trachea and bronchioles are called **epithelial cells**. Some cells have tiny hairs called **cilia** and others make sticky mucus.

- Cigarette smoke stops the cilia from moving and dust and particulates collect and irritate the cells. Smokers cough to move this mess upwards so it can be swallowed.

G–E

D–C

Alcohol

- Drinking alcohol has quick (short-term) effects. A person who has drunk alcohol may lose their balance easily, find it hard to talk clearly and find it difficult to use their muscles.

- There is a legal limit to the amount of alcohol car drivers can have in their bloodstream.

- People can die of alcohol poisoning if they've drunk too much.

- There are long-term effects too, such as damage to the liver and brain.

- The liver breaks down toxic chemicals such as alcohol. Too much alcohol kills the liver cells and causes **cirrhosis**.

- The alcohol content of a drink is measured in **units** of alcohol.

Top Tip!

In the exam you will need to interpret data on alcohol and cigarette smoke. Practice questions will help you with this skill.

G–E

D–C

Questions

Grades G-E

1 What effect do stimulants have on the brain?

Grades D-C

2 Name a class A drug that is also a hallucinogen.

Grades G-E

3 Describe one short-term effect of alcohol.

Grades D-C

4 Describe the effect of cigarette smoke on ciliated epithelial cells.

Staying in balance

Homeostasis

G–E

- Our body makes sure that water, oxygen and carbon dioxide levels are kept steady.

- Body temperature is kept at 37 °C. Body cells work best at this temperature. Our body can be harmed if it gets too hot or too cold.

- You can check your body temperature using a heat-sensitive strip placed on your forehead or a clinical thermometer placed inside your mouth or anus.

- We lose heat by sweating and by more blood flowing near to the surface of our skin.

- We gain or keep heat by exercising, shivering, releasing energy from food and letting less blood flow near to the surface of our skin.

D–C

- Various body systems keep the levels of oxygen, water, carbon dioxide and temperature constant. Keeping a constant internal environment is called **homeostasis**.

- Sweat comes from **sweat glands** in the skin and needs heat energy to evaporate. It takes heat from the body.

- If your body gets too hot, you could suffer from heat stroke or **dehydration**.

- **Hypothermia** occurs if you get too cold.

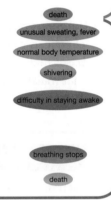

How the change in temperature affects the body.

42?C — death
38-39?C — unusual sweating, fever
37?C — normal body temperature
35?C — shivering
33?C — difficulty in staying awake
28?C — breathing stops
25?C — death

Hormones

G–E

- **Hormones** are made in special **glands** and are carried in the blood to where they have an effect. The part of the body a hormone affects is called the **target organ**.

- Hormone responses are slower than reflexes as it takes time to travel in blood.

- **Insulin** is a hormone made by the **pancreas**. People with **diabetes** don't make enough insulin.

D–C

- Diabetes can be controlled by eating a diet low in sugar or by an injection of insulin. Insulin lowers the level of glucose in the blood.

G–E

- Our bodies also produce **sex hormones**. **Ovaries** produce hormones called **oestrogen** and **progesterone** and **testes** produce a hormone called **testosterone**.

D–C

- Ovaries start producing sex hormones when girls reach **puberty**. The hormones cause breasts to develop and hips to widen. Hair starts to grow in the pubic area and under armpits. Periods start because the ovaries have begun to release an egg every month.

- Boys become more muscular, grow facial hair and their voice breaks. Their testes start to produce sperm and genitals develop.

- All these developments are called **secondary sexual characteristics**.

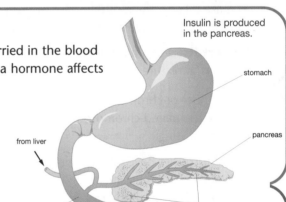

Insulin is produced in the pancreas.

stomach

pancreas

from liver

small intestine

insulin-producing cells

Top Tip!

Lots of people mix up the hormones. Testosterone starts with a t so it's made in the testes.

Questions

Grades G-E

1 Describe two ways the body keeps warm.

Grades D-C

2 Explain what is meant by the term 'hypothermia'.

Grades G-E

3 Name the two hormones produced by the ovaries.

Grades D-C

4 Describe one secondary sexual characteristic of girls and boys.

Gene control

Genes

- The information that makes you who you are is in your **genetic code.** The code is a set of instructions, a bit like a recipe to make a cake.

- The code is carried by your **genes** which are in **chromosomes** in the nucleus of every cell of your body. The chromosomes have all the information to make you.

- Genes are made of a chemical called **DNA** (deoxyribonucleic acid).

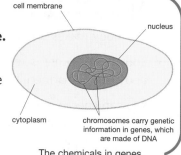

cell membrane

nucleus

cytoplasm

chromosomes carry genetic information in genes, which are made of DNA

The chemicals in genes.

- In DNA the two strands look like a twisted ladder. The shape is called a **double helix**.

- The rungs of the ladder are made of **four** different chemicals called **bases**. The specific arrangement of bases makes up the unique genetic code (or recipe) that makes you.

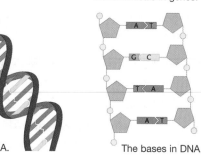

DNA.

The bases in DNA.

G–E

D–C

Chromosomes

- Each of your body cells has 46 chromosomes, arranged in matching pairs.

- To make a baby, the mother makes an **egg** and the father makes **sperm**. Eggs and sperm have half the number of chromosomes each.

- The **fertilised** egg has the correct number of chromosomes, so a baby has a mixture of their mother's and father's characteristics.

- The number of chromosomes in a cell is usually an even number because the paired chromosomes separate when eggs and sperm are formed.

- Different species have different numbers of chromosomes in each of their body cells. The camel has 70; the squirrel has 40; the mosquito has 6; and humans have 46.

- Eggs and sperm (**gametes**) have only one chromosome from each pair (23 in total). They combine to make a fertilised egg that has 46 chromosomes.

Top Tip!

Make sure you write a clearly explained answer to a question. Always read your answer through. If it doesn't make sense to you, it won't make sense to the examiner!

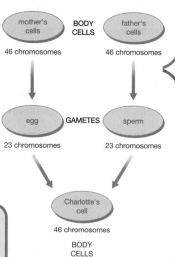

mother's cells — BODY CELLS — father's cells

46 chromosomes   46 chromosomes

egg — GAMETES — sperm

23 chromosomes   23 chromosomes

Charlotte's cell

46 chromosomes

BODY CELLS

How the chromosome number is made.

G–E

D–C

Making clones using asexual reproduction

- Scientists have found a way of making copies of living things without using sexual reproduction. They use a form of **asexual reproduction** called **cloning** which can be carried out in plants and animals. In a clone, all the genes come from only one parent so the clones look exactly like the parent.

G–E

Questions

(Grades G-E)

1 Name the chemical genes are made from.

(Grades D-C)

2 How many different bases are there in a chromosome?

(Grades D-C)

3 How many chromosomes are there in the sperm cell of a camel?

(Grades G-E)

4 Name the type of reproduction that produces a clone.

Who am I?

Characteristics

G–E

- Some of our **characteristics** are **inherited** from our parents, such as earlobe shape, eye colour and nose shape. **Genes** control all these characteristics.

- Scars and spoken language are examples of characteristics that aren't inherited. They have been caused by the environment.

- Height, intelligence and body mass are caused by both inheritance *and* environment.

- Human beings show **variation**; we're all different.

- Sometimes genes controlling characteristics are changed. These changes are known as **mutations**.

D–C

- All humans have 46 chromosomes, arranged in pairs, in their body cells. One pair of chromosomes is called the **sex chromosomes**.

- Females have an identical pair of X sex chromosomes called **XX chromosomes**.

- The male sex chromosomes are called **XY chromosomes**. They aren't identical.

- Variation is caused by genes being mixed up in gametes, fertilisation and changes in genes or chromosomes called mutations.

a X and b Y sex chromosomes highly magnified.

- Mutations can be caused by radiation and chemicals or they can just occur spontaneously.

- Some mutations are harmful, such as **haemophilia**; while others can be advantageous, such as **sickle-cell anaemia** – a mutation that makes people ill but stops them catching a fatal disease called malaria.

- Some characteristics are **dominant** over others and more people will show the dominant characteristic than the **recessive** one. For example, lobed ears are dominant over ears with no lobes.

Comparing characteristics.

lobed ear   ear without lobe (attached lobe)

- **Breeding experiments** can be carried out to find dominant characteristics. For instance, when purple-stemmed tomato plants are crossed with green-stemmed plants, the offspring (F_1 generation) all show the dominant purple colour.

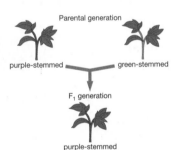

Parental generation

purple-stemmed   green-stemmed

F_1 generation

purple-stemmed

Breeding green- and purple-stemmed tomato plants.

Top Tip!

Genetics uses many new words. Make a list of them and make sure you understand them. If you can't understand the question … you can't answer it!

Inherited disorders

G–E

- People can inherit disorders from their parents because they inherit faulty genes. The following are all inherited:
  - red-green colour blindness
  - cystic fibrosis
  - sickle-cell anaemia
  - haemophilia.

Questions

(Grades G-E)

1 What is meant by the term 'mutation'?

(Grades D-C)

2 Name one cause of a mutation.

3 More people have brown eyes than blue. Which colour is recessive?

(Grades G-E)

4 Name one inherited disorder.

B1 Summary

Diet and exercise

The **Body Mass Index** (BMI) can be used to indicate being under or over weight.

Digested food is absorbed.

Enzymes chemically digest food.

Food is digested physically or chemically.

Our energy comes from **aerobic respiration** or **anaerobic respiration**. Anaerobic respiration releases less energy than aerobic respiration.

Blood is put under pressure by the heart.

Blood pressure has two readings:
– **diastolic** pressure
– **systolic** pressure.

A **balanced diet** contains food such as:
– **carbohydrates**
– **proteins**
– **fats**
– **nutrients** such as **minerals** and **vitamins**.

Hormones, sense organs and reflexes

Insulin controls the blood sugar level.

Endocrine glands produce hormones such as **insulin** and **sex hormones**.

Reflexes are fast reactions that don't involve the brain.

Neurones carry **electrical impulses**.

Eyes, ears, nose, tongue and skin are sense organs.

The body temperature of 37 °C is linked to the **optimum temperature** for enzymes.

Binocular vision is used to **judge distance**.

Drugs

Tobacco and alcohol are called '**social drugs**'. Alcohol affects judgement and causes liver and brain damage. Tobacco smoke contains many **chemicals** such as nicotine and tar.

Harmful drugs are classified as class A, B or C. Any class A drug, such as cocaine, is dangerous and addictive.

New drugs must be tested in trials.

The mosquito is a **vector** that carries the pathogen that causes malaria.

Fungi, bacteria, viruses and protozoa can cause disease. They are **pathogens**.

Infectious diseases are easily passed on.

Our **immune system** and **immunisation** protect against infections.

Genes

Genes control the production of proteins such as enzymes.

The **coded information** is the sequence of bases in DNA.

Cystic fibrosis, red-green colour deficiency and sickle-cell anaemia are inherited genetic disorders.

Inherited disorders are caused by **faulty genes**.

We have **23 pairs** of **chromosomes**.

Some human characteristics are **inherited** and some are caused by the **environment**.

The **genetic code** is coded information in genes which make up chromosomes.

Cooking

Cooking food

- There are different ways to cook food:
  - on a barbeque
  - on a grill
  - on an electric or gas ring (frying, boiling or steaming).
  - in a microwave
  - in an oven

Why do we cook chicken?

- Some foods can be eaten **raw**, but other foods must be **cooked** to make them safer or more attractive. Food is cooked because:
  - the high temperature **kills** harmful **microbes**
  - the **texture** is improved
  - the **taste** is improved
  - the **flavour** is enhanced
  - it's easier to **digest**.

Chemical changes

Eggs change irreversibly when they're cooked.

- When a food is heated and cooked, it **changes**. It can't go back to its raw state.

- Cooking food is a **chemical change** that's **irreversible**. An **energy change** takes place in the food and a **new substance** is made.

- When you cook **eggs**, the colourless, transparent liquid changes into a white, opaque solid.

- **Potatoes** must be cooked. When cooked, their taste and texture changes irreversibly.

- Potatoes and flour are good sources of **carbohydrate**.

- Meat and eggs are good sources of **proteins**. Proteins are large molecules that have definite shapes. When food is cooked, the protein molecules change shape.

Baking powder

- Baking powder gives off **carbon dioxide** that makes cakes rise when it's heated.

- Baking powder is a chemical called **sodium hydrogencarbonate**. When it's heated, it decomposes to give sodium carbonate, carbon dioxide and water:
  - the **reactant** is sodium hydrogencarbonate
  - the **products** are sodium carbonate, carbon dioxide and water.

- The word equation for the reaction is:

$$\text{sodium hydrogencarbonate} \xrightarrow{\text{heat}} \text{sodium carbonate} + \text{carbon dioxide} + \text{water}$$

Testing for carbon dioxide

- The chemical test for **carbon dioxide** is to pass it through **limewater**. It turns the limewater from colourless to milky white.

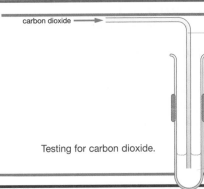

carbon dioxide

delivery tube

Testing for carbon dioxide.

limewater turns from colourless to milky white when carbon dioxide is bubbled through it

Questions

Grades G-E

1 What does the word 'irreversible' mean?

Grades D-C

2 What do protein molecules do when they're heated?

3 When you heat baking powder it decomposes. What does this mean?

Grades G-E

4 What happens to limewater when carbon dioxide is bubbled through it?

Food additives

Food additives

- Foods contain many different **chemicals**. When foods are processed, chemicals called **additives** can be added. The main types of food additive are:
  - **antioxidants**
  - colours
  - **emulsifiers**
  - flavour enhancers.

- Antioxidants stop food from reacting with oxygen and turning bad.

- **Ascorbic acid** (vitamin C) is used in tinned fruit and wine as an antioxidant. Its E number is E300.

- Food additives are added for different reasons:
  - to **preserve** food by stopping it reacting with oxygen, bacteria or mould
  - to give a different **sensory experience**, such as to **enhance** the colour or flavour of food.

Food packaging

- **Labels** are now added to all foods that are sold. This makes sure that people know what they're buying and how much salt, etc., each product has. The ingredients are listed in descending order of their mass.

- Food packaging stops food **spoiling**.
  - **Active packaging** changes the condition of the food to extend its shelf life.
  - **Intelligent packaging** uses sensors to monitor the quality of the food and lets the customer know when the food is no longer fresh.

- These methods remove water, or heat or cool the contents of packs.

Nutrition		
Typical values	Per 30g with 125ml semi-skimmed milk	Per 100g
Energy	738kJ 174kcal	1624kJ 383kcal
Protein	5.8g	5.5g
Carbohydrate of which sugars	31.7g 17.8g	84.8g 38.3g
Fat of which saturates	2.7g 1.7g	2.4g 1.4g
Fibre	0.6g	1.9g
Sodium	0.6g	1.4g

There are 84.8 g per 100 g of carbohydrate in this breakfast cereal.

Emulsions and emulsifiers

- Oil and water don't mix. If **washing-up liquid** is added, oily plates are easily cleaned. This is because oil doesn't attract water, it **repels** it.

- A detergent in washing-up liquid gives 'hooks' between oil and water. The oil is 'hooked' onto the water and pulled off a dirty plate. This is an example of an **emulsion**. The **detergent** in washing-up liquid acts as an **emulsifier**.

- Detergents are long molecules made up of two parts:
  - the **tail** is a 'fat-loving' part
  - the **head** is a 'water-loving' part.

- Examples of **emulsions** are:
  - some **paints**
  - **milk**, which is an emulsion of oil in water
  - **mayonnaise**, which is an emulsion of oil and vinegar with egg. Egg is the emulsifier.

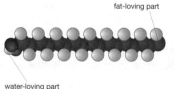

fat-loving part

water-loving part

The fat-loving part of the detergent goes into the grease droplet.

Questions

1 What's added to stop food reacting with oxygen?

2 What's 'intelligent packaging'?

3 What's used to help oil and water mix?

4 Emulsifiers are long molecules that have two parts. Explain why.

Smells

Natural and synthetic cosmetics

- Perfumes and cosmetics can be made from **natural sources**.

- A similar perfume can be made **synthetically**. Chemicals are boiled to make an **ester**.

- Cosmetics must be tested to make sure they're safe. Some cosmetics are tested on animals, but some people strongly disagree with this.

- Cosmetics need to be thoroughly tested to ensure they don't cause rashes, itchiness, skin damage or lead to cancer or other life-threatening conditions.

- **Cosmetic testing** takes many years and is highly controversial.
  – Some people object to testing on animals as the animals may be harmed, and they don't have any control over what happens to them.
  – Other people say they feel safer if the cosmetics have been tested on animals.

Perfumes

- We can smell perfumes because they stimulate **sense cells** in the nose.

- This table shows the **properties** that a perfume needs:

need	evaporate easily	non-toxic	doesn't react with water	insoluble in water	doesn't irritate the skin
why	perfume particles reach nose	doesn't poison	doesn't react with perspiration	isn't washed off the skin	can be sprayed onto skin

Esters

- To make a perfume, **alcohol** is mixed with an **acid** to make an **ester**.

  alcohol + acid ⟶ ester + water

- Look at the diagram on the right.
  – Acid is added to the alcohol and is heated for some time.
  – The condenser stops the gas from escaping and helps it to cool down again.

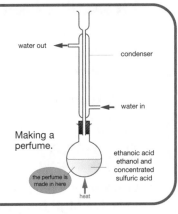

water out

condenser

water in

Making a perfume.

the perfume is made in here

ethanoic acid ethanol and concentrated sulfuric acid

heat

Solvents and solutions

- A substance that **dissolves** in a liquid is **soluble**. The substance is called the **solute** and the liquid that it dissolves in is called the **solvent**.

- A substance that doesn't dissolve in a liquid is **insoluble**.
  – Water doesn't dissolve nail varnish so can't be used to remove it from nails.
  – Nail varnish remover does dissolve nail varnish.

- A **solution** is a solute and a solvent that don't separate.

- Esters are used as solvents, and other solvents can be used as cleaners.

Questions

(Grades G-E)

1 What are the chemicals that make synthetic perfumes?

(Grades D-C)

2 Two different people may have different ideas about cosmetic testing. Explain why.

3 Which two substances combine to make an ester?

(Grades G-E)

4 When a solute dissolves in a solvent, it's said to be _____ .

Making crude oil useful

Fossil fuels

- Coal, gas and crude oil are **fossil fuels**. Fossil fuels have formed from dead animals and plants trapped in the Earth and compressed over millions of years. When these fossil fuels are used up, there will be no more. They're **non-renewable**.

- Fossil fuels are **finite resources** because they're no longer being made.

Fractional distillation

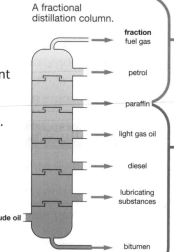

A fractional distillation column.

- Crude oil is separated by heating it up and then cooling it down. This is called **fractional distillation**. The crude oil is separated into different **fractions** (parts). The process works because each fraction has a different **boiling point**.

- Crude oil is a mixture of many types of oil, which are all **hydrocarbons**.

- In fractional distillation, crude oil is heated at the bottom of a tower.
  - Oil that doesn't boil, sinks as a thick liquid to the bottom. This fraction is **bitumen** and is used to make **tar** for road surfaces. Bitumen has a very high boiling point. It 'exits' at the bottom of the tower.
  - Other fractions boil and their gases rise up the tower. Fractions with lower boiling points, such as **petrol** and **LPG**, 'exit' at the top of the tower, where it's colder.

Diagram labels: fraction fuel gas, petrol, paraffin, light gas oil, diesel, lubricating substances, crude oil, bitumen

Problems in extracting crude oil

- When crude oil is found, it comes through the Earth's crust on land or under the sea. This is a dangerous activity. If sea-going tankers run aground and are damaged, the spilt oil forms an **oil slick**.

- Oil slicks can harm animals, pollute beaches and destroy unique habitats. Clean-up operations are extremely expensive and the detergents and barrages used can cause **environmental problems**.

Cracking

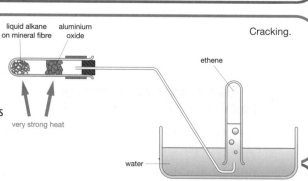

Cracking.

Diagram labels: liquid alkane on mineral fibre, aluminium oxide, ethene, very strong heat, water

- **Cracking** is a process that:
  - needs a **high temperature**
  - needs a **catalyst**
  - turns less useful large hydrocarbon molecules (i.e. paraffin) into more useful smaller hydrocarbon molecules (i.e. petrol).

- Cracking is a process that:
  - turns large alkane molecules into smaller alkane and alkene molecules
  - also makes useful alkene molecules, which can be used to make **polymers**.

- Alkanes have a general formula of: C_nH_{2n+2}.
  Octane has 8 carbon atoms and $2n + 2 = 18$ hydrogen atoms. The formula for octane is C_8H_{18}.

Questions

1 What's a fossil fuel?

2 Where do fractions with the lowest boiling points 'exit' the tower in fractional distillation?

3 Explain what's meant by the process 'cracking'.

4 What's the formula for an alkane with 7 carbon atoms?

Making polymers

G–E

Polymers and polymerisation

- A polymer is a very **big molecule** made up of many small molecules, called **monomers**, joined together in a **chain**. This reaction is called **polymerisation**.

D–C

- You can recognise a polymer from its **displayed formula** by looking out for these features:
  - a long chain
  - the pattern repeats every two carbon atoms
  - there are two brackets on the end with extended bonds through them
  - there's an '*n*' after the brackets.

This is the displayed formula of poly(ethene).

- A **polymerisation reaction** needs **high pressure** and a **catalyst**.

- When a polymer is made from monomers that are the same type, it's called an **addition polymer**.

Hydrocarbons

G–E

- A **hydrocarbon** is made up of **carbon** and **hydrogen** only. **Alkanes** and **alkenes** are hydrocarbons.

- You can recognise a hydrocarbon from its displayed formula as it only has C or H joined together.

One atom of carbon and four atoms of hydrogen chemically combine to make a **hydrocarbon** called **methane**.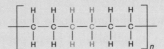

- If the name of the alkane is known, it's easy to predict the name of the alkene.

number of carbon atoms	alkane	displayed formula	alkene	displayed formula
2	ethane		ethene	
3	propane		propene	

D–C

- A hydrocarbon is a compound of carbon and hydrogen atoms only.
  - An **alkane** has a single bond C–C.
  - An **alkene** has one double bond C=C.

Propane, C_3H_8, is a hydrocarbon and an **alkane**.

Propanol, C_3H_7OH, *isn't* a hydrocarbon because it contains an oxygen atom.

Propene is a hydrocarbon, a **monomer** and an **alkene**.

Polypropene is the **polymer** made.

Questions

(Grades G-E)

1 Write down the name of the polymer made from the monomer styrene.

(Grades D-C)

2 What two conditions are needed for polymerisation to take place?

(Grades G-E)

3 What's the name of the alkane that has two carbon atoms?

(Grades D-C)

4 What's the difference between an alkane and an alkene?

Designer polymers

Uses of polymers

clothes   carrier bags   packaging   rope

Polymers are chosen for the job they do best.

- Fabrics for clothes, paint for cars and cases for computers are all made from different **polymers**. Polymers are **chemicals** such as poly(ethene), nylon and polyester.

- Each polymer is chosen carefully for the job that it does best. Some polymers are waterproof and are used to make raincoats. There's also another material used to make raincoats which is 'breathable'. It keeps people dry, not only from the rain but also from their sweat.

- Polymers are better than other materials for some uses.

use	polymer	other material
contact lens	wet on the eye	dry on the eye
teeth filling	attractive	looks metallic
wound dressing	waterproof	gets wet

- **Nylon** is tough, lightweight and keeps rainwater out, but it keeps body sweat in. The water vapour from the sweat **condenses** and makes the wearer wet and cold inside their raincoat.

- If nylon is **laminated** with a PTFE/polyurethane **membrane**, clothing can be made that's waterproof and breathable. Gore-Tex® has all the properties of nylon and is breathable, so it's worn by many active outdoor people. Water vapour from sweat can pass through the membrane, but rainwater can't.

Waterproof walking.

Disposing of polymers

- Most **addition polymers** are **non-biodegradable**. They don't decay and aren't decomposed by bacteria.

- They can be disposed of in **landfill sites**, by **burning** and by **recycling**. However, they're difficult to dispose of and can cause litter and pollution.

- **Disposal problems** for non-biodegradable polymers include the following:
  – landfill sites get filled quickly and waste valuable land
  – burning waste plastics produces toxic gases
  – disposal by burning or landfill sites wastes a valuable resource
  – problems in sorting different polymers makes recycling difficult.

- Scientists are developing addition polymers that are **biodegradable**. These are easily disposed of by **dissolving**. Biopol is a biodegradeable plastic that can be used to make laundry bags for hospitals. It degrades when washed leaving the laundry in the machine.

Questions

(Grades G-E)
1 What two properties are needed in a polymer to make drainpipes?

(Grades D-C)
2 What's the disadvantage of using nylon to make outdoor clothes?

(Grades G-E)
3 What does non-biodegradable mean?

(Grades D-C)
4 What's given off when disposing of plastics by burning?

Using carbon fuels

Choosing a fuel

G–E

- Coal isn't a good fuel for a motor vehicle! **Petrol** or **diesel** are good **fuels** for cars because they're liquids. They flow round the engine easily.

D–C

- A fuel is chosen because of its **characteristics**.

characteristic	coal	petrol
energy value	high	high
availability	good	good
storage	bulky and dirty	volatile
toxicity	produces acid fumes	produces less acid fumes
pollution caused	acid rain, carbon dioxide and soot	carbon dioxide, nitrous oxides

Combustion

G–E

- **Oxygen** is needed for fuels to burn. Burning is called **combustion**.

- Combustion releases **useful heat energy**.

- Lots of oxygen is needed for **complete combustion**.

- Complete combustion of a **hydrocarbon fuel** makes **carbon dioxide** and **water**.

- If a fuel burns in a **shortage of oxygen**, it's called **incomplete combusion**. Unwanted gases are given off that contain **soot** and are **toxic**.

- One of the toxic **fumes** is a gas called **carbon monoxide**. This is a **poisonous** gas.

- A **Bunsen burner** flame produces **energy** from burning gas.
  - If the air hole is **open**, a **blue** flame is seen. The fuel is burning in **plenty of oxygen**: combustion is complete.
  - If the air hole is **closed**, a **yellow** flame is seen. The fuel is burning in a **shortage of oxygen**: combustion is incomplete.

> **Top Tip!**
> **Complete** combustion gives off **carbon dioxide** and **water**. **Incomplete** combustion gives off **carbon monoxide** and **water**.

D–C

- The word equation for a fuel burning in air is:

  fuel + oxygen ⟶ carbon dioxide + water

- This reaction can be shown by an experiment in the laboratory.
  - **Cobalt chloride** paper or **white copper sulphate** powder is used to test for water.
  - **Limewater** is used to test for carbon dioxide.

- Complete combustion is better than incomplete combustion because:
  - less soot is made
  - more heat energy is released
  - toxic carbon monoxide gas isn't produced.

When a fuel burns in air, what's produced?

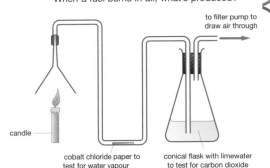

to filter pump to draw air through

candle

cobalt chloride paper to test for water vapour

conical flask with limewater to test for carbon dioxide

> **Top Tip!**
> Remember: gas appliances should be checked regularly! A heater in a poorly ventilated room is burning fuel in a shortage of oxygen. It will give off poisonous carbon monoxide.

Questions

Grades G-E

1 What gas is needed for fuels to burn?

2 Which colour flame in a Bunsen burner releases more useful energy?

Grades D-C

3 Which liquid is used to test for carbon dioxide?

4 Complete combustion is better than incomplete combustion. Explain why.

Energy

Chemical reactions

- **Chemical reactions** can make:
  - heat
  - light
  - sound
  - electricity.

- A chemical reaction happens when **reactants** change into **products**.

- If things get hotter or cooler, **energy** has been transferred.

> **Top Tip!**
>
> Remember that:
> - energy is measured in joules (J)
> - temperature is measured in degree Celsius (°C).

- Chemical reactions can be divided into two groups.
  - When energy is **transferred** to the surroundings in a chemical reaction, it's an **exothermic** reaction (energy is released). This is shown by a **temperature increase**, for example a lit firework.
  - When energy is **taken from** the surroundings in a chemical reaction, it's an **endothermic** reaction (absorbs energy). This is shown by a **temperature decrease**, for example in photosynthesis.

Fuels

- **Fuels** need oxygen to burn.

- **Ethanol** burns in oxygen to make carbon dioxide and water:
  - the **reactants** are ethanol and oxygen
  - the **products** are carbon dioxide and water.

ethanol + oxygen ⟶ carbon dioxide + water

- You could use this experiment to compare two different fuels.
  - Place the same mass of fuel in two spirit burners.
  - Place the same mass of water in two test tubes.
  - When all the fuel has burnt, measure the increase in temperature of the water in each test tube using a thermometer.

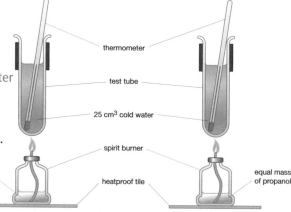

thermometer

test tube

25 cm³ cold water

spirit burner

equal mass of ethanol

heatproof tile

equal mass of propanol

An experiment to compare two different fuels.

Comparing the energy from different flames

- The flame of a Bunsen burner changes colour depending on the amount of oxygen it burns in.
  - Blue flames are seen when the gas burns in plenty of oxygen (**complete combustion**).
  - Yellow flames are seen when the gas burns in limited oxygen (**incomplete combustion**).

- You need to know how to design your own experiment to compare the energy transferred in the two different flames. Here are some hints:
  - remember the apparatus used to compare fuels
  - the amount of gas used needs to be measured
  - remember to make the tests fair.

Questions

Grades G-E

1 Name two types of energy that can be made during a chemical reaction.

Grades D-C

2 What's an exothermic reaction?

Grades G-E

3 Name two things that must be kept constant (stay the same) to make it a fair test when you compare fuels by heating water.

Grades D-C

4 What type of flame is seen during incomplete combustion?

C1 Summary

Food and additives

All foods are chemicals. Cooking is a **chemical change**. A chemical change is irreversible and a new substance is made.

Intelligent packaging helps with storage of food.

Oil and water don't mix. **Emulsifiers** help water and oil to mix. Emulsifiers have a water-loving end and a water-hating end.

Egg and meat are **proteins**. Proteins in eggs and meat change shape when cooked.

Food is cooked to:
– **kill microbes**
– improve **texture**
– improve **flavour**
– make it **easier to digest**.

Additives may be added as:
– **antioxidants**
– **colours**
– **emulsifiers**
– **flavour enhancers**.

Smells and crude oil

Perfumes are **esters** that can be made from acids and alcohols. Perfumes must evaporate easily and be non-toxic.

Crude oil is a **fossil fuel** made by dead animals being compressed over millions of years. It's **non-renewable**.

Crude oil is separated by **fractional distillation**. The fractions with the lower boiling points exit at the top of the tower.

Nail varnish doesn't dissolve in water but it does in remover. Solutes **dissolve** in solvents to make solutions.

There's not enough petrol made to meet the demand. There's more heavy oil distilled than needed. These **larger alkane molecules** can be cracked to make smaller, more useful ones, like those of petrol.

Polymers

Polymers are large, long-chain molecules made from small monomers.

Nylon and Gore-Tex® can be used in coats because they're **waterproof**. Gore-Tex® has the advantage that it's also **breathable**.

Monomers are **alkenes**, such as ethene and propene. Alkenes are **hydrocarbons** made of carbon and hydrogen only.

Poly(ethene) is used for plastic bags because it's waterproof and flexible. **Poly(styrene)** is used for packaging and insulation.

Fossil fuels and energy

If there's a good supply of oxygen, there's **complete combustion**. If not, there's **incomplete combustion**.

An **exothermic** reaction **transfers heat out** to the surroundings. An **endothermic** reaction **transfers heat in**.

When choosing a fuel to use for a particular purpose, several factors need to be considered:
– energy value and availability
– storage and cost
– toxicity and how much pollution they cause
– how easy they're to use.

Fuels can be compared by using the same mass of fuel to heat a fixed amount of water and **measuring the change in temperature**.

Heating houses

Heat

- **Hot** objects have a high temperature and usually cool down; cold objects have a lower temperature and usually warm up.

- The unit of **temperature** is the **degree Celsius** (°C).

- **Heat** is a form of energy. The unit of energy (heat) is the **joule** (J).

- Energy, in the form of heat, flows from a warmer to a colder body. When energy flows away from a warm object, the temperature of that object decreases.

- Temperature is a measure of 'hotness'. It allows one object to be compared to another.

Specific heat capacity

- The **energy** needed to change the temperature of a substance depends on:
  – **mass**
  – the **material** it's made from
  – the **temperature change**.

- When you heat a solid, its temperature rises until it changes to a liquid. The temperature stays the same until all of the solid has changed to a liquid. The temperature of the liquid then rises until it changes into a gas. The temperature stays the same until all of the liquid has changed to a gas.

- Heat is needed to **melt** a solid at its **melting point**.

- Heat is needed to **boil** a liquid at its **boiling point**.

- All substances have a property called **specific heat capacity**, which is:
  – the energy needed to raise the temperature of 1 kg by 1 °C
  – measured in joule per kilogram degree Celsius (J/kg°C)
  – different for different materials.

- When an object is heated and its temperature rises, energy is transferred.

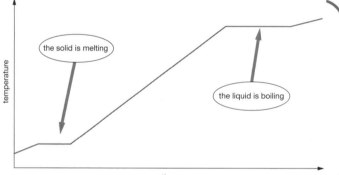

Why does the line flatten out during changes of state?

the solid is melting

the liquid is boiling

temperature

time

Specific latent heat

- **Latent heat** is the heat needed to change the state of a material without a change in temperature.

- **Specific latent heat** is:
  – the energy needed to melt or boil 1 kg of the material
  – measured in joule per kilogram (J/kg)
  – different for different materials and each of the changes of state.

- When an object is heated and it changes state, energy is transferred.

Top Tip!

Remember that heat and temperature are different. Energy transfer doesn't always involve a rise or fall in temperature.

Questions

Grades G-E

1 What is the difference between temperature and heat?

Grades D-C

2 When you put an ice cube on your hand, your hand gets colder. Suggest why.

Grades G-E

3 Describe what happens to a solid at its melting point.

Grades D-C

4 The syrup in a steamed syrup pudding always appears to be hotter than the sponge even though they're at the same temperature. Why is this?

Keeping homes warm

Energy

- **Insulation** reduces energy loss from a home.

- Insulation contains a lot of **trapped air** because air is a good insulator.

- Energy loss from uninsulated homes can be reduced by:
  - injecting **foam** into the cavity between the inner and outer walls
  - laying **fibreglass** or a similar material between the joists in the loft
  - replacing single glazed windows with **double** (or triple) **glazed windows**
  - drawing the **curtains**
  - placing **shiny foil** behind radiators
  - **sealing gaps** around doors.

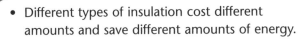

curtains reduce radiation
loft insulation
porch to reduce warm air loss
double-glazed windows insulate
carpet underlay acts as insulation
wall cavity filled with insulation
draught excluder on door

- Different types of insulation cost different amounts and save different amounts of energy.

- Most energy is lost from the **walls** of an uninsulated house.

- To work out the most cost-effective type of insulation, the **payback time** is calculated:

$$\text{payback time} = \frac{\text{cost of insulation}}{\text{annual saving}}$$

Draught proofing costs £80 to install and saves £20 per year on heating bills.

$$\text{payback time} = \frac{80}{20}$$
$$= 4 \text{ years}$$

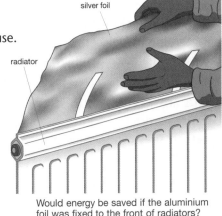

silver foil

radiator

Would energy be saved if the aluminium foil was fixed to the front of radiators?

- Different energy sources each have their advantages and disadvantages. Cost can be compared by using a consistent unit – **kWh**.

- The formula for energy efficiency is:

$$\text{efficiency} = \frac{\text{useful energy output}}{\text{total energy input}}$$

For every 100 J of energy in coal, 27 J are transferred to a room as heat by a coal fire.

$$\text{efficiency} = \frac{27}{100}$$
$$= 0.27 \text{ or } 27\%$$

- Coal fires are very inefficient because so much heat is *lost* via the chimney.

Questions

Grades G-E

1 Why is fibreglass a good material to insulate a loft?

2 Why does shiny foil behind a radiator help to reduce energy loss?

Grades D-C

3 Doug spends £3000 fitting double glazing. It saves him £50 each year on his heating bills. Calculate the payback time.

4 A coal fire has an efficiency of 0.35 (35%). Mrs Tarantino spends £150 per year on coal. How much money does she waste heating the surroundings instead of the room?

How insulation works

Insulators

- Air is a good **insulator** because it doesn't allow energy to transfer from a warm body to cooler surroundings.

- Fur coats keep us warm because they have a lot of trapped air.

Convection and radiation

- **Convection** in air takes place when hot air rises and cooler air falls to take its place.

- This movement of air is called a **convection current**.

- **Infrared radiation** from the Sun can be reflected by a shiny surface. The heat can be used for cooking or producing electricity.

House insulation

- Double glazing reduces energy loss by **conduction**. The gap between the two pieces of glass is filled with a gas or contains a **vacuum**.

warm end of solid, where particles have gained energy and vibrate a lot, transferring their energy to neighbouring particles

cool end of solid, where particles are not vibrating very much

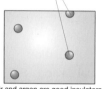

particles of gas are far apart, so energy cannot easily be transferred

no particles, so no energy transfer

a solid is a good conductor

air and argon are good insulators

a vacuum is the best insulator

- **Solids** are good conductors because particles are close together. They can transfer energy easily.

Why is air a better insulator than a solid?

- Particles in a **gas** are far apart, so it's difficult to transfer energy.

- There are no particles in a **vacuum**, so it's impossible to transfer energy by conduction.

- **Loft insulation** reduces energy loss by **conduction** and **convection**:
  - warm air in the home rises
  - energy is transferred through the ceiling by conduction
  - air in the loft is warmed by the top of the ceiling
  - the warm air is trapped in the loft insulation
  - both sides of the ceiling are at the same temperature so no energy is transferred.

snow does not melt on a well insulated house

cold air in loft
loft insulation
ceiling
warm air in room

- Without loft insulation:
  - the warm air in the loft can move by convection and heat the roof tiles
  - energy is transferred to the outside by conduction.

- **Cavity wall insulation** reduces energy loss by conduction and convection:
  - the air in the foam is a good insulator
  - the air can't move by convection because it's trapped in the foam.

- **Insulation blocks** used to build new homes have shiny foil on both sides so:
  - energy from the Sun is reflected back to keep the home cool in summer
  - energy from the home is reflected back to keep the home warm in winter.

Top Tip!

Remember, hot air will only rise into the loft if the loft-hatch is open.

Questions

1 Why does a woollen jumper keep us warm?
2 Write down two ways in which radiated energy from the Sun can be used.

3 Suggest why a vacuum-sealed double glazed unit is better than having thicker glass in a window.
4 Debbie says that snow doesn't melt as quickly on the roof of a well-insulated house. Explain why.

Cooking with waves

Infrared and microwave radiation

G–E

- The **electromagnetic spectrum** is a family of waves that have different **frequencies** and **wavelengths**. **Microwaves** and **infrared** radiation are part of the **electromagnetic spectrum**. They have wavelengths that are **longer** than the wavelength of visible light.

- All warm and hot bodies **emit infrared** radiation. Hotter bodies emit more radiation than cooler bodies.
  – Dark, dull surfaces emit more radiation than light shiny surfaces.

- Infrared radiation is **absorbed** by all bodies, which then become warmer.
  – Dark, dull surfaces absorb more radiation than light shiny surfaces.

- Water molecules in food absorb microwaves.

Top Tip!

Black surfaces absorb radiation; they don't attract heat.

D–C

- Microwaves penetrate up to 1 cm into food but infrared radiation doesn't penetrate food very easily.

- Microwaves can penetrate glass or plastic but are reflected by shiny metal surfaces. The door of a microwave oven is made from a special reflective glass.

Communication

G–E

- **Mobile phones** use microwaves for communication.

- There's some evidence that microwaves from mobile phones can affect the body. Young people are advised not to use mobile phones unless they have to.

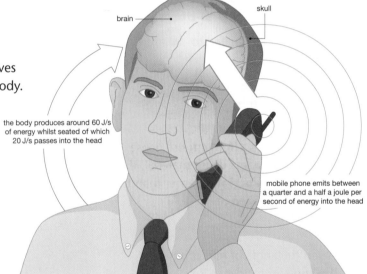

skull

brain

the body produces around 60 J/s of energy whilst seated of which 20 J/s passes into the head

mobile phone emits between a quarter and a half a joule per second of energy into the head

The science of mobile phones.

D–C

- Microwave radiation is used to communicate over long distances. The transmitter and receiver must be in **line of sight**. Aerials are normally situated on the top of high buildings.

- **Satellites** are used for microwave communication. The signal from Earth is received, amplified and re-transmitted back to Earth. Satellites are in line of sight because there are no obstructions in space. The large aerials can handle thousands of phone calls and television channels at once.

The Telecom Tower. Why are microwave aerials on high buildings?

Questions

(Grades G-E)

1 Which emits most infrared radiation – an electric fire or an electric iron?

(Grades D-C)

2 Suggest why microwave ovens need to have a special glass door.

(Grades G-E)

3 How can young people use a mobile phone more safely?

(Grades D-C)

4 Some areas of the country have very poor mobile phone reception. Suggest why.

Infrared signals

Signals

- **Infrared signals** can be used for **remote controllers**, such as television and other audio-visual equipment; a cordless mouse; and household equipment like garage doors and blinds.

- **Passive infrared sensors** detect body heat and are used in burglar alarms.

- Signals can be **digital** or **analogue**.

- **Digital** signals have two values – **on** and **off**.

- **Analogue** signals can have any value and are continuously **variable**. The analogue signal changes both its **amplitude** and **wavelength**.

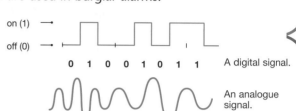

on (1) →
off (0) →

0 1 0 0 1 0 1 1

A digital signal.

An analogue signal.

G–E

D–C

Total internal reflection and critical angle

- Light can be reflected inside materials such as glass, water and perspex. This process is called **total internal reflection**.

- Laser beams and infrared radiation can travel along optical fibres.

- Telephone conversations and computer data are transmitted long distances along **optical fibres**.

- Some fibres are coated to improve reflection.

- When light travels from one material to another it's **refracted**.

- If light is passing from a more dense material into a less dense material, the **angle of refraction** is larger than the **angle of incidence**.

- When the angle of refraction is 90°, the angle of incidence is called the **critical angle**.

- If the angle of incidence is **bigger** than the critical angle, the light is reflected. This is **total internal reflection**.

Top Tip!

Remember optical fibres are solid, not hollow!

What happens to light when it meets the boundary with air in this optical fibre?

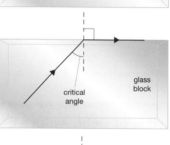

angle of refraction

angle of incidence

glass block

critical angle

glass block

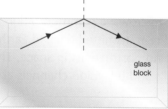

glass block

G–E

D–C

Questions

1 What type of radiation is produced when you use the remote control for your DVD player?

2 Draw a diagram of the scale of an analogue voltmeter that can read up to 5 V.

3 Write down two types of radiation that can travel along an optical fibre.

4 The critical angle for light passing from glass into air is 41°. Draw a diagram to show what happens if the angle of incidence is 30°.

Wireless signals

Radio waves

- **Wireless technology** means that computers and phones can be used anywhere because they're portable, which makes them very convenient.

- Wireless technology means what it says – there are no wires, radio waves are used instead.

- **Radio waves** are part of the **electromagnetic spectrum**.

- Radio waves can be reflected, which means that a signal can be received even if the aerial is not in line of sight.

- Sometimes an **aerial** receives a reflected signal as well as a direct signal. On a television picture this appears as **ghosting**.

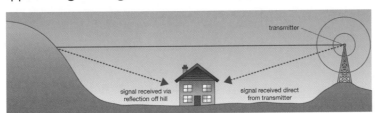

Radio waves can be reflected off solid obstacles such as a hill.

- Radio waves are refracted in the upper atmosphere. The amount of **refraction** depends on the frequency of the wave. There's less refraction at higher frequencies.

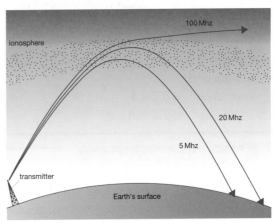

What type of wave shows most refraction?

- Radio stations broadcast signals with a particular frequency. The same frequency can be used by more than one radio station because the distance between the stations means that only one will be received. However, in unusual weather conditions, the radio waves can travel further and the broadcasts **interfere**.

Questions

(Grades G-E)

1 What's the main advantage of wireless technology?

(Grades D-C)

2 Radio stations that broadcast on FM use frequencies of about 100 MHz or higher. Suggest why there's less interference when you listen to a radio station broadcasting on FM.

Light

Transverse waves

- When a pebble is dropped into a pool of water, a **circular wave** spreads out. The water particles move up and down as the wave spreads out.

- Water waves are **transverse** waves. A transverse wave travels at **right angles** to the wave vibration.

- The speed of light, and all waves in the electromagnetic spectrum, is 300 000 km/s.

Wave properties

- The **amplitude** of a wave is the maximum displacement of a particle **from** its rest position.

- The **trough** of a wave is the maximum displacement of a particle **below** its rest position.

- The **crest** of a wave is the maximum displacement of a particle **above** its rest position.

- The **wavelength** of a wave is the distance **between** two adjacent points of similar displacement on the wave.

- The **frequency** of a wave is the **number of complete waves** passing a point in one second.

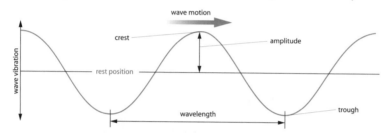

The parts of a transverse wave.

- The formula for calculating wave speed is:
  wave speed = frequency × wavelength

  When Katie throws a stone into a pond, the distance between ripples is 0.3 m and four waves reach the edge of the pond each second.
  wave speed = 0.3 × 4
              = 1.2 m/s

Top Tip!

Remember to always give the units in your answer:
– wavelength – **metre** (m)
– frequency – **hertz** (Hz)
– speed – **metre per second** (m/s)

Sending messages

- Early messages, such as smoke signals, beacons and semaphore, relied on **line of sight**. Runners and horsemen relayed messages over longer distances.

- Signalling lamps need a code to represent letters.

- Lasers produce a very intense beam of light. Laser light can be used along optical fibres for communication.

- The **Morse code** uses a series of dots and dashes to represent letters of the alphabet. This code is used by signalling lamps as a series of short and long **flashes of light**.

Questions

Grades G-E

1 What's the speed of infrared radiation?

Grades D-C

2 A sound wave has a frequency of 200 Hz and a wavelength of 1.5 m. Calculate the speed of sound.

Grades G-E

3 What's the advantage of using a signalling lamp instead of sending a runner?

Grades D-C

4 How does Morse code work?

Stable Earth

Grades

Earthquakes

G–E

- Earthquakes happen at a **fault**.

- **Shock waves** travel through and round the surface of the Earth.

- We detect earthquakes using a **seismometer**.
  – A heavy weight, with a pen attached, is suspended above a rotating drum with graph paper on it. The base is bolted to solid rock.
  – During an earthquake, the base moves and the pen draws a trace on the graph paper.

D–C

- The **focus** is where the earthquake happens below the surface.

- The **epicentre** is the point on the surface above the focus.

- **L waves** travel round the surface very slowly.

- **P waves** are **longitudinal** pressure waves:
  – P waves travel through the Earth at between 5 km/s and 8 km/s
  – P waves can pass through solids and liquids.

- **S waves** are **transverse** waves:
  – S waves travel through the Earth at between 3 km/s and 5.5 km/s
  – S waves can only pass through solids.

- A **seismograph** shows the different types of earthquake wave.

A seismograph. Which type of wave travelled fastest during the earthquake?

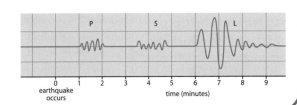

Weather effects

G–E

- The Earth is getting warmer because there are more **greenhouse gases** in the atmosphere.

- **Carbon dioxide** is the main greenhouse gas produced whenever a fuel burns. The more energy we use, the more carbon dioxide there'll be.

- Trees and plants use carbon dioxide *but* large areas of **forest** are being destroyed.

D–C

- **Natural events** and **human activity** affect our weather.
  – Dust from **volcanoes** can reflect energy from the Sun back into the atmosphere – it becomes cooler on Earth.
  – Dust from **factories** can reflect radiation from towns back to Earth – it becomes warmer on Earth.

G–E

- **Ultraviolet** radiation causes suntan. Too much exposure to ultraviolet radiation can cause sunburn or skin cancer. Sunscreen filters out ultraviolet radiation.

- Ultraviolet light on the skin causes the cells to make **melanin**, a pigment that produces a tan. People with dark skin don't tan easily because ultraviolet radiation is filtered out.

D–C

- Use a sunscreen with a high **SPF** (sun protection factor) to reduce risks. The formula for calculating a safe length of time to spend in the Sun is:
  safe length of time to spend in the Sun = published normal burn time × SPF

Questions

Grades G-E
1 What's a seismometer?

Grades D-C
2 What's the difference between the focus and the epicentre of an earthquake?

Grades G-E
3 Write down two ways in which human activity is contributing to climate change.

Grades D-C
4 Kate sees that on a hot day the normal burn time is 5 minutes. How long can she stay in the sun, without burning, if she uses sunscreen with SPF 30?

P1 Summary

Heat and temperature

Hot objects have high temperatures and tend to cool down.
Cold objects have low temperatures and tend to warm up.
Energy is **transferred** from a hotter to a colder object.

Temperature is a measure of **hotness** in degree Celcius (°C). Heat is a measure of **energy transfer** in joules (J).

Energy is **transferred** when a substance **changes temperature**. The amount of energy transferred depends on:
– the mass
– temperature change
– specific heat capacity.

Energy is **transferred** when a substance **changes state**. The amount of energy transferred depends on:
– the mass
– the specific latent heat.

Energy transfer

Air is a good **insulator** and reduces energy transfer by **conduction**.

$$\text{efficiency} = \frac{\text{useful energy output}}{\text{total energy input}}$$

Trapped air reduces energy transfer by **convection**.

Shiny surfaces **reflect** infrared radiation to reduce energy transfer.

Energy saving in the home can be achieved by:
– double glazing
– cavity wall insulation
– draught strip
– reflecting foil
– loft insulation
– curtains
– careful design.

Waves carrying energy

Warm and hot objects emit **infrared radiation**. Infrared radiation is used for cooking and remote controllers.

Microwaves can be used for **cooking** and for **communication** when transmitter and receiver are in line of sight.

Digital and **analogue** signals are used for **communication**.

Radio waves are used for **communication**.

Waves in the electromagnetic spectrum are:
– **radio waves**
– **microwaves**
– **infrared**
– **visible light**
– **ultraviolet**.
All electromagnetic waves can be **reflected** and **refracted**.

The stable Earth

Earthquakes occur at plate boundaries. Earthquake waves travel through the Earth.

Climate change is a result of both **human activity**, such as burning fossil fuels, and **natural phenomena**, such as volcanoes.

Exposure to **ultraviolet radiation** causes **sun burn** and **skin cancer**. Sunscreen and sunblock reduce damage caused by ultraviolet waves.

Ecology in our school grounds

Ecosystems

- A garden is an example of an **ecosystem**. All the living things in the garden and their surroundings make up the ecosystem. Ecosystems can be **natural** such as an aquarium, or **artificial** such as a lake.

- All the animals and plants living in the garden make up the **community**.

- Where an animal lives is called its **habitat**. For example, in a garden, a worm's habitat is the soil.

Top Tip!

An **ecosystem** describes living things and the environment. A **habitat** describes the place where living things live.

- We know more about the surface of the Moon than we know about the deepest ecosystems of our oceans.

- Animals from the deep can't live near the surface and are rarely seen. For example, the giant squid can grow up to 20 m long but suffocates in warm surface water. Many new species may exist at depths that humans can't reach.

The giant squid.

Collecting living things

- Animals living in an ecosystem can be caught using these methods.

pooters   nets   pitfall traps

- Animals and plants can be identified using **keys**.

- To find out which plants are growing, square frames called **quadrats** are placed on the ground. The plants inside them are identified and counted.

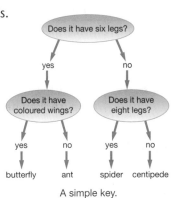

A simple key.

Counting animals

- To estimate a **population**, scientists can use a method called 'mark and recapture'.
  - The animals are trapped and marked in some harmless way.
  - They are then released and the traps are set again a few days later.

- To estimate the population the following formula is used.

$$\frac{\text{number of animals caught first time} \times \text{number of animals caught second time}}{\text{number of marked animals caught second time}} = \text{population}$$

- Population sizes will always be changing because:
  - animals are being born and others are dying
  - there is movement of animals in and out of the ecosystem.

Top Tip!

A **population** is a group of animals or plants of the same species. A **community** is lots of different species living in the same ecosystem.

Questions

Grade G-E

1 Name one example of a natural ecosystem and one of an artificial ecosystem.

Grade D-C

2 What happens to a giant squid in warm surface water?

Grade G-E

3 Which catching method would you use to catch ants?

Grade D-C

4 What is meant by the term 'population'?

Grouping organisms

Plant and animal kingdoms

- Organisms can be sorted into the **plant kingdom** and the **animal kingdom**.

- The animal kingdom is split into two groups:
  - **vertebrates** with a backbone
  - **invertebrates** with no backbone.

- There are five vertebrate groups.
  - **Fish** have wet scales and gills to get oxygen from the water.
  - **Amphibians** have a moist permeable skin.
  - **Reptiles** have dry scaly skin.
  - **Birds** all have feathers and beaks, but not all of them can fly.
  - **Mammals** have fur and produce milk.

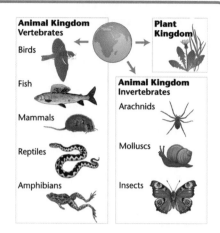

Top Tip!

You may be asked about a vertebrate you've never heard of. Don't worry! It will fit into one of the five groups.

- This table shows the main differences between plants and animals.

	food	shape	movement
plants	make their own food using chloroplasts to trap energy from the Sun	spread out to collect plenty of water and nutrients from soil	stay in one place, they cannot get up and move somewhere else
animals	cannot make their own food, so they need to eat	more compact than plants to help them move around	able to move around to find food

Species

- Dogs and cats are both **mammals** and share characteristics such as fur. But they're also very different because they're different **species**.

- All the dogs we keep as pets belong to the same species. But they can look very different. This is because humans have **bred** lots of different types of dogs.

labrador   poodle   labradoodle

- A tiger and a lion are both cats. However, they're two different **species**. Members of the same species can breed. Lions breed with other lions to make young lions. These young lions will be **fertile**.

How have humans made lots of different types of dog species?

- All cats belong to the same **family**. The family is called Felidae. Each species of cat is given its own scientific name. Lions have the name *Panthera leo*. Tigers are called *Panthera tigris*. They both have the same first name because they are closely related.

- The lion and the tiger share a recent ancestor but have evolved to live in different **habitats**. Lions live in open grassland while tigers prefer forest.

- Cheetah and leopards aren't closely related. However, they're very similar because they're **adapted** to the same habitat.

Questions

1 Name the five vertebrate groups.

2 Explain why plants need chloroplasts.

3 One characteristic that both cats and dogs have is their fur. Name another characteristic they have in common.

4 What is the family name for cats?

The food factory

Photosynthesis

- Plants make their own food by photosynthesis. Photosynthesis means using light (photo-) to make food (-synthesis).

- Plants carry out photosynthesis in the following way.
  - Plant leaves contain chlorophyll which is a green-coloured substance. The green leaves use the chlorophyll to trap light.
  - The light energy is used to turn **carbon dioxide** and **water** into **glucose**.

- During photosynthesis, a plant makes **glucose** and **oxygen**.
  - Oxygen is very important to both plants and animals because they need it for respiration.
  - Glucose is used for **energy** for the plant to grow, or it can be stored. To store the glucose it has to be first turned into **starch**.

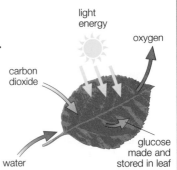

How plants photosynthesise.

- Glucose is transported as **soluble** sugars to parts of the plant where it's needed.

- The glucose can be used by the plant in many ways:
  - in respiration to release energy
  - converted into **insoluble** starch, fats or oils for storage
  - converted into **cellulose** to make new cell walls
  - converted into **proteins** for growth and repair of cells.

- Photosynthesis can be described using this word equation:

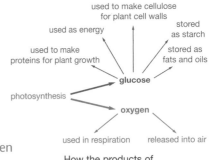

How the products of photosynthesis are used.

$$\text{carbon dioxide} + \text{water} \xrightarrow[\text{(chlorophyll)}]{\text{(light energy)}} \text{glucose} + \text{oxygen}$$

Speeding up photosynthesis

- Plants grow faster in the summer because:
  - it's warmer
  - there's more light.

- These actions increase the rate of photosynthesis:
  - keeping the plants warm
  - providing the plants with extra carbon dioxide
  - increasing the amount of light for the plant.

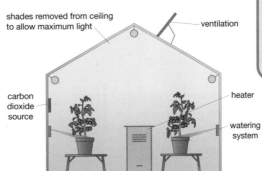

Increasing the rate of photosynthesis.

Plants and respiration

- **Respiration** uses oxygen to release energy from glucose. At the same time it releases carbon dioxide and water. Respiration is the reverse of photosynthesis.

Questions

(Grade G-E)

1 Name four things a plant needs for photosynthesis.

(Grade D-C)

2 Name three uses of glucose in a plant.

(Grade G-E)

3 Explain why plants grow slower on cold winter days.

(Grade D-C)

4 Name three actions that increase the rate of photosynthesis.

Compete or die

Plant and animal competition

- Plants and animals **compete** to survive. Animals also compete to breed. If they don't, their species will die out.

- Plants compete for **light**, **water** and **minerals**.

- Animals compete for **food**, **water**, **shelter** and **mates**.

- Swallows and martins are two birds that compete for the same insect food. The **population** size of these birds never stays the same. In summer, you will see lots of them because there is plenty of food. In winter, they must fly south to find food.

- Bluebells flower in spring to catch as much light as possible before the leaves are fully out on the trees, causing shade. In summer, the bluebells find it difficult to grow as the larger trees take most of the light, water and minerals. The bluebells and trees are in **competition** with each other.

Top Tip!
If you're asked about animals or plants you have never heard of, don't be put off.
All animals and plants compete for similar things.

- Animals often compete to attract a mate so that they can breed. Animals need to breed so that the species survives. Male elephant seals fight each other in order to keep their mates.

Animal relationships

- In any habitat there are lots of different animals living together. Some of these animals help each other out – they are **friends**. Other animals hunt another animal for food – they are **foes**.

- Lions, buffaloes, oxpeckers and antelopes all live in the same habitat. The oxpecker and buffalo are friends. The oxpecker feeds on insects that live in the buffalo's skin. The lion and the antelope are foes. Lions will hunt and eat antelopes. The lion is called a **predator** and the antelope is its **prey**.

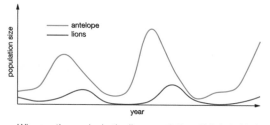

- The relationship between predator and prey can be shown in a food chain.

- There are many ways in which animals of different species interact.
  - Lions eat antelopes. If there are lots of lions, antelope numbers will go down as more get eaten. When there are fewer antelopes, lion numbers go down as there is not enough food.

Why are the peaks in the lion population slightly behind the peaks in the antelope population?

  - The tapeworm is a **parasite**. It lives in the digestive system of other animals including humans. The tapeworm takes food away from its **host** so that it can grow.
  - The sharksucker is a fish that attaches itself to sharks. It cleans the shark's skin by eating its parasites. In return, the shark protects the sharksucker from predators. Relationships like this in which both animals benefit is called **mutualism**.

Questions

Grade G-E

1 Name one thing that both plants and animals compete for.

Grade D-C

2 Explain why animals need to compete for a mate and breed.

Grade G-E

3 Give two examples of predators.

Grade D-C

4 What is meant by the term 'mutualism'?

Adapt to fit

Adapting to habitats

- Every living thing is **adapted** to live in its habitat.
  - Birds have feathers, lightweight bones and strong flight muscles so they can fly.
  - Fish have gills so they can live in water.
  - Earthworms can move soil through their bodies so they can make underground burrows.
  - Cacti have stems that store water enabling them to survive the heat of the desert.

- Brown bears are **predators**. They're adapted to **hunt** salmon.
  - Eyes at the front of their head judge distance.
  - Sharp claws grab the salmon.
  - Sharp teeth tear into the salmon's flesh.

- The salmon are **prey**. They're adapted to **escape** from bears.
  - Their **streamlined** shape helps them swim fast.
  - Their colour gives them **camouflage** in the water.
  - They swim up river together in large numbers so only a few get caught.
  - Eyes on the side of their heads give them a wide field of view.

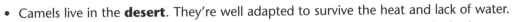

eyes at the side of the head give a large range of vision (and a smaller area of binocular vision)

Salmon have a large range of vision. How does this help them escape from bears?

- Camels live in the **desert**. They're well adapted to survive the heat and lack of water.
  - All their body fat is in the hump, so heat can be lost from the rest of the body.
  - Stored fat in the hump can be used when there is no other food available.
  - Their body temperature can rise above normal, so they don't need to sweat.
  - Bushy eyelashes and hair-lined nostrils stop sand getting in.
  - Large feet spread out their weight to stop them sinking into the sand.

- Polar bears live in the **Arctic**. They're well adapted to the cold.
  - They have thick white fur for camouflage and insulation.
  - A layer of fat over their body called **blubber** keeps them insulated.
  - A large body compared to their surface area stops them losing too much heat.
  - Small ears reduce the surface area from which heat can be lost.
  - Sharp claws and teeth help them to seize and eat their prey.
  - Strong legs help them run and swim.
  - Large feet spread their weight on the snow.
  - Fur-covered soles on their paws help them to grip and insulates them against the cold.

- Brown bears and polar bears live in different habitats. Brown bears would find it difficult to exist in the polar bears' habitat because they aren't adapted for the cold.

Top Tip!

Make sure you know the different meanings of 'describe' and 'explain'.
- The camel has large feet – is to 'describe' an adaptation.
- The camel has large feet to spread the load on sand – is to 'explain' an adaptation.

Questions

Grade G-E

1 Name an animal adapted to fly that is *not* a bird.
2 Explain why a bear's eyes are on the front of its head, not the side.

Grade D-C

3 Explain why camels have bushy eyelashes.
4 Apart from the cold, why else would the brown bear find it difficult to survive in the Arctic?

Survival of the fittest

Fossils

- **Fossils** are the preserved parts of dead plants and animals that have turned to stone over millions of years. Scientists use the fossils to decide what a dinosaur may have looked like.

- Scientists study fossils of animals found in rocks of different ages. The deepest rocks in the Earth contain the oldest fossils.

- By comparing old and newer fossils, scientists can see how animals have changed over time. This change is called **evolution**.

The fossilised skull of a dinosaur.

- Fossils form in different ways.
  - Hard parts such as shells and bones can be replaced by minerals, which turn to stone.
  - Some organisms sink into mud and then **casts** or **impressions** form when they decay.
  - Organisms can be preserved in **amber**, peat bogs, tar pits or ice.

- The **fossil record** shows how organisms have changed over time.

- Not all living things have such a complete fossil record. This is because:
  - some body parts decay quickly before they can be fossilised
  - fossilisation is rare and most living things will completely decay
  - there may still be fossils we haven't found.

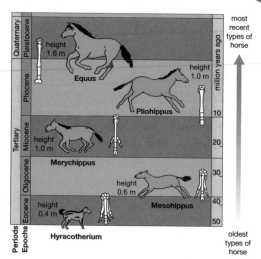

How the shape of the horse's foot has evolved over time.

Adapt or die

- Large numbers of penguins live together in the Antarctic. Not all the penguins are the same. Some will be better adapted, giving them more chance of survival. For example, some penguins are better swimmers and can catch more fish. The faster swimmers also have more chance of getting away from predators. Being better adapted for swimming helps penguins to survive.

- Environments can change. To survive these changes a species needs to adapt and evolve, otherwise it will become **extinct**. In any species, it's only the best adapted that survive.

- This **survival of the fittest** is called **natural selection**. This means that **genes** pass on the successful characteristics of a species to the next generation.

- There are examples of natural selection occurring today.
  - Peppered moths are dark or pale in colour. Dark moths are better camouflaged in polluted areas, so more of them survive.
  - Rats have evolved to become resistant to the poison warfarin.
  - Bacteria are becoming resistant to antibiotics.

Top Tip!

You need to be able to use natural selection to explain how bacteria have become resistant. Remember, it's all about survival of the fittest and passing on genes.

Questions

(Grade G-E)

1 Which rocks contain the oldest fossils?

(Grade D-C)

2 Write down one reason why the fossil record is incomplete.

(Grade G-E)

3 Why are some penguins better at escaping from predators?

(Grade D-C)

4 How do rats pass on resistance to warfarin to the next generation?

Population out of control?

Resources and pollution

- The world population has increased by about 5 billion in the last 200 years.

- All these people are using more and more of the Earth's resources.
  - **Fossil fuel** resources such as coal, oil and gas are burned for energy and heat.
  - **Mineral** resources such as limestone are used for building.

- The more resources used, the more waste is produced.

- All this waste is **polluting** the Earth.
  - Household rubbish is piling up in landfill sites.
  - Sewage can end up in rivers, killing fish.
  - Burning fossil fuels releases carbon dioxide and sulphur dioxide.

- Increasing levels of carbon dioxide causes **climate change** and sulphur dioxide causes **acid rain**.

- An increase in the use of chemicals called CFCs has led to a depletion of the ozone layer.

Top Tip!

Try not to mix up the three main effects of pollution. It's CFCs that deplete the ozone layer, *not* carbon dioxide.

rise in sea levels

increased carbon dioxide levels

acid rain

carbon dioxide sulphur dioxide CFCs

climate change

dead trees

dead fish

produce pollutants

ozone layer depleted

Sun

UV rays

FACTORIES   CARS   LORRIES

CFCs (lost from old freezers and refrigerators)

used by

increased incidence of skin cancers

FOSSIL FUELS

The main effects of pollution.

Pollution and habitats

- Rivers in Britain were often polluted by factory waste. The fish couldn't survive in the polluted water. Animals that fed on the fish also left the river. Many rivers have been cleaned up. There's a lot more fish in the clean rivers. Otters and herons have returned to these rivers as they now provide food.

Indicator species

The water louse is an indicator species. Can it live in polluted water?

Top Tip!

You only need to remember that indicator species are used. You don't have to remember the level of pollution that each species tolerates.

- The presence or absence of an **indicator species** is used to estimate levels of pollution.
  - The stonefly larva is an insect that can only live in clean water.
  - The bloodworm, water louse, sludge worm and rat-tailed maggot are animals that can live in polluted water.
  - Lichen grows on trees and rocks but only when the air is clean. It's unusual to find lichen growing in cities. This is because it's killed by the pollution from cars.

Questions

(Grade G-E)

1 Name the two gases released when fossil fuels burn.

(Grade D-C)

2 Which gas causes acid rain?

(Grade G-E)

3 Why are otters only found in clean rivers?

(Grade D-C)

4 Name two indicator species that can live in polluted water.

Sustainability

Endangered and extinct species

- Animals that no longer exist are called **extinct**. Examples are the dodo, sabre-toothed tiger and mammoth.

- Many animals and plants are in danger of becoming extinct. A species is **endangered** when its numbers are low.

- In Britain, people are protecting endangered species such as the red squirrel, red kite and osprey. This is called **conservation**. It's important to save these animals so future generations can see and enjoy them. In other countries the panda and gorilla are endangered.

- Animals become endangered or extinct because:
  – their climate changes and they cannot adapt fast enough
  – their habitat is destroyed or becomes polluted
  – they're hunted by humans or outcompeted by better adapted animals.

- Animals can be saved from extinction by:
  – protecting habitats or setting up **artificial ecosystems** and **captive breeding** in zoos
  – making hunting illegal and educating people about the reasons to save them.

The dodo.

G–E

D–C

Whales

- Different whale species are found in different seas. This is because they eat different food.

- Some whales are close to extinction because they are still hunted.

- Whales, fish and trees are all **sustainable resources**. If only a few are taken they will never die out because the ones left behind will be able to reproduce enough so they don't become extinct.

- Live whales are also important as people can make money from the tourist trade.

- Some whales are kept in captivity for research or captive breeding programmes or just for our entertainment. However, many people object when whales lose their freedom.

skin: used in belts, shoes, handbags and luggage

sinews: used in tennis rackets

spermacetti: used in high-grade machine oil

oil: sperm whale oil taken from bone and skin used in high-grade alcohol, shoe cream, lipstick, ointment, crayons, candles, fertiliser, soap and animal feeds

whalemeat: used in pet food and human food

teeth: used in buttons, piano keys and jewellery

liver: used in oil

bone: used in fertiliser and animal feeds

ambergris: from intestine, used in perfumes

Whale parts have many uses.

G–E

D–C

Sustainable development

- **Sustainable development** is a way of taking things from the environment but leaving enough behind to ensure a supply for the future and to prevent permanent damage.
  – People are educated about the need to maintain species' numbers for future generations.
  – Woods are re-planted to keep up the supply of trees.

- Sustainable resource and sustainable development are easy to confuse. We use fish, so they're the resource. Development is how we plan to maintain their numbers, for example by setting quotas.

D–C

Questions

(Grade G-E)

1 Explain why the gorilla is an endangered animal.

(Grade D-C)

2 Explain why 'climate change' could lead to the extinction of some species.

(Grade G-E)

3 Why do whales live in different seas?

(Grade D-C)

4 Suggest a reason why people object to keeping whales in captivity.

B2 Summary

Ecosystems

Animal and plant populations can be counted using:
– **pooters**
– **nets**
– **pitfall traps**
– **quadrats**.

All the living things and their surroundings make up an ecosystem.

Keys can be used to identify the animals and plants in a habitat.

Ecosystems can be **artificial** (e.g. fish pond) or **natural** (e.g. lake).

Many ecosystems are still unexplored and could contain new species.

Classification

The **animal kingdom** is split into two groups:
– **vertebrates**
– **invertebrates**.

Plants can make their own food by a process called **photosynthesis**:

carbon dioxide + water $\xrightarrow[\text{(chlorophyll)}]{\text{(light energy)}}$ glucose + oxygen

There are five vertebrate groups:
– **fish**
– **amphibians**
– **reptiles**
– **birds**
– **mammals**.

Competition and survival

Some animals are **adapted** to be successful **prey**.

Animals and plants adapt to their **habitats**. Those better adapted are more able to **compete** for resources. Species that cannot adapt may become **extinct**. **Fossils** provide evidence of extinct species.

The **survival** of a species depends on how well it can adapt to changes in the environment. The number of predators can affect population numbers of prey and vice versa.
Survival may also depend on the presence of another organism:
– **mutualism**
– **parasitism**.

Some animals are **adapted** to be successful **predators**.

Animals and plants within a habitat **compete** for limited resources such as food and water.

The increase in human population is leading to an increase in pollution and loss of habitat. As habitats become smaller, species are unable to compete and become extinct. Species can be protected from extinction if resources are carefully managed – **sustainable development**.

Paints and pigments

What is paint?

- Paint is a mixture called a **colloid**. The ingredients of paint are:
  - a **pigment** – a coloured substance often made of ground-up rock
  - a **binding medium** – glue or oil
  - a **solvent** – thins the paint, making it easier to use.

- In oil paints:
  - the pigment is spread in oil
  - the oil is dissolved in a solvent if it's too thick.

- We use paints:
  - to **protect** wood against rain; the oil sticks to the wood and forms a skin
  - to **decorate** pictures or walls in a house; the binder is used to stick the pigment to the canvas or walls.

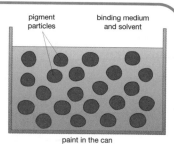

pigment particles

binding medium and solvent

paint in the can

G–E

- A paint is a colloid where small solid particles are dispersed through the whole liquid, but aren't dissolved.

- When **oil paint** is painted on a surface, the solvent **evaporates** leaving the binding medium to dry and form a skin, which sticks the pigment to the surface.

- An **emulsion paint** is a water-based paint. It's made of tiny droplets of one liquid in water, which is called an **emulsion**. When emulsion paint has been painted on to a surface as a thin layer, the water evaporates leaving the binding medium and pigment behind. As it dries it joins together to make a continuous film.

pigment particles / oil and solvent · pigment particles · Oil paint drying. · solvent evaporates · oil forms a protective skin

paint in the can · painted surface · Emulsion paint drying.

pigment particles · pigment particles · oil droplets spread out and join up · pigment particles · oil forms a protective skin

water · oil droplet · water evaporates

paint in the can · wet paint on a surface · painted surface

D–C

Pigments

- There are two types of pigment, which are shown in the table.

thermochromic pigment	phosphorescent pigment
when it gets hot, it changes colour	takes in light energy during the day
when it cools down, it changes back to the original colour	gives out light energy at night
used in some paints that are chosen for their colour and also for the temperature at which their colour changes, e.g. a thermochromic pigment that changes colour at 45 °C can be used to paint cups or kettles to act as a warning	stores the energy that it absorbs and can release it slowly as light

G–E

D–C

Dyes

- Dyes are used to colour fabrics. Some dyes are **natural** such as juice from coloured berries. Others are **synthetic** and made from chemicals.

- Synthetic dyes have increased the number of colours available.

G–E

D–C

Questions

Grades G-E

1 What's the job of a solvent in paint?

Grades D-C

2 What's a colloid?

Grades G-E

3 What's a thermochromic pigment?

Grades D-C

4 The range of colours for fabrics has increased over the last 150 years. Explain why.

Construction materials

G–E

The raw materials

- These materials are used in construction:
  - granite, marble and limestone
  - aluminium and iron (steel)
  - brick, cement, concrete and glass.

D–C

- Limestone is easier to cut into blocks than marble or granite. Marble is much harder than limestone. Granite is harder still and is very difficult to shape.

- Brick, concrete, steel, aluminium and glass come from materials in the ground, but they need to be manufactured from raw materials. This is shown in the table.

raw material	clay	limestone and clay	sand	iron ore	aluminium ore
building material	brick	cement	glass	iron	aluminium

Mining and quarrying

G–E

- Many modern buildings are made from materials dug out of the Earth.

- Stone such as **limestone**, **marble** and **granite** is cut out of the ground and used in buildings. Blocks of stone are expensive to quarry and are only used for special buildings.

- There are many environmental problems caused by removing rocks from the ground:
  - quarries and mines take up land-space
  - quarrying means an increase in noise, traffic and dust
  - landscapes are destroyed and have to be reconstructed.

Cement and concrete

G–E

- Limestone and marble are both forms of **calcium carbonate**. When calcium carbonate is heated, it **thermally decomposes** to form **calcium oxide** and **carbon dioxide**.

- **Cement** is made from limestone. To make cement, the limestone is heated and clay is added.

- **Concrete** is made when cement, sand and gravel are mixed with water and left to set.

- Concrete can be **reinforced**. It has steel rods inside it and is much stronger than normal concrete. The concrete is poured around steel rods and left to set.

D–C

- Calcium carbonate thermally decomposes at a very high temperature. This is shown in the word equation:

$$\text{calcium carbonate} \xrightarrow{\text{heat}} \text{calcium oxide} + \text{carbon dioxide}$$

- **Thermal decomposition** is the chemical breakdown of a compound into at least two other compounds under the effect of heat.

- **Cement** is made when limestone and clay are heated together.

- Reinforced concrete has steel rods or steel meshes running through it and is stronger than concrete. It is a **composite** material.

Questions

Grades G-E

1 Name three construction materials.

Grades D-C

2 What's cement made from?

Grades G-E

3 What's the chemical name for marble and limestone?

Grades D-C

4 What are the products of heating limestone?

Does the Earth move?

The structure of the Earth

- The Earth is a sphere with an **iron core** surrounded by a **mantle**. On the outside is a thin, rocky **crust**. The mantle is made of molten rock.

- The outer layer of the Earth is made of **tectonic plates**, which move very slowly over the molten rock. At the **plate boundaries** this movement causes **earthquakes** and **volcanoes**.

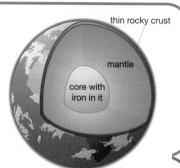

- The outer layer of the Earth is called the **lithosphere**. It's relatively cold and rigid and is made of the crust and the part of the mantle that lies just underneath.

- The tectonic plates that make up the Earth's crust are **less dense** than the mantle, which they 'float' on. There are two kinds of plate:
  - **continental plates** that carry the continents
  - **oceanic plates** that lie underneath the oceans.

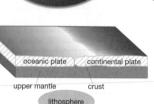
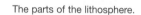
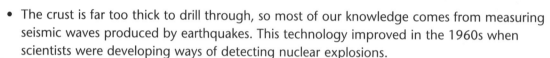

The parts of the lithosphere.

- The crust is far too thick to drill through, so most of our knowledge comes from measuring seismic waves produced by earthquakes. This technology improved in the 1960s when scientists were developing ways of detecting nuclear explosions.

Magma and rocks

- Underneath the surface of the Earth, most of the rock is solid. However, some of the rock does melt and is called **magma**. It slowly moves up to the surface of the Earth. Eventually it cools down and **solidifies** to make **igneous** rock.

- **Molten rock** that reaches the surface of the Earth through weaknesses is called **lava**. It comes out in a **volcano**.
  - Volcanoes that produce runny lava are often fairly safe.
  - If the lava is thick and sticky then an eruption can be explosive.
  - The ash from volcanoes makes a rich soil that's good for growing things.
  - Most volcanic eruptions aren't that dangerous, so people think it's worth moving back to the area.

- Magma rises through the Earth's crust because it's less dense than the crust. It cools and solidifies into igneous rock either after it comes out of a volcano as lava, or before it even gets to the surface.

- By looking at crystals of **igneous rock**, geologists can tell how quickly the rock cooled.
  - Igneous rock that **cools rapidly** (close to the surface) has small crystals.
  - Igneous rock that **cools slowly** (further from the surface and better insulated) has large crystals.

rock type	small crystal	large crystal
iron-rich magma	basalt	gabbro
silica-rich magma	rhyolite	granite

- Geologists study volcanic rocks to decide what previous eruptions were like. They also use seismic measurements to help them predict future eruptions and learn more about the Earth's structure.

Questions

1 The Earth is made up of three parts. Can you name them?

2 Why do the tectonic plates 'float' on the molten rock?

3 What type of rock is made when magma cools down?

4 Explain why the size of crystals changes when magma cools.

Metals and alloys

Copper

- Rocks containing copper ore are mined. Copper is a metal **element**. An ore is a **compound**.

- In the **laboratory**, copper is extracted from its ore by heating it with **carbon**.

- **Electrolysis** is used to purify copper.

- More than a third of all copper is **recycled**, saving resources and money.
  - It's cheaper to recycle copper than to extract new copper from the ground.
  - Recycling also saves energy needed to crush rock and to operate smelters and electrolysis cells.

- Copper has a fairly **low melting point** that makes it easy to melt down and recycle. However, copper that's been used already may be contaminated with other elements, such as solder. This means that it can't be used for purposes where the copper must be very pure, such as electric wiring.

- Copper used for recycling has to be sorted carefully so that valuable 'pure' copper scrap isn't mixed with less pure scrap.

- When impure copper is used to make **alloys**, it must first be analysed to find out how much of each element is present. If the scrap copper is very impure, it has to be electrolysed again before it can be used.

Electrolysis

- Impure copper can be purified in the laboratory using an **electrolysis cell**.
  - The **anode** is impure copper and dissolves into the **electrolyte**.
  - The **cathode** is 'plated' with new copper.

An electrolysis cell.

Alloys

- An **alloy** is a mixture of a metal element with another element.

- By adding another element to a metal its properties can be changed to make it more useful. For example, **steel** is a useful alloy of **iron**.

- Examples of alloys are: amalgam, brass, bronze, solder and steel.
  - **Amalgam** is used by dentists to fill cavities in teeth.
  - **Brass** is used to make taps and door handles.
  - **Solder** is used to join metals.

- Most **metals** form alloys.
  - Amalgam contains mercury.
  - Brass contains copper and zinc.
  - Solder contains lead and tin.

Top Tip!

Alloys are often more useful than the metals they're made from.

Questions

Grades G-E

1 Copper is recycled where possible. Explain why.

Grades D-C

2 Which electrode becomes pure copper in electrolysis?

Grades G-E

3 What's an alloy?

Grades D-C

4 Which metals form the alloy brass?

Cars for scrap

Rusting and corrosion

- **Rust** is a brownish solid that forms when iron is in contact with **oxygen** and **water**. Rust flakes off the surface of the iron.

Top Tip!

Oxygen and water are needed for rusting.

- Most cars have a metal body made of steel or aluminium.
  - **Steel** is an **alloy** that contains mostly iron; all cars made with steel rust.
  - Cars made with **aluminium** don't **corrode** when oxygen and water are present.

- **Acid rain** and **salt water** accelerate rusting.

- Aluminium doesn't corrode in moist air because it has a protective layer of **aluminium oxide** which doesn't flake off the surface.

G–E

D–C

Materials and their properties

- A material is chosen because of its **properties**. For example, a car is made of: **metals** and **alloys** (copper, iron, steel, lead and aluminium), **plastics**, **glass** and **fibres**.

- **Aluminium** and **iron** are: good **conductors** of **electricity**; **malleable** (easily beaten into thin sheets); and not very strong (they only become strong when they're made into **alloys**).

- There are important differences between aluminium and iron:
  - it's easy to separate iron from aluminium because iron is magnetic and aluminium isn't
  - iron is more dense than aluminium
  - iron corrodes easily and aluminium doesn't.

- Alloys often have different and more useful properties than the pure metals they're made from. **Steel** (an alloy made of iron and carbon) is stronger and harder than iron and doesn't rust as easily as pure iron.

- Steel and aluminium can both be used to make **car bodies**, but each material has its advantages:
  - iron is stronger and harder   – aluminium is lighter   – aluminium corrodes less.

G–E

D–C

Recycling

Recycling car material using an electromagnet.

- The advantages of recycling in the car industry are:
  - aluminium and iron are **finite resources** (they will eventually run out)
  - it avoids environmental damage due to mining and quarrying
  - it reduces the amount of rubbish that goes into landfill sites

  - more recycling of metals means that less metal ore needs to be mined
  - recycling of iron and aluminium saves money and energy compared to making them from their ores.

- European Union law requires 85% (increasing to 95% in the future) of a car to be recyclable. Technology has to be developed to separate all the different materials used in making a car.

- Benefits of recycling other materials used in a car include:
  - less crude oil is used to make **plastics** and less non-biodegradeable waste is dumped
  - recycling **batteries** reduces the dumping of toxic materials into the environment.

G–E

D–C

Questions

(Grades G-E)

1 Which two chemicals are both needed for iron to rust?

(Grades D-C)

2 Explain how aluminium is protected from corrosion in moist air.

(Grades G-E)

3 Which metal is more dense: iron or aluminium?

(Grades D-C)

4 Give two reasons why a car should be made from aluminium.

Clean air

G–E

Clean air

- **Air** is a mixture of different gases:
  - **oxygen** – **nitrogen** – **water vapour** – **carbon dioxide**

- The amount of water vapour in the air changes, but the amounts of the other gases in the air remain almost constant.

- The levels of gases in the air depend on:
  - **combustion** and **respiration**, which increase the level of carbon dioxide and decrease the level of oxygen
  - **photosynthesis**, which decreases the level of carbon dioxide and increases the level of oxygen.

D–C

- 'Clean air' is made up of 78% nitrogen, 21% oxygen and of the remaining 1%, only 0.035% is carbon dioxide.

- There's a balance between processes that use up carbon dioxide and make oxygen, and processes that use up oxygen and make carbon dioxide. These processes are shown in the **carbon cycle**.

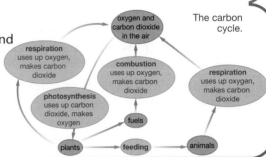

The carbon cycle.

The atmosphere

D–C

- Scientists **know** that gases trapped in liquid rock under the surface of the Earth are always escaping. This happens in volcanoes.

- Scientists **guess** about the original atmosphere of the Earth. It's known that at some point in the Earth's history, microbes developed that could photosynthesise. These organisms could remove carbon dioxide and add oxygen. Eventually the level of oxygen reached what it is today.

Pollution

G–E

- **Pollutants** are substances made by human activity that harm the environment. The atmosphere contains a large number of pollutants. The main ones are shown in the table.

pollutant	carbon monoxide	oxides of nitrogen	sulphur dioxide
environmental problem	a poisonous gas	photochemical smog and acid rain	acid rain kills plants and aquatic life, erodes stonework
origin of pollutant	incomplete combustion of petrol	formed in the internal combustion engine	sulphur impurities in fossil fuels

D–C

- **Atmospheric pollution** also affects people's health. The EU and the UK government have introduced many laws about pollution control, but still more controls are needed.

- A car fitted with a **catalytic converter** changes carbon monoxide into carbon dioxide. At the same time oxides of nitrogen are converted into nitrogen.

Questions

Grades G-E

1 What does combustion do to the levels of gases in the air?

Grades D-C

2 Which process in the carbon cycle uses up carbon dioxide?

Grades G-E

3 Which pollutant dissolves in water to produce acid which erodes statues?

Grades D-C

4 What does a catalytic converter do?

Faster or slower (1)

Rates of reaction

- A **chemical reaction** takes place when reactant **particles** hit or collide with each other.

- In a chemical reaction, **reactants** are made into **products**: reactants ———▶ products

- The **rate of reaction** measures how much product is made each second. Some reactions are very **fast** (**burning**) and others are very **slow** (**rusting**).

- If you measure the rate of reaction between magnesium and dilute hydrochloric acid, the **reaction time** is the time taken for all the magnesium to react.
  – The shorter the reaction time, the faster the reaction.
  – When the reaction stops, no more gas is made.
  – The reaction stops when one of the reactants is used up.

Changing rates of reaction

- The speed of a reaction can be increased by increasing the:
  – **concentration** of the reactants
  – **temperature** of the reactants
  – **pressure** of the reactants that are gases
  – **surface area** of the reactants.

- The more collisions there are in a reaction, the faster the reaction. The particles must be moving very fast and have lots of **kinetic energy** for collisions to occur.

The rate of a chemical reaction can be increased by increasing the **concentration**.
– As the concentration increases the particles become more crowded.
– Instead of four particles of **A**, there are ten particles of **A** in the same volume.
– The particles are more crowded, so there are more collisions and the rate of reaction increases.
– Graph A shows that a higher concentration of acid reacted with magnesium results in a quicker reaction rate, with the same amount of hydrogen collected. The gradient of the blue line is greater than the red line.

low concentration   high concentration

○ reacting particle of substance **A**
● reacting particle of substance **B**

Graph A. time (seconds)

The rate of a chemical reaction can be increased by increasing the **temperature**.
– Particles move faster as the temperature increases.
– The reacting particles have more kinetic energy (shown by the thicker arrows) so the number of collisions increases and the rate of reaction increases.
– Graph B shows that in the same experiment between magnesium and acid a higher temperature results in a quicker reaction rate, with the same amount of hydrogen collected. The gradient of the blue line is greater than the red.

low temperature   high temperature

○ reacting particle of substance **A**
● reacting particle of substance **B**

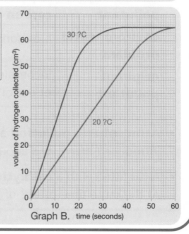

Graph B. time (seconds)

Questions

1 Write down three ways that the rate of a reaction can be altered.

2 Use ideas about particles to explain how the rate of a reaction can be altered.

3 How can the time taken for a reaction between magnesium and acid be measured?

4 If a reaction between the same mass of magnesium and excess acid is measured at two different temperatures, the total volume of gas produced doesn't change. Explain why.

Faster or slower (2)

Explosions

- An **explosion** happens when a reaction takes place very quickly. Explosions can include:
  - burning hydrogen
  - custard powder
  - TNT or dynamite.

- During an explosion, a large volume of gaseous products are released, moving outwards from the reaction at great speed causing the explosive effect.
- **Combustible powders** often cause explosions.
  - A powder reacts with oxygen to make large volumes of carbon dioxide and water vapour.
  - A factory using combustible powders such as sulphur, flour, custard powder or even wood dust must be very careful. The factory owners must ensure that the powders can't reach the open atmosphere and that the chance of producing a spark is very small.

Rates of reaction

- Powdered reactants always react faster than lumps.

  - A powdered reactant has a much larger **surface area** than the same mass of a block of reactant.
  - As the surface area of a solid reactant increases, so does the rate of reaction.

Fewer reacting particles of **B** can be in contact with reacting particles of **A**. As the surface area increases there are more collisions which means the rate of reaction increases.

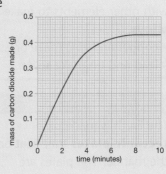

○ reacting particle of substance **A**
○ reacting particle of substance **B**   small surface area   large surface area

The graph shows how the rate of reaction between calcium carbonate and dilute hydrochloric acid is measured.
- As the reaction takes place, the mass on the balance (where the reacting substances are placed) decreases. This is because carbon dioxide gas is escaping.

$$CaCO_3 + 2HCl \longrightarrow CaCl_2 + H_2O + CO_2$$

- The **gradient** of the graph is a measure of the rate of reaction. As the reaction takes place, the rate of reaction becomes less and less because the concentration of acid and the mass of calcium carbonate decrease.
- As the reaction proceeds there are fewer collisions between reactants.

Catalysts

- A **catalyst** is a substance added to a chemical reaction to make the reaction go faster.

- A catalyst:
  - increases the rate of a reaction
  - is unchanged at the end of a reaction
  - is needed in small quantities to catalyse a large mass of reactants.

Questions

(Grades D-C)
1 Give two examples of combustible powders.

(Grades G-E)
2 Which reacts faster: powdered reactants or lumps of a reactant?

(Grades D-C)
3 Why is only 50 cm³ of hydrogen gas produced when using a 0.135 g lump of zinc with acid, compared to 100 cm³ of gas produced when using a 0.27 g lump of zinc?

(Grades G-E)
4 What's a catalyst?

C2 Summary

Paints and pigments

Paints are made from:
- **coloured rock** (pigment) particles
- **solvent**
- **binding medium**.

Paint is a **colloid**. It dries when the solvent evaporates.

Thermochromic pigments change colour on heating. **Phosphorescent pigments** glow in the dark. They store energy and release it as light over time.

Building materials

Building materials come from the ground. We use them directly or we turn the rock into concrete, glass and brick. Sand is turned into glass.

Huge amounts of **limestone** are quarried to make cement. Limestone is heated to thermally decompose it.

Metals

Iron and aluminium are used in cars. Iron rusts, but aluminium doesn't. Iron is more dense than aluminium.

Metals from cars are easy to recycle. Plastics need more legislation.

Metals are extracted from metal ores. When they corrode, they change into oxides again.

Pure metals can be mixed with other elements to make **alloys**.
- copper and zinc make brass
- lead and tin make solder.

Rusting is the chemical reaction between iron, oxygen and water. Acid rain accelerates this.

Earth and atmosphere

The Earth is made of **tectonic plates** that float on the mantle. The plates are moving all the time.

Moving tectonic plates trigger volcanic eruptions.

The atmosphere used to be poisonous, but plants produced oxygen. The composition of the atmosphere is now 21% oxygen and 78% nitrogen.

If molten rock cools slowly the crystals that are formed are bigger.

Carbon dioxide is given out in **combustion** but taken in during **photosynthesis**.

The Earth's original atmosphere came from gases escaping from the interior of the Earth.

Fast or slow?

Rates of reaction are affected by:
- **temperature**
- **surface area**
- **concentration**
- **catalysts**.

Explosions are chemical reactions that happen very quickly.

The higher the temperature, the faster the particles move. This increases the rate of reaction.

Collecting energy from the Sun

Unlimited energy

- The **Sun** is the **renewable** source of energy for the Earth.
- **Light** from the Sun allows plants to **photosynthesise** and **heat** from the Sun provides the warmth living things need.

Photocells

- **Photocells** use **light**, and **solar cells** use **light from the Sun** to produce **direct current** (dc) electricity. This means they can be used in remote locations.
  - The **larger** the area of the **photocell**, the more electricity is produced.
  - The **greater** the **light intensity**, the more electricity is produced.

Why do you think there's a photocell on top of the parking meter?

- The **advantages** of **photocells** are:
  - they're robust and don't need much maintenance
  - they don't need any fuel or long power cables
  - they don't cause pollution or contribute to climate change
  - they use a renewable energy resource.

- The only **disadvantage** is that they don't produce electricity when it's dark.

Renewable energy

- **Solar panels** use energy from the Sun to heat water. Solar panels are black to absorb as much **radiation** as possible and the warmed water in their tubes passes to a storage tank by **convection**.

- **Convection currents** are formed in the air when there are differences in land temperature. This is known as **wind**.

- Wind can be used to turn a **wind turbine** and produce **electricity**.

cool dense air

warm less dense air

cool surface

warm surface

What causes a convection current?

- Moving air has **kinetic energy** which is transferred into electricity by a wind turbine.

- A house that uses **passive solar heating** makes use of direct sunlight. It has large windows facing the Sun (South) and small windows facing North.
  - During the **day**, energy from the Sun warms the walls and floors.
  - During the **night**, the walls and floors radiate energy back into the room.

- Curved solar reflectors **focus** energy from the Sun.

Top Tip!

In the Southern Hemisphere, the larger windows will need to face North.

Questions

Grades G-E

1 What's the difference between a photocell and a solar cell?

Grades D-C

2 Some roadside warning signs are powered using photocells. Suggest why.

Grades G-E

3 Why is a solar panel coloured black?

Grades D-C

4 Why do the large windows in a solar-heated house have to face North in Australia but South in England?

Generating electricity

The dynamo effect

- A **dynamo** is one example of a **generator**. A **magnet** rotates inside a coil of wire to produce **alternating current** (ac).

- If a wire is moved near a magnet, or vice versa, alternating current is produced in the wire.

- The **current** from a dynamo can be increased by:
  - using a **stronger** magnet
  - **increasing** the number of **turns** on the coil
  - **rotating** the magnet **faster**.

- The voltage and frequency from a dynamo can be displayed on an **oscilloscope**.

- The formula to work out the frequency is:
  frequency (in hertz, Hz) = 1 ÷ period (in seconds, s)

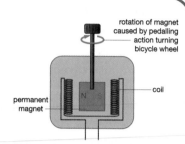

rotation of magnet caused by pedalling action turning bicycle wheel

coil

permanent magnet

What changes could you make to this dynamo to increase the current output?

Generators

- The **generator** at a power station works like a dynamo.

- A simple generator consists of a coil of wire rotating between the poles of a magnet to produce a current in the coil.

Top Tip!
It's the relative movement of the magnet and coil that's important.

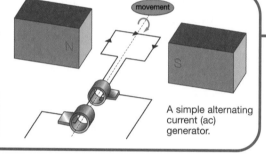

movement

A simple alternating current (ac) generator.

Distributing electricity

- Most power stations use **fossil fuels** as their energy source.

- The **National Grid** distributes electricity to **consumers**.

- Energy is lost from the overhead power lines to the surroundings as heat.

- In a **power station**, **fuel** is burned to heat water to produce **steam**. Steam at high pressure turns a **turbine** which then drives a **generator**.

Transformers

Top Tip!
A transformer *doesn't* change alternating current to direct current.

- A **transformer** changes the size of an alternating voltage.

- Some transformers increase (**step-up**) voltages, others decrease (**step-down**) voltages.

- The **National Grid** distributes electricity around the country at high voltages. This means that:
  - there's less energy loss
  - the distribution costs are lower
  - electricity prices are cheaper.

Questions

Grades G-E

1 What type of current is produced by **a** a battery **b** a dynamo?

2 Write down two examples of fossil fuels used in power stations.

Grades D-C

3 Suggest why steam is used to turn a turbine at most power stations.

4 What are the advantages of distributing electricity around the country at high voltages?

Fuels for power

Energy sources

- Most **power stations** use **non-renewable fossil fuels** as their energy source: coal, gas and oil.

- Some modern power stations use **renewable biomass** as their energy source: wood, straw and manure.

- **Nuclear power stations** use **non-renewable uranium** as their energy source.

- A **fuel** burns in air to release energy in the form of heat.

- **Biomass** can be burned. It's usually allowed to **ferment** to produce **methane**, which is then burned.

- **Nuclear fuels** don't burn. In a nuclear reactor, uranium atoms split and release lots of energy in the form of heat.

- Nuclear reactions in power stations have to be controlled to avoid an explosion.

Nuclear waste

- **Nuclear power stations** don't produce carbon dioxide or smoke, and they don't contribute to climate change.

- Waste from a nuclear power station is **radioactive**.
  – Low-level radioactive waste can be pumped out to sea.
  – High-level waste has to be stored in steel drums deep underground.

- **Radiation** from nuclear waste causes **ionisation**, which causes a change in the structure of any atom exposed to the radiation.
  – The cells of our bodies are made of many different atoms. DNA is an important chemical in a cell and can be changed when it's exposed to radiation. The cell behaves differently to normal and this is called **mutation**.
  – One effect of mutation is for a cell to divide in an uncontrolled way. This can lead to **cancer**.

- **Waste** from a nuclear reactor can remain radioactive for thousands of years.

- **Plutonium**, one of the waste products, can be used to make nuclear weapons. Nuclear bombs destroy everything in a very large area and make that area unusable for a long time.

Power

- **Power** is a measure of the rate at which energy is used. The unit is the **watt** (W). The formula for power is: power = voltage × current

- **Electrical consumption** is the amount of energy that's been used. The unit is the **kilowatt hour** (kWh). The formula for energy used is:
  energy used = power × time

- The formula to work out the **cost** of using an electrical appliance is:
  cost of electricity used = energy used × cost per kWh

Questions

Grades G-E

1 What's meant by a non-renewable energy source?
2 Write down one advantage of producing electricity from a nuclear power station.

Grades D-C

3 Explain how exposure to nuclear radiation can cause cancer.
4 How much does it cost to use a 2 kW toaster for $\frac{1}{4}$ hour if electricity costs 10p per kWh?

Nuclear radiations

Background radiation

- The nuclear radiation that's always around us is called **background radiation**.

- Radioactivity is measured with a Geiger-Müller (GM) tube connected to a **ratemeter** – a **Geiger counter**.

- Most background radiation is naturally occurring.

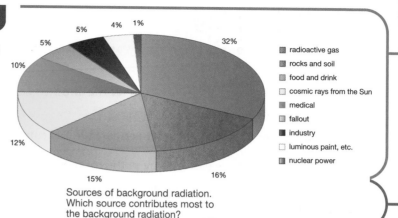

- radioactive gas
- rocks and soil
- food and drink
- cosmic rays from the Sun
- medical
- fallout
- industry
- luminous paint, etc.
- nuclear power

Sources of background radiation. Which source contributes most to the background radiation?

G–E

D–C

Properties of ionising radiations

- The three main types of **ionising radiations** are: **alpha** (α), **beta** (β) and **gamma** (γ).

- Alpha, beta and gamma radiations come from the nucleus of an atom. **Alpha** radiation causes the **most** ionisation and **gamma** radiation the **least**. Ionisation produces **charged particles**.

type of ionising radiation	range	penetration through materials
alpha	short – a few centimetres	easily absorbed by a sheet of paper or card
beta	about 1 metre	absorbed by a few millimetres of aluminium
gamma	theoretically infinite	can pass through metres of lead or concrete

G–E

D–C

Handling radioactivity

- When handling radioactivity, you should:
  - wear suitable protective clothing
  - not handle it directly
  - keep a safe distance: handle with tongs
  - use shielding to absorb radiation
  - use for the minimum time necessary.

- **Radioactive waste** is disposed of at sea, buried in landfill sites or stored deep underground.

G–E

D–C

Uses of radioactivity

- Ionising radiation kills cells and living organisms. **Cobalt-60** is a radioactive material used to treat **cancers**.

- Radiation kills bacteria and microbes, so medical instruments are **sterilised** by gamma radiation.

- Some radioactive waste can be **reprocessed** into new, useful radioactive material.

- **Alpha radiation** is used in **smoke alarms**.

- **Beta** or **gamma** sources are used in **rolling mills** to conrol **thickness**.

- **Gamma** sources are injected into the body as **tracers**.

G–E

D–C

Questions

1 What is meant by the term 'background radiation'?

2 What fraction of background radiation comes from natural sources?

3 Suggest two reasons why a school teacher always handles a radioactive source with tongs.

4 A rolling mill uses beta radiation to control the thickness of cardboard. Explain why alpha radiation and gamma radiation aren't used.

Our magnetic field

Magnetic fields

- The Earth behaves as if it has a large magnet at its centre. The **magnetic field** around the Earth is similar to the field due to a **bar magnet**.

- The Earth's magnetic field is strongest at the North and South **poles**.

- A **compass** points towards magnetic North along the direction of the magnetic field.

- The **outer core** of the Earth is mainly **molten iron**; it's too hot to be magnetic.

- An **electric current** in a wire or a coil has a magnetic field around it too.

Top Tip!
The model of Earth's magnetic field has a magnetic South pole at geographic North.

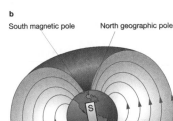

South magnetic pole   North geographic pole

- The magnetic field around a coil of wire is similar to the field around a bar magnet.

- A magnet shouldn't be brought close to a **television** or **computer monitor** because it causes the electron beam in the tube to change direction. The beam strikes the wrong part of the screen giving a distorted picture.

Compare the shape of the magnetic fields around **a** a bar magnet and **b** the Earth.

Satellites

- The Moon is a **natural satellite** that orbits the Earth.

- The Moon and the Earth were probably formed by two planets colliding 4.6 billion years ago.

- **Artificial satellites** orbit the Earth. They provide information about **weather**, are used as **navigation aids**, and for **communication** and **spying**.

Solar effects

- The **Sun** is a source of **ionising radiation**.

- **Solar flares** erupt from the Sun's surface and cause disruption to communication signals.

- The **energy** from a solar flare is equivalent to that from a million hydrogen bombs.

- Large numbers of charged particles are emitted at very high speeds. These produce magnetic fields that interact with the Earth's magnetic field.

Origin of the Moon

- When the Solar System was formed, there were probably more planets than today.

- Scientists believe there was another planet in the same orbit as the Earth.
  - The two planets collided and were both almost totally destroyed.
  - Iron became concentrated at the core of the new Earth, less dense rocks started to orbit.
  - These rocks clumped together to form the Moon.
  - The Earth and the Moon were rotating much faster than they do now – the Moon caused the speed of rotation to slow down.

Questions

(Grades G-E)

1 Draw a diagram to show the magnetic field around a bar magnet. Show clearly the magnetic poles and the direction of the magnetic field.

(Grades D-C)

2 A television screen is coated with red, blue and green dots. What happens to the dots when they're hit by a beam of electrons?

(Grades G-E)

3 What's a satellite?

(Grades D-C)

4 How do scientists believe the Moon was formed?

Exploring our Solar System

The Universe

- Our **galaxy** is called the **Milky Way**, and the Milky Way is one of the galaxies that make up the **Universe**.

- **Stars** are very hot and produce their own light – that's why we can see them.

- Sometimes we can see **meteors**, **comets** and **orbiting satellites** because they reflect light.

- **Meteorites** are large rocks that don't burn up as they fall to Earth.

- We can't see **black holes**.

- The Earth is one of the planets in our Solar System orbiting the Sun.

- There may be another planet, three times further away than Pluto and larger.

- In August 2006, scientists decided that Pluto shouldn't be considered a planet because of its size and orbit shape.

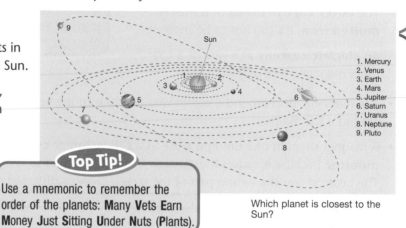

Sun

1. Mercury
2. Venus
3. Earth
4. Mars
5. Jupiter
6. Saturn
7. Uranus
8. Neptune
9. Pluto

Which planet is closest to the Sun?

Top Tip!

Use a mnemonic to remember the order of the planets: **M**any **V**ets **E**arn **M**oney **J**ust **S**itting **U**nder **N**uts (**P**lants).

Exploration

- **Radio signals** have been sent into space since 1901.

- A coded signal about life on the Earth was sent towards another star system in 1974 – it will be at least 40 000 years before we can expect a reply!

- Spacecraft showing pictures of life on the Earth and containing records of sounds from the Earth have also been sent into space.

- Unmanned spacecraft (**probes**) have explored the surface of the Moon and Mars. They can go to places where humans can't survive.

- The **Hubble Space Telescope** orbits the Earth collecting information from distant galaxies.

- The Moon is the only body in space visited by humans. **Astronauts** can wear normal clothing in a pressurised spacecraft, but outside the spacecraft they need to wear special **spacesuits**.
  – A dark visor stops an astronaut being blinded.
  – The suit is pressurised and has an oxygen supply for breathing.
  – The surface of the suit facing towards the Sun can reach 120 °C.
  – The surface of the suit facing away from the Sun may be as cold as -160 °C.

- When travelling in space, astronauts experience **lower gravitational forces** than on the Earth.

It will be a long time before we can expect a reply!

Questions

1 Write down three things we can see in the sky because they reflect light.

2 Write down the names of the planets in the Solar System in order from the Sun.

3 How many years will it take for the radio message, sent in 1974, to reach the star system at which it was aimed?

4 Why do astronauts have to wear special spacesuits when outside their spacecraft?

Threats to Earth

Asteroids

G–E

- When an **asteroid** hits the Earth, it leaves a large **crater**.

- The asteroid that collided with the Earth 65 million years ago caused more than just a crater:
  - hot rocks rained down
  - there were widespread fires
  - **tsunamis** flooded large areas
  - clouds of dust and water vapour spread around the world in the upper atmosphere
  - sunlight couldn't penetrate and temperatures fell
  - 70 per cent of all species, including dinosaurs, became extinct.

D–C

- Asteroids are **mini-planets** or **planetoids** orbiting the Sun in a 'belt' between Mars and Jupiter. They're large rocks that were left over from the formation of the Solar System.

- **Geologists** have examined evidence to support the theory that asteroids have collided with the Earth.
  - Near to a crater thought to have resulted from an asteroid impact, they found quantities of the metal **iridium** - a metal not normally found in the Earth's crust but common in meteorites.
  - Many **fossils** are found below the layer of iridium, but few fossils are found above it.
  - **Tsunamis** have disturbed the fossil layers, carrying some fossil fragments up to 300 km inland.

Comets

G–E

- **Comets** are lumps of ice filled with dust and rock.

- When a comet orbits close to the Sun, the ice warms up and a **glowing tail** is thrown out. The tail is made up of the dust and rocks freed from the ice.

D–C

- Compared to the near circular orbits of the planets, the orbit of a comet is very **elliptical**. Most comets pass inside the orbit of Mercury and well beyond the orbit of Pluto.

- Solar winds blow the dust into the comet's tail so the tail always points away from the Sun.

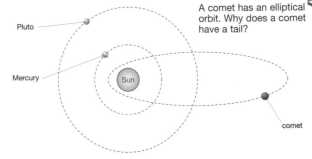

Pluto

Mercury

Sun

comet

A comet has an elliptical orbit. Why does a comet have a tail?

NEOs

G–E

- Some comets and asteroids have orbits that pass close to the orbit of the Earth. These are known as near-Earth-objects (**NEOs**) and some can be seen with a telescope. A small change in their direction could bring them on a collision course with the Earth.

D–C

- Scientists are constantly monitoring and plotting the paths of comets and other NEOs.

Top Tip!

The longer we study and plot the path of a NEO, the more accurate our prediction about its future movement and the risk of collision will be.

Questions

Grades G-E

1 What could happen if a large asteroid hit Earth?

Grades D-C

2 What's an asteroid?

Grades G-E

3 What forms the tail of a comet?

Grades D-C

4 Why is it important to constantly monitor the paths of comets and NEOs?

The Big Bang

The Universe

- Fifteen billion years ago, all of the matter in the Universe was in a single point. It was incredibly hot – millions upon millions of degrees Celsius.

- The Universe suddenly exploded; scientists call this the **Big Bang**. It expanded rapidly and cooled down. Within three seconds, electrons, protons, neutrons and the elements **hydrogen** and **helium** had formed.

- Almost all of the **galaxies** in the Universe are **moving away** from each other. The furthest galaxies are moving fastest. The Universe is expanding all the time.

- **Microwave signals** are constantly reaching Earth from all parts of the Universe.

How does this model show that the Universe is expanding?

G–E

D–C

Stars

A star is born!

- **New stars** are being formed all the time. They start as a swirling cloud of gas and dust.

- Eventually all stars will die and some stars become **black holes**. Light can't escape from a black hole.

- A medium-sized star, like the Sun, becomes a **red giant**: the core contracts, the outer part expands and cools, and it changes colour from yellow to red. During this phase, gas shells, called **planetary nebula**, are thrown out.

- The core becomes a **white dwarf** shining very brightly, but eventually cools to become a **black dwarf**.

- Large stars become **red supergiants** as the core contracts and the outer part expands.

- The core suddenly collapses to form a **neutron star** and there's an explosion called a **supernova**. Remnants from a supernova can merge to form a **new star**. The dense core of the neutron star continues to collapse until it becomes so dense it forms a **black hole**.

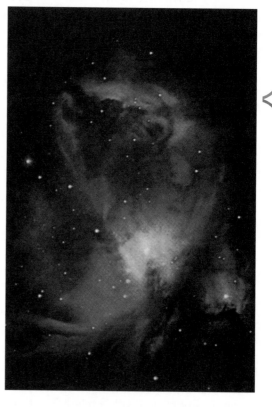

G–E

D–C

Questions

Grades G-E

1 What were the first elements formed after the Big Bang?

Grades D-C

2 Which galaxies in the Universe are moving fastest?

Grades G-E

3 Why can't we see a black hole?

Grades D-C

4 Our Sun is about 4.6 billion years old. Patrick says it may have been a star before that. Explain how this is possible.

P2 Summary

Energy sources

Kinetic energy from moving air turns the blades on a wind turbine to produce electricity.

The **Sun** is a stable energy source. It **transfers energy** as light and heat to Earth.

Photocells use the Sun's light to produce electricity.

Passive solar heating uses glass to help keep buildings warm.

Electricity generation

A **dynamo** produces electricity when coils of wire rotate inside a magnetic field. The size of the current depends on:
– the number of turns
– the strength of the field
– the speed of rotation.

Transformers change the size of the voltage and current. The National Grid transmits electricity around the country at **high voltage** and **low current**. This reduces energy loss.

Nuclear fuels are radioactive. The radiation produced can cause cancer. Waste products remain radioactive for a long time.

Fossil fuels and **biomass** are burned to produce heat.
Nuclear fuels release energy as heat. Water is heated to produce steam:
– the steam drives turbines
– turbines turn generators
– generators produce electricity.

The main forms of **ionising radiation** are:
– **alpha**
– **beta**
– **gamma**.
Their uses depend on their penetrative and ionisation properties.

The Earth's field

The **Earth** is surrounded by a **magnetic field** similar in shape to that of a coil of wire. The core of the Earth contains molten iron.

Solar flares are the result of clouds of charged particles being emitted from the Sun at high speed disturbing the magnetic field around Earth.

When two planets collide, a new planet and a moon may be formed.

The Earth and Universe

Planets, **asteroids** and **comets** orbit the Sun in our **Solar System**. The Universe consists of many galaxies.

Most **asteroids** are between Mars and Jupiter but some pass closer to Earth. They are constantly being monitored. An asteroid strike could cause climate change and species extinction.

Scientists believe that the Universe started with a **Big Bang**. **Stars** have a **finite life** depending on their size.

The **Universe** is explored by telescopes on Earth and in space. Large distances mean that it takes a long time for information to be received and inter-galactic travel is unlikely.

Molecules of life

Cells

- An **animal cell** has the following parts.

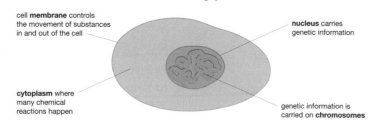

cell **membrane** controls the movement of substances in and out of the cell

nucleus carries genetic information

cytoplasm where many chemical reactions happen

genetic information is carried on **chromosomes**

An animal cell.

G–E

> **Top Tip!**
> Animal cells don't have a cell wall – they have a cell membrane. Remember your skin is soft, not hard like a stem!

- **Cell respiration** is carried out inside **mitochondria**. During respiration, energy is released from glucose in the presence of oxygen.

D–C

DNA

- **DNA** is a chemical found inside the **nucleus**. It forms structures called **chromosomes** with sections called **genes**. Each gene is a code for making **proteins**. Our bodies need to make proteins to grow and to repair cells. Everyone has his or her own unique **DNA code**.

G–E

- The structure of DNA helps it to copy itself every time a cell divides. This is called **DNA replication**.

- Each gene in DNA holds the code for making a protein that our bodies need by using amino acids from our food. Proteins are made by joining amino acids into a chain. The DNA controls the order of amino acids and the production of proteins is called **protein synthesis**.

- DNA can be used to identify people by **DNA fingerprinting**, which produces a pattern of unique bands like a barcode.

D–C

Enzymes

- Many chemical reactions are slow. **Enzymes** can be added to speed up reactions.

G–E

- An enzyme is a protein that acts as a biological catalyst. It speeds up reactions within the cell such as respiration, photosynthesis and protein synthesis.

- Each enzyme is **specific** to a **substrate**. In an enzyme-catalysed reaction, substrate molecules are changed into **product** molecules. For example, the enzyme amylase changes starch (substrate) into sugar (product).

D–C

- pH and temperature affect enzyme-controlled reactions.

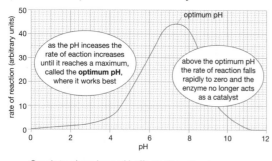

as the pH increases the rate of reaction increases until it reaches a maximum, called the **optimum pH**, where it works best

above the optimum pH the rate of reaction falls rapidly to zero and the enzyme no longer acts as a catalyst

Graph to show how pH affects the rate of an enzyme-catalysed reaction.

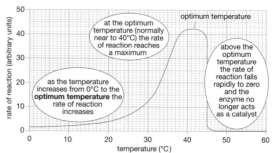

at the optimum temperature (normally near to 40°C) the rate of reaction reaches a maximum

as the temperature increases from 0°C to the **optimum temperature** the rate of reaction increases

above the optimum temperature the rate of reaction falls rapidly to zero and the enzyme no longer acts as a catalyst

Graph to show how temperature affects the rate of an enzyme-catalysed reaction.

Questions

Grades G-E

1 In which part of the cell would you find DNA?

Grades D-C

2 Describe how proteins are made.

Grades G-E

3 Why are enzymes added to reactions?

Grades D-C

4 What is meant by the term 'enzyme'?

Diffusion

Human body

- The body moves different substances in and out of cells across the **cell membrane**.

- When we **breathe in**, **oxygen** moves from the **lungs** into the red blood cells, then from the red blood cells into body tissue. **Carbon dioxide** moves from body tissue into the blood, then from the blood into the lungs.

- After **eating**, digested food molecules move from the **small intestine** into the blood. From the blood they go into body tissue.

- Food and oxygen pass from the **mother's** blood to the **foetus's** blood by **diffusion**. The foetus makes carbon dioxide and other wastes in its body which pass into the mother's blood.

- **Diffusion** is the movement of a substance from a region of **high concentration** to a region of **low concentration.**

- **Alveoli** in the **lungs** have a higher concentration of oxygen than the blood that surrounds them. The oxygen diffuses into the blood and carbon dioxide diffuses from the blood into the alveoli. To maintain this **gas exchange**, breathing takes place.

- After **eating** there is a high concentration of digested food molecules in the small intestine, which causes them to diffuse through the cells of the small intestine wall into the blood.

- A **foetus** needs to be supplied with food and oxygen from its mother so it can develop. The mother's blood contains dissolved food such as glucose and amino acids. The mother's blood and the foetus's blood come close together in the **placenta**, but they don't mix since they may be different blood groups and mixing would be fatal.

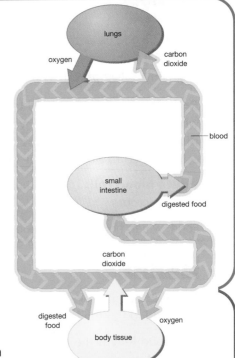

The movement of substances in and out of the body.

Top Tip!

High concentration = orange squash before the water.
Low concentration = orange squash with lots of water added.

Plants

- Plants use carbon dioxide for **photosynthesis**. They get carbon dioxide from the air by moving it in through the leaves. At the same time, oxygen moves out of the leaves. Plants lose **water** by **evaporation** from the surface of the leaves.

- Carbon dioxide **diffuses** into the leaf through small pores called **stomata** and oxygen diffuses out. Water is lost through stomata by diffusion and evaporation.

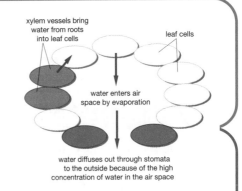

xylem vessels bring water from roots into leaf cells

leaf cells

water enters air space by evaporation

water diffuses out through stomata to the outside because of the high concentration of water in the air space

The movement of water in plants.

Questions

1 When oxygen leaves the blood, where does it go?

2 Exactly where in the lungs does gas exchange take place?

3 By which process is water lost from the surface of the leaf?

4 Describe how water is lost from the leaf.

Keep it moving

Blood

- Blood is made up of the following components: a yellow liquid called **plasma**; tiny **red blood cells** that transport oxygen; **white blood cells** that defend against disease; and tiny cell fragments called **platelets** which help to clot the blood.

- **Red blood cells** are adapted to carry as much oxygen as possible. They contain **haemoglobin**, which joins to oxygen, and have **no nucleus** so there's more room to store oxygen. They are **disc-shaped** and have a **dent** on both sides to help absorb oxygen. They are **tiny** so they can carry oxygen to all parts of the body.

- **White blood cells** change shape so they can wrap around (**engulf**) microbes. They don't fight or kill microbes.

- Food, water, hormones, antibodies and waste products are carried in the **plasma**.

Heart

- The **heart** pumps blood around the body. There are two sides to a heart: the **right** side pumps blood to the **lungs** and the **left** side pumps blood to the **rest of the body**.

- The blood **leaves** the heart in **arteries** where the **pressure** is **high**, and **returns** to the heart at **low pressure** in **veins**.

- Cholesterol can build up in arteries, which can slow blood flow and cause a heart attack. The heart or parts of the heart can be replaced either mechanically or biologically.

- The **valves** of the heart prevent the backflow of blood.

- **Coronary arteries** supply the heart with **food** and **oxygen**.

- Too much **cholesterol** in the diet can cause serious **heart problems** and even the need for a **heart transplant**. There are some problems with heart transplants such as: shortage of donors, rejection, dependency on drugs, and difficulty in matching tissue to age and size.

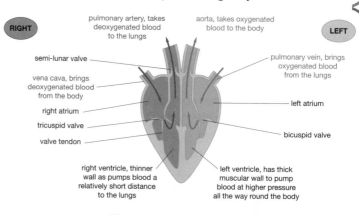

The structure and function of the heart.

Using **mechanical replacements** also has problems, such as the size of the replacement, the power supply needed and the chance of rejection.

Circulatory system

- The vessels of the **circulatory system** work together to transport substances around the body.
  - **Arteries** transport blood away from the heart.
  - **Veins** transport blood to the heart.
  - **Capillaries** join arteries to veins. Materials such as oxygen are exchanged between the capillaries and the body tissue.

Questions

Grades D–C

1 Name the chemical in blood that joins to oxygen.

Grades G–E

2 Name the chemical that can slow blood flow in arteries.

Grades D–C

3 Suggest one advantage and one disadvantage mechanical replacements have over heart transplants.

4 Name the three types of blood vessels.

Divide and rule

Cells

- Every day thousands of skin cells are lost from the skin as they are continuously rubbed off. All of these cells need to be replaced. To make new cells the body carries out **cell division**. Cells divide whenever the body needs to:
  - **grow**
  - **replace** worn out cells
  - **repair** damaged tissue.

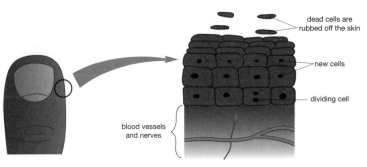

dead cells are rubbed off the skin

new cells

dividing cell

blood vessels and nerves

Skin cells dividing to make new skin.

- Humans are made up of millions of cells: they are **multi-cellular**. This gives them many advantages.
  - Multi-cellular organisms can grow large.
  - Cell **differentiation** takes place. Cells change shape or size to carry out different jobs.
  - Organisms become more complex and develop different organ systems.

- Humans have **23 pairs** of **chromosomes**. The chromosomes in a pair look the same and carry similar information. They are called **homologous** pairs. When a cell has pairs of chromosomes it's called a **diploid** cell (i.e. it has the full set of chromosomes).

- During growth a type of cell division called **mitosis** makes new cells. The new cells are exact copies and contain 23 pairs of chromosomes.

Sex cells

- **Eggs** and **sperm** are called sex cells or reproductive **gametes**. Gametes join during **fertilisation**. Eggs and sperm are specially adapted to do their jobs.
  - An egg is much larger than a sperm because it contains food for the developing embryo.
  - A sperm has a tail to help it move.
  - A male releases millions of sperm to increase the chance of one reaching an egg.
  - The nucleus of an egg and sperm contains genes.

- Gametes have half a set of chromosomes called the **haploid number**. During fertilisation the gametes join to form a **zygote**. The zygote is diploid and can develop into an embryo.

- **Meiosis** is a special type of cell division that produces gametes. Reproduction using meiosis results in a lot of genetic **variation** within a species.

Top Tip!

Body cells are **diploid**. **Gametes** are **haploid** (they only have half the number of chromosomes).

- Sperm are specially adapted to swim a long way. Each sperm has lots of **mitochondria** to release energy for motion.

A sperm cell.

acrosome contains enzymes to digest the egg cell membrane

many mitochondria in cells release energy

nucleus

Questions

Grades G-E

1 Write down three reasons why the body needs to make new cells.

Grades D-C

2 How many chromosomes are there in a diploid human cell?

Grades G-E

3 What is meant by the term 'fertilisation'?

Grades D-C

4 Name the type of cell division that produces haploid cells.

Growing up

Cells

- A **plant cell** has the following parts.

- For a fertilised egg to grow into a foetus, the cells need to divide and change. The cells change so they can carry out different jobs. Some cells turn into nerve cells and others change into bone cells. This change is called cell **differentiation**.

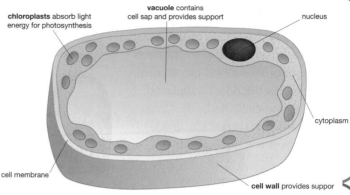

chloroplasts absorb light energy for photosynthesis

vacuole contains cell sap and provides support

nucleus

cytoplasm

cell membrane

cell wall provides suppor

A plant cell.

- A few days after an egg is fertilised it contains a group of cells called **stem cells**. Stem cells all have the same simple cell structure. They divide and then differentiate to form all the different specialised cells in the body. As the embryo grows, all the specialised cells form **tissues** and **organs**.

- This table shows how plant and animal cells are similar and different.

plant cell	animal cell
has nucleus, cytoplasm and cell membrane	has nucleus, cytoplasm and cell membrane
cellulose cell wall for support	no cell wall
most have chloroplasts for photosynthesis	no chloroplasts
large vacuole containing cell sap	may have a small vacuole but no cell sap

Growth

- There are five main stages in human growth:

  infancy　　**childhood**　　**adolescence (puberty)**　　**adulthood (maturity)**　　**old age**

- Animals and plants grow in different ways. Animals tend to grow to a certain size and then stop. Plants can continue to grow.

Gestation

- **Gestation** is the length of time from fertilisation to birth. The larger the animal the longer gestation tends to be. This is because the animal needs time to develop enough to survive outside the uterus. An elephant has a gestation of 700 days but a rat only has 22 days.

- Different parts of the **foetus** and **baby** grow at different rates. The brain and head develop quickly to co-ordinate the complex human structure and chemical activity.

- After a baby is born it has regular growth checks. The baby's weight and head size are recorded to check that the baby is growing at a normal rate.

Questions

1 Name the part of a plant cell that absorbs light energy.

2 Name two structures found in plant cells but *not* in animal cells.

3 List the five stages of human growth.

4 Explain why elephants have a longer gestation period than mice.

Controlling plant growth

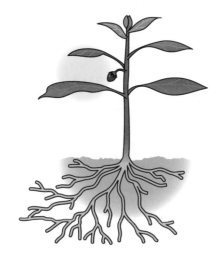 *(decorative title underline)*

Grades

Plant hormones

G–E

- Plants make special chemicals called **hormones**. Hormones control different processes in a plant:
  - growth of **shoots** towards light
  - growth of **roots** downwards into the soil, in response to **gravity**
  - growth of **flowers**
  - ripening of **fruit**.

- Farmers can spray their crops with hormones to make the plants grow fruit, or use hormones to slow down growth.

D–C

- Farmers, gardeners and fruit growers mostly use man-made plant hormones such as **synthetic auxin**. This is sprayed on selected crops to kill weeds and is known as a **selective weedkiller**.

- **Rooting powder** is used to stimulate roots to grow from plant cuttings.

- Hormones are used to make fruit grow without the flowers being fertilised. This means the fruits have no pips, such as seedless grapes.

- A hormone called **ethene** is sprayed on bananas to ripen them ready for sale.

- The seeds taken from a parent plant are **dormant**, which means **germination** won't take place. Hormones are used to break the dormancy and make the seed germinate.

Responses

D–C

- A plant is **sensitive** and responds to different **stimuli**.

- A hormone called **auxin** controls the response. This is made in the tips of roots and shoots and travels through a plant in **solution**.
  - Plant **shoots** grow **towards light** – **positive phototropism**.
  - Plant **roots** grow **away from light** – **negative phototropism**.
  - Plant **shoots** grow **away from** the pull of **gravity** – **negative geotropism**.
  - Plant **roots** grow **with** the pull of gravity – **positive geotropism**.

Shoots are positively phototropic and negatively geotropic.
Roots are negatively phototropic and positively geotropic.

Top Tip!

The 'positive' and 'negative' terms are difficult to remember. If it's positive it grows towards the stimulus. Imagine being positively attracted to someone!

Questions

Grades G-E

1 Name the chemical used to ripen fruit in plants.

2 Suggest why farmers may use hormones to slow down the growth of fruit.

Grades D-C

3 Describe the effect of rooting powder on plant cuttings.

4 Which part of the plant shows positive geotropism?

New genes for old

Selective breeding

- Farmers choose an animal or plant with the **characteristics** they want so that they produce more, for example, cows that make lots of milk. Then they **breed** them to produce **offspring** that have the desired characteristics.

- **Selective breeding** is used to breed a cow that has a high **yield** of creamy milk.
  – Choose types of cows that produce lots of milk (Friesians) or creamy milk (Jerseys).
  – **Cross-breed** them by mating a cow with a bull.
  – Select the best offspring that produce large quantities of creamy milk.
  – Repeat the selection and breeding process for a number of generations.

Mutation

- Plants and animals can also change by a process called **mutation**, which happens when there is a change in their genes.

- Changes to genes, called **mutations**, usually cause harm to the organism. For example, in **haemophilia** the blood doesn't clot.

- Some mutations can be advantageous and give a better chance of survival, such as bacteria that can mutate and become resistant to antibiotics.

- Mutations can be caused by radiation (X-rays), chemicals in cigarette smoke or by chance.

Transferring genes

- Scientists can take **genes** from one organism and put them into a different organism. This is called **genetic engineering** or **genetic modification (GM)**.

- Genetic engineering involves adding a gene to the DNA of an organism. For example, a bacterium has been genetically engineered to make human insulin for people with diabetes.

- Rice doesn't contain vitamin A. Scientists have taken the gene to make **beta-carotene** from carrots and put it into rice plants. Humans eating this rice can then convert the beta-carotene into vitamin A.

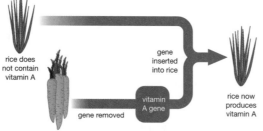

- Scientists are developing crops that are resistant to herbicides, frost and disease. This will enable more crops to grow in difficult places, but the gene may have harmful effects on humans who eat the plants.

Questions

1 Suggest a characteristic in chickens that a farmer may want.

2 Describe the main processes in selective breeding.

3 What is meant by the term 'genetic modification'?

4 Suggest one disadvantage of genetically modified crops.

More of the same

Cloning animals

- **Cloning** is used to make copies of animals and plants. The copies are called **clones** and are **genetically identical**. Cloning involves only one parent. It is an example of **asexual reproduction**. Dolly the sheep was the first mammal to be cloned from an adult.

- Sometimes clones are produced naturally, such as human twins, which are called **natural clones**.

- **Embryo transplantation** can be used to clone cows. Embryo calves are placed in surrogate mothers to develop in the normal way.

- Scientists are hoping to **clone pigs** to supply organs for transplants into humans.

- **Human embryos** could also be cloned to provide **stem cells**. These could be transplanted into people suffering from diabetes to make their own insulin. However, people are concerned that this would be unethical because the embryo is a living thing. Some people are also afraid that scientists will clone adult humans.

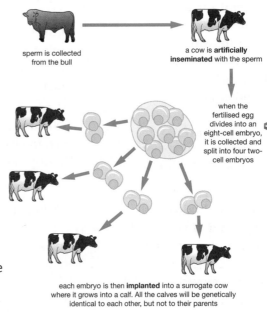

sperm is collected from the bull

a cow is **artificially inseminated** with the sperm

when the fertilised egg divides into an eight-cell embryo, it is collected and split into four two-cell embryos

each embryo is then **implanted** into a surrogate cow where it grows into a calf. All the calves will be genetically identical to each other, but not to their parents

Embryo transplantation in cows.

Cloning plants

- Many plants reproduce by asexual reproduction where there is no fertilisation between male and female gametes. New plants are produced using **cell division** only. The new plants are **clones** of the parent plant.
  - The part of the **potato** we eat is the potato **tuber**. Left long enough, it will grow shoots and roots from the 'eye' (bud).
  - **Strawberries** grow stems called **runners**. The runners spread over the ground and have buds that grow into new strawberry plants.

- Gardeners can clone plants by taking **cuttings**. The cutting is dipped into a hormone powder which helps it to grow roots.

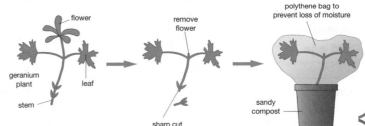

flower

remove flower

polythene bag to prevent loss of moisture

geranium plant

leaf

stem

sharp cut

sandy compost

Taking a cutting.

- Here are some **advantages** of cloning plants:
  - all the plants are genetically identical
  - cloning produces lots of identical plants more quickly
  - cloning enables growers to produce plants that are difficult to grow from seed.

- And some **disadvantages**:
  - the plants are all genetically identical so if the environment changes or a new disease breaks out, it's unlikely that any of the plants will survive
  - cloning plants over many years has resulted in little genetic variation.

Questions

(Grades G-E)

1 Explain what is meant by the term 'genetically identical'.

(Grades D-C)

2 Name the process used to clone cows.

(Grades G-E)

3 Describe how strawberry plants reproduce asexually.

(Grades D-C)

4 Suggest one disadvantage of cloning plants.

B3 Summary

Molecules of life

Chromosomes are made of **DNA**. A section of DNA is called a **gene**. Each gene codes for a particular **protein**.

Animals and plant cells have the following parts:
– **membrane**
– **nucleus**
– **cytoplasm**
– **mitochondria**.
Plant cells also have:
– **cell wall**
– **vacuole**
– **chloroplasts**.

DNA is found in the **nucleus** of the cell. DNA carries **coded information**; individuals have their own unique DNA.

DNA fingerprints can be used to identify individuals.

Enzymes are **biological catalysts**, they catalyse chemical reactions in the body.

Proteins are made up of chains of **amino acids**. When the cell makes a new protein it has to join the amino acids together in the correct order.

Blood and diffusion

Carbon dioxide and **oxygen diffuse** in and out of plants through the leaves.

Diffusion of substances takes place in the **placenta**. Food and oxygen diffuses into the foetal blood. Carbon dioxide and waste diffuses into the mother's blood.

Blood is moved around the body in:
– **arteries**
– **veins**
– **capillaries**.
The heart pumps the blood to the lungs and body.

In the lungs **oxygen** diffuses into **red blood cells**. **Carbon dioxide** diffuses from the blood into the **lungs**.

Food diffuses from the s**mall intestine** into the **blood**.

Cell division and growth

There are five stages in human growth:
– **infancy**
– **childhood**
– **adolescence**
– **maturity**
– **old age**.

Eggs and sperm are special cells called **gametes**. A type of cell division called **meiosis** produces them. Gametes contain the **haploid** number of chromosomes. **Fertilisation** takes place when an egg and sperm join. The result is a diploid cell called a **zygote**.

After cells divide they become specialised. This is called **differentiation**. Undifferentiated cells are called **stem cells**. Stem cells can develop into different types of cells, tissues and organs.

Cells divide by **mitosis** so that organisms can grow and replace old cells.

Plant hormones

Hormones are chemicals that control:
– **growth of shoots and roots**
– **flowering**
– **ripening of fruit**.
Hormones have commercial uses such as:
– **weedkillers**
– **rooting powder**.

The hormone called **auxin** is involved in the plant's response to light (**phototropism**) and the plant's response to gravity (**geotropism**).

Using cells and DNA

Selective breeding involves breeding organisms with the best characteristics.

Cloning involves producing genetically identical copies.

Genetic engineering involves taking **genes** from one organism and putting them into another.

What are atoms like?

Atoms

- An **atom** is a **nucleus** surrounded by **electrons**.
  - The **nucleus** carries a **positive charge**.
  - The **electrons** carry a **negative charge**.

- An atom is **neutral** because it has the same number of positive charges in the nucleus as there are negatively charged electrons around it.

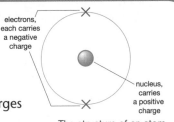

electrons, each carries a negative charge

nucleus, carries a positive charge

The structure of an atom.

- The nucleus of an atom is made up of **protons** and **neutrons**.
- The **atomic number** is the number of protons in an atom.
- The **mass number** is the total number of protons and neutrons in an atom.

	relative charge	relative mass
electron	−1	0.0005 (zero)
proton	+1	1
neutron	0	1

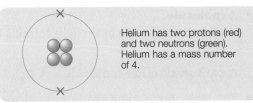

Helium has two protons (red) and two neutrons (green). Helium has a mass number of 4.

- The same number of electrons occupies the space around the protons of the nucleus.

- Electrons occupy **shells**. The electron shell nearest to the nucleus takes up to 2 electrons. The second shell takes up to 8 electrons.

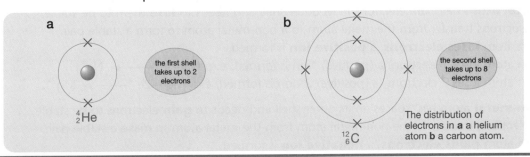

a

the first shell takes up to 2 electrons

$^4_2$He

b

the second shell takes up to 8 electrons

The distribution of electrons in **a** a helium atom **b** a carbon atom.

$^{12}_6$C

The periodic table

- Each atom has an **atomic number**. This number is written next to the **symbol** of an element in the **periodic table**. If the atomic number of an element is known, it can be identified by looking on the periodic table.

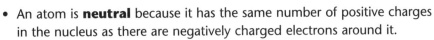

the atomic number of Lithium is 3

							H hydrogen 1									He helium 2
Li lithium 3	Be beryllium 4		B boron 5	C carbon 6	N nitrogen 7	O oxygen 8	F fluorine 9	Ne neon 10
Na sodium 11	Mg magnesium 12		Al aluminium 13	Si silicon 14	P phosphorus 15	S sulfur 16	Cl chlorine 17	Ar argon 18
K potassium 19	Ca calcium 20							

- An **element** is a substance that can't be broken down chemically. There are just over 100 **elements** in the **periodic table**. An element contains the same type of atom.

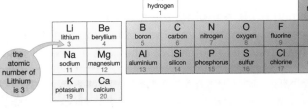

element   +   element   =   compound

- A **compound** is a substance that contains at least two elements that are chemically joined together.

- The elements in the periodic table are arranged in **ascending** atomic number.
- **Isotopes** are elements that have the same atomic number but different mass numbers.

Questions

Grades G-E

1 What's the charge on a proton?

Grades D-C

2 What's the mass of one proton?

3 How many electrons does an atom of sodium have?

Grades G-E

4 Write down the names of the elements in copper sulphide.

Ionic bonding

Forming ions and molecules

- An **atom**:
  - is the smallest particle that can bond with another particle
  - can be recognised from its symbol, which has one capital letter and one lower case letter
  - has no numbers and no charge in its symbol.

  The symbol for a **magnesium atom** is: **Mg**

- An **ion**:
  - is a **charged atom** or **group of atoms**
  - has a positive or negative charge on it.

  A **calcium ion** has two positive charges: **Ca^{2+}**

- A **molecule**:
  - has more than one atom in its formula and no charge.

  A **carbon dioxide molecule** is: **CO_2**

Atom	Ion	Molecule
H	H^+	H_2
O	O^{2-}	H_2O
Mg	Mg^{2+}	MgO
Cl	Cl^-	$MgCl_2$
Na	Na^+	NaOH
S	SO_4^{2-}	$MgSO_4$

- The table shows some examples of elements as atoms, ions and molecules.

Ionic bonding

- A **metal atom** has extra electrons in its outer shell and needs to **lose** them to be stable. The electrons transfer from the metal atom to a non-metal atom to form a stable pair.
  - If an atom **loses electrons**, a **positive ion** is formed.
  - If an atom loses 1 electron, a (positive) $^+$ion is formed, e.g. $Na - e^- \longrightarrow Na^+$.
  - If an atom loses 2 electrons, a (positive) 2^+ ion is formed, e.g. $Mg - 2e^- \longrightarrow Mg^{2+}$.

- A **non-metal** atom has 'spaces' in its outer shell and needs to **gain** electrons to be stable. The electrons transfer to the non-metal atom from the metal atom to make a stable pair.
  - If an atom **gains electrons**, a **negative ion** is formed.
  - If an atom gains 1 electron, a (negative) $^-$ion is formed, e.g. $F + e^- \longrightarrow F^-$.
  - If an atom gains 2 electrons, a (negative) 2^- ion is formed, e.g. $O + 2e^- \longrightarrow O^{2-}$.

- During **ionic bonding**, the metal atom becomes a positive ion and the non-metal atom becomes a negative ion. The positive ion and the negative ion then attract one another. They attract to a number of other ions to make a solid **lattice**.

Properties of sodium chloride and magnesium oxide

- **Sodium chloride**:
  - has a high **melting point**
  - dissolves in water
  - doesn't conduct electricity when solid.

- **Magnesium oxide**:
  - has a very high melting point
  - doesn't conduct electricity when solid.

- Sodium chloride **solution** conducts electricity.

- **Molten** (melted) magnesium oxide and sodium chloride conduct electricity.

Questions

Grades G-E

1 Is Mg^{2+} an atom, a molecule or an ion?

Grades D-C

2 Explain how a negative ion is made from a neutral atom.

3 Explain the difference between how a metal atom and a non-metal atom transfer electrons.

Grades G-E

4 Describe the melting point of magnesium oxide.

Covalent bonding

Molecules

- A **molecule** forms when two or more non-metal **atoms** bond together.

- If a molecule has the formula O_2, it has two oxygen atoms in its **molecular formula**, so the total number of atoms is two.

  Displayed formula: O＝O   Model:

- If a molecule has the formula CO_2, it has one carbon atom and two oxygen atoms in its molecular formula, so the total number of atoms is three.

  Displayed formula: O＝C＝O Model:

Covalent bonding

- There are two types of bonding:
  - **ionic bonding** leads to large crystals
  - **covalent bonding** leads to molecules; examples are carbon dioxide (gas) and water (liquid), which have low melting points.

- Non-metals combine together by sharing **electrons**. This is called **covalent bonding**.

A molecule of **water** is made up of three atoms: two hydrogen and one oxygen. – Oxygen has six electrons in its outer shell; it needs two more electrons to be complete. – Hydrogen atoms each have one electron in their only shell, so the oxygen outer shell is shared with each of the hydrogen electrons. – Now each of the hydrogen atoms has a share of two more electrons making the shell full.	A molecule of **carbon dioxide** is made up of three atoms: two oxygen and one carbon. – Carbon has four electrons in its outer shell; it needs four more electrons to be complete. – Oxygen atoms each have six electrons in their outer shell, so they each need two more electrons to be complete. – The oxygen outer shell is shared with two of the electrons of the carbon outer shell each. – Now each of the oxygen atoms has a share of two more electrons making the shell full.

- Carbon dioxide and water don't conduct electricity because they're covalently bonded.

The periodic table

- Look at part of the periodic table, right.
  - elements in the same **group** are in the same vertical **column**. They have similar **chemical properties**.
  - elements in the same **period** are in the same horizontal **row**.

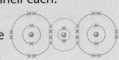

this column has the elements of group 1

H hydrogen 1							He helium 2
Li lithium 3	Be beryllium 4	B boron 5	C carbon 6	N nitrogen 7	O oxygen 8	F fluorine 9	Ne neon 10
Na sodium 11	Mg magnesium 12	Al aluminium 13	Si silicon 14	P phosphorus 15	S sulfur 16	Cl chlorine 17	Ar argon 18
K potassium 19	Ca calcium 20						

this row has the elements of period 3

- This is how to tell which **group number** an element belongs to:
  - group 1 elements have 1 electron in the outer shell
  - group 7 elements have 7 electrons in the outer shell
  - group 8 elements have 8 electrons in the outer shell.

Group 1   Group 7   Group 8

element	electron	period
H	1	1
Li	2,1	2
Na	2, 8, 1	3

- This is how to tell which **period** an element belongs to:
  - electrons in only **one shell**, it's in the **first period**
  - electrons in **two shells**, it's in the **second period**
  - electrons in **three shells**, it's in the **third period**.

Questions

Grades G-E

1 How many different types of atom are there in a molecule of KNO_3?

Grades D-C

2 Draw a model showing the bonding of a water molecule.

Grades G-E

3 Name two elements in group 7.

Grades D-C

4 Sulphur has an electron pattern of 2, 8, 6. To which period does it belong?

The group 1 elements

Alkali metals

- Group 1 metals are called the **alkali metals**.
  - Alkali metals are stored under oil because they react with air and water.
  - Alkali metals react vigorously with water.

- The order of **reactivity** of the alkali metals with water is:
  - sodium is more reactive than lithium
  - potassium is more reactive than sodium.

lithium, sodium and potassium are metals in group 1

			H hydrogen 1				He helium 2
Li lithium 3	Be beryllium 4	B boron 5	C carbon 6	N nitrogen 7	O oxygen 8	F fluorine 9	Ne neon 10
Na sodium 11	Mg magnesium 12	Al aluminium 13	Si silicon 14	P phosphorus 15	S sulfur 16	Cl chlorine 17	Ar argon 18
K potassium 19	Ca calcium 20						

G–E

- When lithium, sodium and potassium react with water:
  - they float on the surface because their **density** is less than the density of water
  - hydrogen gas is given off
  - the metal reacts with water to form an **alkali** – the **hydroxide** of the metal.

D–C

Lithium reacts quickly and vigorously with water.

lithium + water $\longrightarrow$ lithium hydroxide + hydrogen

Sodium reacts very quickly and vigorously with water and forms sodium hydroxide.

sodium + water $\longrightarrow$ sodium hydroxide + hydrogen

Potassium reacts extremely vigorously with water and produces a lilac flame and forms potassium hydroxide.

potassium + water $\longrightarrow$ potassium hydroxide + hydrogen

- Reactivity of the alkali metals with water increases down group 1.

reactivity increases down the group

	melting point in °C	boiling point in °C
$_3$Li	179	1317
$_{11}$Na	98	892
$_{19}$K	64	774

- These group 1 metals have **1 electron** in their **outer shell**. This is why group 1 metals have similar properties.

Flame tests

G–E

- If you burn compounds in a flame:
  - the flame turns **red** for **lithium**
  - the flame turns **yellow** for **sodium**
  - the flame turns **lilac** for **potassium**.

- If you want to test the flame colours of the chemicals:
  - put on safety goggles; moisten a flame test wire with dilute hydrochloric acid
  - dip the flame test wire into the sample of solid chemical
  - hold the flame test wire in a blue Bunsen burner flame
  - record the colour of the flame in a table.

D–C

Questions

Grades G-E

1 Why are group 1 metals kept under oil?

Grades D-C

2 Why does potassium float on water?

3 Explain why group 1 metals have similar properties.

Grades G-E

4 Which alkali metal compound produces a lilac flame?

The group 7 elements

The halogens

- Group 7 elements are called the **halogens** and include fluorine, chlorine, bromine and iodine. They have many uses:
  – **chlorine** is used to sterilise water
  – **iodine** is used to sterilise wounds
  – **sodium chloride** is used as a preservative, a flavouring and in the manufacture of chlorine.

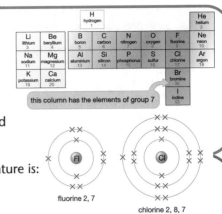

this column has the elements of group 7

- The **physical appearance** of the halogens at room temperature is:
  – chlorine is a green gas
  – bromine is an orange liquid
  – iodine is a grey solid.

- Group 7 elements have similar properties as they all have **7 electrons** in their **outer shell**.

fluorine 2, 7

chlorine 2, 8, 7

bromine (outer shell only shown) 7

iodine (outer shell only shown) 7

Halogens and reactivity

- There's a **trend** in the **reactivity** of halogens.
  – Fluorine is more reactive than chlorine.
  – Chlorine is more reactive than bromine.
  – Bromine is more reactive than iodine.

reactivity

- Halogens react vigorously with **alkali metals**.

- When a halogen reacts with an alkali metal, a **metal halide** is made.

When lithium reacts with chlorine, the metal halide made is lithium chloride.
lithium + chlorine ⟶ lithium chloride

When potassium reacts with iodine, the metal halide made is potassium iodide.
potassium + iodine ⟶ potassium iodide

When sodium reacts with bromine, the metal halide made is sodium bromide.
sodium + bromine ⟶ sodium bromide

Displacement reactions of halogens

- The **reactivity** of the halogens decreases down the group.

- If halogens are bubbled through **solutions of metal halides**, there are two possibilities:
  – **no reaction**: if the halogen is less reactive than the halide in solution.
  – a **displacement reaction**: if the halogen is more reactive than the halide in solution.

Chlorine displaces the bromide to form bromine solution.
chlorine + potassium bromide ⟶ potassium chloride + bromine (orange solution)

Chlorine also displaces iodides from sodium iodide solution.
chlorine + sodium iodide ⟶ sodium chloride + iodine (red-brown solution)

Bromine displaces iodides from solutions.
bromine + potassium iodide ⟶ potassium bromide + iodine

Questions

Grades G–E

1 What are the elements of group 7 collectively known as?

2 Which element is more reactive: chlorine or iodine?

Grades D–C

3 Write down the word equation for the reaction between potassium and bromine.

4 Why does iodine *not* displace bromine from potassium bromide?

Electrolysis

Conducting liquids

- **Electrolysis** is the **decomposition** of a liquid using electricity. During electrolysis:
  - the **electrolyte** is a liquid that conducts electricity
  - the **anode** is the positive electrode
  - the **cathode** is the negative electrode
  - **anions** are negative ions attracted to the anode
  - **cations** are positive ions attracted to the cathode.

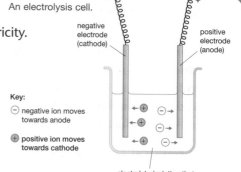

An electrolysis cell.

negative electrode (cathode)

positive electrode (anode)

Key:
⊖ negative ion moves towards anode
⊕ positive ion moves towards cathode

electrolyte (solution that conducts electricity)

The electrolysis of dilute sulphuric acid

Electrolysis of sulphuric acid in the laboratory.

- The key features of the electrolysis of dilute sulphuric acid are:
  - the **electrolyte** is a dilute solution of sulphuric acid
  - two **electrodes** are connected to a dc source of electric current, between 6 V and 12 V, and placed into the electrolyte
  - the electrode connected to the negative terminal is the **cathode**
  - the electrode connected to the positive terminal is the **anode**.

- When the current is switched on, bubbles of gas appear at both electrodes. Water splits into two ions: H^+ is the positive ion and OH^- is the negative ion.
  - H^+ is attracted to the negative cathode and discharged as hydrogen gas, H_2.
  - OH^- is attracted to the positive anode and discharged as oxygen gas, O_2.

- Twice the volume of hydrogen gas is given off as oxygen gas because the formula of the compound breaking up is H_2O.

Testing for hydrogen and oxygen

- Sulphuric acid solution can be broken down into hydrogen and oxygen.

- To test for the two gases: a lighted splint burns with a **'pop'** in **hydrogen**, a glowing splint **relights** in **oxygen**.

Electrolytic decomposition

- Aluminium is extracted from its **mineral** using electricity. The mineral is called **bauxite**.

- The key features in the production of aluminium by electrolytic decomposition are:
  - the use of molten aluminium oxide
  - aluminium is formed at the graphite cathode; oxygen is formed at the graphite anode
  - the anodes are gradually worn away by **oxidation**
  - the process requires a high electrical energy input.

- The word equation for the **decomposition of aluminium oxide** is:

  aluminium oxide ⟶ aluminium + oxygen

Questions

1 Which electrode is the positive electrode?

2 The ratio of hydrogen gas to oxygen gas made during the electrolysis of water is 2:1. Explain why.

3 What's the mineral from which aluminium is extracted?

4 What happens to the anodes during the process of electrolysis of aluminium?

Transition elements

Transition elements

G–E

- Transition elements are **metals** and have typical metallic properties. They:
  - conduct heat
  - are shiny
  - conduct electricity
  - are sonorous (ring when struck)
  - are malleable
  - are ductile.

- **Copper** and **iron** are examples of transition elements.

				H\nhydrogen\n1	Key												8\n4\nHe\nhelium\n2

The periodic table with the transition elements shaded in grey.

D–C

- A **compound** that contains a transition element is often coloured:
  - copper compounds are blue
  - iron(II) compounds are pale green
  - iron(III) compounds are orange/brown.

- A transition element and its compounds are often **catalysts**:
  - iron is used in the **Haber process** to make ammonia, which is used in fertilisers
  - nickel is used to harden the oils in the manufacture of margarine.

Top Tip!

A catalyst is an element or compound that changes the rate of a chemical reaction without taking part in the reaction. Catalysts are unchanged during the reaction.

Precipitation reaction

G–E

- **Precipitation** is a reaction between solutions that makes an **insoluble solid**. When a yellow solution of potassium chromate is added to a colourless solution of silver nitrate, a precipitate (solid) is formed. The **precipitate** is orange-coloured silver chromate.

Thermal decomposition

G–E

- **Thermal decomposition** is a reaction in which a substance is broken down into at least two other substances by heat.

D–C

- If a transition metal carbonate is heated, it **decomposes** to form a metal oxide and carbon dioxide. On heating:
  - $FeCO_3$ decomposes forming iron oxide and carbon dioxide
  - $CuCO_3$ decomposes forming copper oxide and carbon dioxide
  - $MnCO_3$ decomposes forming manganese oxide and carbon dioxide
  - $ZnCO_3$ decomposes forming zinc oxide and carbon dioxide.

- The metal carbonates change colour during decomposition.

Top Tip!

The test for carbon dioxide is that it turns limewater milky.

Sodium hydroxide solution

D–C

- Sodium hydroxide solution is used to identify the presence of transition metal ions in solution:
  - Cu^{2+} ions form a blue solid
  - Fe^{2+} ions form a grey/green solid
  - Fe^{3+} ions form an orange **gelatinous** solid.

Questions

Grades G-E

1 What are the symbols for copper and nickel?

Grades D-C

2 What colour are iron(III) compounds?

Grades G-E

3 What's a precipitation reaction?

Grades D-C

4 There's a difference between Fe^{2+} ions and Fe^{3+} ions. How would you show this using sodium hydroxide.

Metal structure and properties

Properties of metals

G–E

- Most metals:
  - are lustrous
  - are hard
  - have a high density
  - are good conductors of heat and electricity
  - have a high melting point and a high boiling point.

- The uses of a metal depend on its properties:
  - **Iron** is used to make **steel**. Steel is very strong and is used to make bridges.
  - **Copper** is used to make **brass**. Brass conducts electricity well and is used to make electrical wires.

D–C

- **Physical properties** of metals include:
  - having high thermal conductivity
  - being good conductors of heat
  - being malleable
  - being ductile
  - having high melting points and boiling points because of strong metallic bonds.

  Copper is often used for the base or the whole of saucepans because it has high thermal conductivity.

- **Chemical properties** of metals include:
  - resistance to attack by oxygen or acids.

  Copper is also resistant to chemicals, which is another reason why it's used for saucepans.

The structure of metals

G–E

- A metal is made of particles held together by **metallic bonds**.

- The particles in **solid metals** are:
  - close together
  - in a regular arrangement.

- A metal has a structure that contains crystals.

Metallic bonds hold the metal together.

Conductors and superconductors

G–E

- At very low temperatures some metals become **superconductors**.

D–C

- When metals conduct electricity, the electrons in the metal move. Superconductors are materials that conduct electricity with little or no resistance.

- When a substance goes from its normal state to a superconducting state, it no longer has any magnetic field. This is called the Meissner effect.

- The potential benefits of superconductors are:
  - loss-free power transmission
  - super-fast electronic circuits
  - powerful electromagnets.

The permanent magnet levitates above the superconductor.

Questions

(Grades G-E)

1 Write down three properties of metals.

(Grades D-C)

2 Metals have high melting points. Explain why.

(Grades G-E)

3 What happens to some metals at very low temperatures?

(Grades D-C)

4 What happens if a small permanent magnet is put above a superconductor?

C3 Summary

Atoms and bonding

Atoms have a **positive nucleus** surrounded by **negative electrons**. The electrons are arranged in shells. The outer shell of electrons needs to be full to be **stable**.

Atoms **join together** to make **molecules** or large crystal structures. There are two ways in which atoms can bond, by **making ions** or by **sharing electrons**.

Ions are made when atoms **lose** or **gain electrons**. Ions are either positive or negative. If electrons are lost, a positive ion is made.

Atoms can share electrons to make molecules containing two or more atoms. This bonding is called **covalent bonding**.

Periodic table

Group 1 metals react vigorously with water to make alkaline solutions.

Group 7 elements are called the **halogens**. They have seven electrons in their outer shell.

The periodic table lists all elements in order of their **atomic number**.

The periodic table lists elements in **groups**. The elements have similar properties. They're in groups according to the pattern of their electrons.

Electrolysis

Pure water doesn't conduct electricity. If sulphuric acid is added, it decomposes to give hydrogen and oxygen gases.

Electrolysis is the decomposition of a substance using electricity.

Aluminium is made by the electrolysis of bauxite. The mineral has to be purified before it's used. The aluminium is deposited at the cathode.

Transition metals and metal structure

Iron, gold, silver, copper, nickel and chromium are all **transition metals**. They're used in a wide range of objects. Mercury is used in thermometers as it's a liquid metal at room temperature.

Metals **conduct electricity** easily because electrons move through the structure easily. At low temperatures some metals can become **superconductors**. These show little or no resistance when conducting electricity.

Transition metal compounds are usually coloured. The compounds often dissolve in water to make coloured solutions. The solutions react with sodium hydroxide to make **coloured precipitates**.

Speed

Measuring speed

- **Speed** is a measure of how fast something is going.

- To determine speed you need to measure **distance** and **time**. Faster objects cover more distance in a given time.

- The unit of speed is **metres per second** (m/s) or **kilometres per hour** (km/h). So, if a car is travelling at 80 km/h it goes a distance of 80 km in a time of 1 hour.

- In everyday situations a **tape measure** or **trundle wheel** and **stopwatch** can be used to measure speed. On roads, a speed camera takes a photograph as a car passes. A second photograph is taken 0.5 seconds later. There are white lines painted on the road 1.5 m apart which show how far the car travels in 0.5 seconds.

  A car passing over six lines travels:
  1.5 × 6 = 9 m in 0.5 seconds
  This means the average speed of the car was 18 m/s or 65 km/h.

> **Top Tip!**
> Remember! 1 km = 1000 m, 1 hour = 60 × 60 = 3600 seconds.

- The formula for speed is: $\text{average speed} = \dfrac{\text{distance}}{\text{time}} = \dfrac{d}{t}$

  We write 'average speed' because the speed of a car changes during a journey.

  An aircraft travels 1800 km in 2 hours.

  $\text{Average speed} = \dfrac{1800}{2} = 900 \text{ km/h} = 900 \times \dfrac{1000}{3600} = 250 \text{ m/s}.$

- Increasing the speed means increasing the distance travelled in the same time. Increasing the speed reduces the time needed to cover the same distance.

Distance-time graphs

- Drawing a graph of distance against time shows how the distance moved by an object from its starting point changes over time.

- In graph **a**, the distance doesn't change over time, so the car is stationary. In graph **b**, the distance travelled by the car increases at a steady rate. It's travelling at a constant speed.

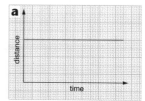 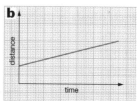 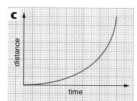

- The **gradient** of a distance-time graph tells you about the speed of the object. A higher speed means a steeper gradient.

- In graph **b**, the distance travelled by the object each second is the same. The gradient is constant, so the speed is constant.

- In graph **c**, the distance travelled by the object each second increases as the time increases. The gradient increases, so there is an increase in the speed of the object.

Questions

(Grades G-E)

1 What is the unit of speed?

(Grades D-C)

2 A car travels 600 m in 20 seconds. What is its average speed?

(Grades G-E)

3 Sketch distance-time graphs for **a** a stationary train **b** a train travelling at a steady speed.

(Grades D-C)

4 What can you say about the gradient of a distance-time graph for a car journey if **a** the car is travelling at a steady speed **b** the speed of the car is decreasing?

Changing speed

Speed-time graphs

- A speed-time graph shows how the **speed** of an object, for example a car, changes with **time**.

- The **gradient** (slope) of a line tells us how the speed is changing. In graph **a**, the line is horizontal so the speed is constant. In graph **b**, the line has a positive gradient so the speed is increasing. In graph **c**, the line has a negative gradient so the speed is decreasing.

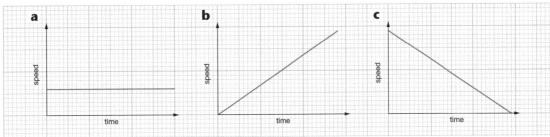

- If the speed is increasing, the object is **accelerating**. If the speed is decreasing, the object is **decelerating**.

- The area under a speed-time graph is equal to the **distance** travelled.
  - The speed of car B in the graph is increasing more rapidly than the speed of car A, so car B is travelling further than car A in the same time.
  - The area under line B is greater than the area under line A for the same time.
  - The speed of car D is decreasing more rapidly than the speed of car C, so car D isn't travelling as far as car C in the same time.
  - The area under line D is smaller than the area under line C for the same time.

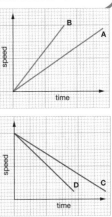

Top Tip!

Don't confuse distance-time and speed-time graphs. Always look at the axes carefully.

Acceleration

- A change of speed is called **acceleration**.
- Acceleration is measured in **metres per second squared** (m/s^2).
- In graph **a**, the car has a constant acceleration of 5 m/s^2. In graph **b**, the car has a constant deceleration of 5 m/s^2.

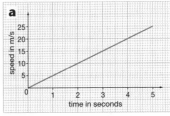

- The formula for measuring acceleration is:

$$acceleration = \frac{change\ in\ speed}{time\ taken}$$

- A negative acceleration shows the car is decelerating.

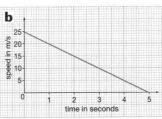

A new car boasts a rapid acceleration of 0 to 108 km/h in 6 seconds.

A speed of 108 km/h is $\dfrac{108 \times 1000}{60 \times 60} = 30$ m/s

Acceleration $= \dfrac{change\ in\ speed}{time\ taken} = \dfrac{(30 - 0)}{6} = 5$ m/s^2

This means the speed of the car increases by 5 m/s every second.

Top Tip!

An object at a constant acceleration is different to an object at a constant speed.

Questions

1 Sketch a speed-time graph for a car that speeds up and then travels at a constant speed.

2 What can be found from the area under a speed-time graph?

3 The speed of a car changes from 20 m/s to 10 m/s. Is it accelerating or decelerating?

4 Find the acceleration of a cat that goes from 0 to 5 m/s in 2 seconds when chasing a mouse.

Forces and motion

What do forces do?

- To **accelerate** in a car, the driver presses on the accelerator pedal.
  - This increases the pull of the engine (forward **force**).
  - If the pedal is pressed down further, the pull of the engine is greater.
  - The **acceleration** increases.

for the same forward force:	for the same mass:	for the same acceleration:
more mass has less acceleration	more forward force causes more acceleration	a large mass needs a large forward force
less mass has more acceleration	less forward force causes less acceleration	a small mass needs a small forward force

Force, mass and acceleration

- If the forces acting on an object are balanced, it's at rest or has a constant speed.
  If the forces acting on an object are unbalanced, it speeds up or slows down.

- The unit of force is the **Newton** (N).

- $F = ma$, where F = unbalanced force in N, m = mass in kg and a = acceleration in m/s^2.

  Marie pulls a sledge of mass 5 kg with an acceleration of 2 m/s^2 in the snow. The force needed to do this is: $F = ma$ $F = 5 \times 2 = 10$ N

Top Tip!

Remember the correct units when using $F = ma$; F in N, m in kg, a in m/s^2.

Car safety

- A car driver cannot stop a car immediately. It takes the driver time to react to danger.
  - **Thinking distance** is the distance travelled between a driver seeing a danger and taking action to avoid it.
  - **Braking distance** is the distance travelled before a car comes to a stop after the brakes have been applied.

- The formula for **stopping distance** is:

  stopping distance = thinking distance + braking distance

- **Thinking time**, and therefore thinking distance, may increase if a driver is:
  - tired
  - under the influence of alcohol or other drugs
  - distracted or lacks concentration.

- For safe driving, it is important to:
  - keep an appropriate distance from the car in front
  - have different speed limits for different types of road
  - slow down when road conditions are poor.

Top Tip!

For an alert driver, thinking time (or **reaction time**) is about 0.7 seconds.

Questions

1 Two cars, A and B, have the same engine. Car A has a larger mass than car B. Which car has the greater acceleration?

2 Calculate the unbalanced force needed to give a car of mass 1200 kg an acceleration of 5 m/s^2.

3 What do we call the distance travelled by a car in stopping after the brakes have been applied?

4 Tim's reaction time is 0.7 seconds. Calculate his thinking distance when travelling at 20 m/s.

Work and power

Work

G–E

- **Work** is done when a **force** moves. For example, when a person climbs stairs, the force moved is their weight.

- The amount of work done depends on:
  - the **size** of the force acting on an object
  - the **distance** the object is moved.

- **Energy** is needed to do work. The more work is done, the more energy is needed.

- Work and energy are measured in **joules** (J).

- **Work** is done when a force moves in the direction in which the force acts.

D–C

- The formula for work done is:
  work done = force × distance moved (in the direction of the force)

  If a person weighs 700 N, the work he does against gravity when he jumps 80 cm is:
  work done = force × distance moved = 700 × 0.8 = 560 J

Power

G–E

- **Power** is the rate at which work is done.

- If two lifts, one old and one new, do the same amount of work but the new one does it more quickly, the new lift has a greater power.

- Power is measured in **watts** (W). A large amount of power is measured in **kilowatts** (kW). 1 kW = 1000 W.

Top Tip!

Always check the units when doing calculations on work, power and energy.

D–C

- The formula for power is:
  $$\text{power} = \frac{\text{work done}}{\text{time taken}}$$

- A person's power is greater when they run than when they walk.

Fuel

G–E

- Some cars are more powerful than others. They travel faster and cover the same distance in a shorter time and require more fuel. They have greater **fuel consumption**.

- Fuel is expensive and a car with high fuel consumption is expensive to run.

D–C

- Fuel pollutes the environment.
  - Car exhaust gases, especially carbon dioxide, are harmful.
  - Carbon dioxide is also a major source of **greenhouse gases**, which contribute to climate change.

Questions

(Grades G-E)

1 Sam lifts an 8 N weight a height of 3 m. Ali lifts a 10 N weight a height of 4 m. Who does more work?

(Grades D-C)

2 How much work does Lee do when he pushes a car 20 m with a force of 80 N?

(Grades G-E)

3 Jan and Meera both run up a flight of stairs in 8 seconds. Meera is more powerful than Jan. Explain.

(Grades D-C)

4 Find the power of a crane that can lift a load of 500 N through a height of 12 m in 15 seconds.

Energy on the move

Kinetic energy

- Moving objects have **kinetic energy**. Different fuels can be used to gain kinetic energy.
  - The fuel for all animals, including humans, is their food.
  - The fuel for a wind turbine is moving air (wind).
  - The fuel for a car is **petrol** or **diesel** oil.

- **Kinetic energy** increases with:
  - increasing **mass**
  - increasing **speed**.

Fuel

- **Petrol** and **diesel oil** are **fossil fuels** made from **oil**. Petrol is more **refined** than diesel oil.

- Petrol cars and diesel cars need different engines. The same amount of diesel oil contains more **energy** than petrol. A diesel engine is more **efficient** than a petrol engine.

- Some cars use more petrol or diesel oil than others and:
  - cause more **pollution**
  - cost more to run
  - decrease supplies of **non-renewable** fossil fuels.

Top Tip!

Make sure you can interpret fuel consumption tables.

- **Fuel consumption** data are based on ideal road conditions for a car driven at a steady speed in urban and non-urban conditions.

car	fuel	engine in litres	miles per gallon (mpg)	
			urban	non-urban
Renault Megane	petrol	2.0	25	32
Land-Rover	petrol	4.2	14	24

Electrically powered cars

- **Electric cars** are battery driven or solar-powered.

- Exhaust fumes from petrol-fuelled and diesel-fuelled cars cause serious pollution in towns and cities.

- Battery-driven cars do not pollute the local environment, but their batteries need to be recharged. Recharging uses electricity from a power station. Power stations pollute the local atmosphere and cause acid rain.

This hybrid electric car has solar panels on its roof that convert sunlight into additional power to supplement its battery.

Questions

1 Name the energy source for **a** a bird **b** a barbecue **c** a hydroelectric power station.

2 Suggest why a car uses more fuel per kilometre when carrying a heavy load.

3 A petrol-driven car does 40 mpg (miles per gallon) and a similar diesel-driven car does 56 mpg. Which car is more efficient?

4 Electric milk floats have been used for many years. Suggest why more people don't use electric cars.

Crumple zones

Car safety

- A moving car has **kinetic energy**. If a car is involved in a collision it has to lose kinetic energy very quickly.

- Modern cars have safety features that **absorb energy** when a vehicle stops suddenly. These are:
  - **brakes** that get hot
  - **crumple zones** that change shape
  - **seat belts** that stretch a little
  - **air bags** that inflate and squash

- Safety features can be **active** or **passive**. These are shown in the table.

active safety features	passive safety features
ABS (anti-lock braking system) brakes	electric windows
	cruise control
traction control	paddle shift controls
safety cage	adjustable seating

- All safety features must be kept in good repair.
  - Seat belts must be replaced after a crash in case the fabric has been overstretched.
  - The safety cage must be examined for possible damage after a crash.
  - Seat fixings should be checked frequently to make sure they are secure.

- On impact:
  - **crumple zones** at the front and rear of the car absorb some of its energy by changing shape or 'crumpling'
  - a **seat belt** stretches a little so that some of the person's kinetic energy is converted to elastic energy
  - an **air bag** absorbs some of the person's kinetic energy by squashing up around them.

An air bag and seat belt in action during a car accident. What parts of the man are protected?

- All these safety features:
  - absorb energy
  - change shape
  - reduce injuries.

- Active safety features include:
  - **ABS brakes** which give stability and maintain steering during hard braking. The driver gets the maximum braking force without skidding and can still steer the car.
  - **Traction control** which stops the wheels on a vehicle from spinning during rapid acceleration.
  - A car **safety cage** which is a **rigid** frame that prevents the car from collapsing and crushing the occupants in a roll-over crash.
  - Crumple zones at front and rear which keep damage away from the internal safety cage.

Top Tip!

ABS brakes don't stop a car more quickly. They give improved control and prevent skidding.

- Passive safety features help the driver to concentrate on the road.

Questions

(Grades G-E)

1 Suggest two forms of energy that a car's kinetic energy may be changed to in an accident.

2 Explain how electric windows can help to prevent car accidents.

(Grades D-C)

3 Which two car safety features protect a driver's chest in an accident?

4 Explain why cruise control is a passive safety feature.

Falling safely

Falling objects

- A falling object:
  - gets faster as it falls
  - is pulled towards the centre of Earth by a force called **weight** which is caused by the force of **gravity**.

> **Top Tip!**
> The net force acting on a parachutist = weight – air resistance.

- Objects that have a large **area of cross-section** fall more slowly. For example, if a ball and a feather are dropped, the ball hits the ground first. This slowing down **force** is called **air resistance** or **drag**.

- All objects fall with the same **acceleration** as long as the effect of **air resistance** is very small.

- The size of the air resistance force on a falling object depends on:
  - its cross-sectional area – the larger the area the greater the air resistance
  - its speed – the faster it falls the greater the air resistance.

- Air resistance has a significant effect on motion only when it is large compared to the weight of the falling object.

- The speed of a **free-fall** parachutist changes as he falls to Earth.
  - In picture 1, the weight of the parachutist is greater than air resistance. He accelerates.
  - In picture 2, the weight of the parachutist and air resistance are equal. The parachutist has reached **terminal speed** because the forces acting on him are **balanced**.
  - In picture 3, the air resistance is larger than the weight of the parachutist. He slows down and air resistance decreases.
  - In picture 4, the air resistance and weight of the parachutist are the same. He reaches a new, slower terminal speed.

1
600 N

2
600 N
600 N

3
1000 N
600 N

4
600 N
600 N

- Free-falling objects:
  - don't experience air resistance
  - accelerate downwards at the same rate irrespective of mass or shape.

- Examples of free-falling objects are:
  - objects falling above the Earth's atmosphere
  - objects falling on the Moon   – the Moon itself.

> **Top Tip!**
> On the Moon and in outer Space there is no drag because there is no atmosphere.

Friction

- All **friction** forces slow an object down.

- Friction forces on vehicles can be reduced by **streamlining** their shapes by:
  - shaping car roof boxes
  - making cars wedge-like in shape
  - angling lorry deflectors.

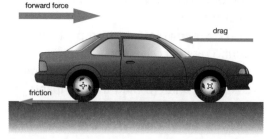

forward force
drag
friction

Streamlining reduces drag and increases the top speed.

Questions

(Grades G-E)

1 Why does a feather fall more slowly than a ball?

(Grades D-C)

2 Name the two forces acting on a parachutist. What can you say about these forces **a** at the start of the descent **b** when terminal speed is reached **c** when the parachute opens.

(Grades G-E)

3 What effect does a streamlined shape have on the motion of a car?

(Grades D-C)

4 Describe how air resistance changes with the speed of a falling object.

The energy of theme rides

Gravitational potential energy

- An object held above the ground has **gravitational potential energy**.

- The amount of gravitational potential energy an object has depends on:
  – its **mass** – its **height** above the ground.

Energy transfers

- A bouncing ball converts gravitational potential energy to kinetic energy and back to gravitational potential energy. It does not return to its original height because energy is transferred to other forms such as **thermal energy** and **sound energy**.

- In the diagram, the gravitational potential energy at D is less than at A.

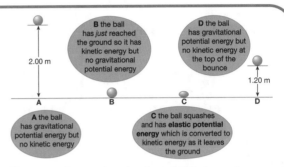

B the ball has *just* reached the ground so it has kinetic energy but no gravitational potential energy

D the ball has gravitational potential energy but no kinetic energy at the top of the bounce

A the ball has gravitational potential energy but no kinetic energy

C the ball squashes and has **elastic potential energy** which is converted to kinetic energy as it leaves the ground

The stages of energy transfer when a ball is dropped.

- A water-powered **funicular railway** has a carriage that takes on water at the top of the hill giving it extra gravitational potential energy.
  – As the carriage travels down the hillside it transfers gravitational potential energy to **kinetic energy**.
  – At the same time, it pulls up another carriage with an empty water tank on a parallel rail.

- A moving object has **kinetic energy**.

- The amount of kinetic energy an object has depends on:
  – its **mass** – its **speed**.

A funicular railway.

How a roller coaster works

- A roller coaster uses a motor to haul a train up in the air. The riders at the top of a roller coaster ride have a lot of gravitational potential energy.

- When the train is released it converts **gravitational potential energy** to **kinetic energy** as it falls. This is shown by the formula:
  loss of gravitational potential energy (PE) = gain in kinetic energy (KE)

- Each peak is lower than the one before because some energy is transferred to heat and sound due to friction and air resistance. This is shown by the formula:
  PE at top = KE at bottom + energy transferred (to heat and sound) due to friction

- kinetic energy = $\frac{1}{2} mv^2$
  – If **speed doubles, KE quadruples** (KE $\propto v^2$).
  – If **mass doubles, KE doubles** (KE $\propto m$).

Top Tip!

Remember! Energy is always conserved.

Questions

1 Alfie, on the 3rd floor, and Jo, on the 8th floor, each hold similar balls out of a window. Whose ball has the greater gravitational potential energy?

2 Describe the energy changes for a girl on a swing.

3 Why does a funicular railway pull up a carriage with an empty water tank?

4 Why does a roller coaster travel more slowly at the top than at the bottom of each hill?

P3 Summary

Distance-time graphs

The object **isn't moving**.

The object has a **constant speed**.

Speed and acceleration

$$\text{speed} = \frac{\text{distance}}{\text{time}}$$

$$\text{acceleration} = \frac{\text{change in speed}}{\text{time}}$$

Speed-time graphs

The speed is **constant**.

The speed is **increasing**.

Forces for transport

Force, mass and acceleration are linked by the equation:
$F = ma$

Fossil fuels – for example, petrol and diesel – are the main fuels used in road transport. Some cars use more petrol or diesel than others so cause more pollution. Diesel engines usually have better **fuel consumption** figures than petrol engines.

Forces can make things speed up or slow down.

When a car stops the:
total stopping distance = thinking distance + braking distance
The higher the speed of the car, the greater the distance it travels in stopping.

Work, energy and power

Work is done when a force moves an object.
$W = F \times d$
Work is measured in joules (J).

Roller coasters use **gravitational potential energy** as the source of movement.

Power is a measure of how quickly work is done.
$P = \frac{W}{t}$
Power is measured in watts (W).

Modern cars have lots of safety features that absorb energy when the cars stop:
– crumple zones
– seatbelts
– air bags.
Cars also have:
– **active safety features** (e.g. ABS brakes)
– **passive safety features** (e.g. cruise control).

Moving objects possess **kinetic energy**.
– The faster they travel, the more kinetic energy they possess.
– The greater the mass of an object, the more kinetic energy it possesses.
kinetic energy (KE) = $\frac{1}{2} mv^2$

Energy is needed to do work. Energy is measured in joules (J).

Falling safely

Terminal speed is the maximum speed reached by a falling object. It happens when the forces acting on the object are balanced.

Falling objects get faster as they fall. They're pulled towards the centre of the Earth by their weight (**gravity**).

A parachute provides a large upward force, bigger than the weight of the parachutist. This slows him down. As he slows down the air resistance gets less until it equals his weight. He then falls at a terminal speed and lands safely.

Who planted that there?

Plant cells

G–E

- Most plant leaves and some plant stems are **green**.

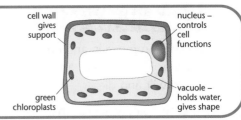

The structure of a plant cell.

cell wall gives support

nucleus – controls cell functions

vacuole – holds water, gives shape

green chloroplasts

Photosynthesis

G–E

- The **green** colour of plants is caused by green **chloroplasts** inside plant cells. Chloroplasts absorb light energy from the Sun to use in **photosynthesis**, which takes place mainly in the leaves.

- Photosynthesis requires:
  - **light** from the Sun
  - **carbon dioxide** which enters the leaf through small pores on the underside of the leaves
  - **water** which enters through the root hairs.

- **Oxygen** is made by photosynthesis and some of it's released into the atmosphere through the pores in the leaves.

D–C

- A **leaf** is adapted for photosynthesis by:
  - being **broad** so it has a large **surface area** to absorb light
  - being **thin** so gases don't have far to travel and light can reach all the way through it
  - having **chlorophyll** in most of its cells
  - having a **network** of specialised **cells in veins** to support it and carry water and sugars to different parts of the plant
  - having **stomata** to allow **gas exchange**: carbon dioxide to **diffuse** into it and oxygen to diffuse out of it.

The structure of a leaf

D–C

- When you cut through a leaf and look at it under a microscope you'll see many different cells.

- A **palisade** cell contains many **chloroplasts**. Photosynthesis occurs at a high rate in these cells and lots of sugars and starch are produced.

A stained section through a green leaf, magnified.

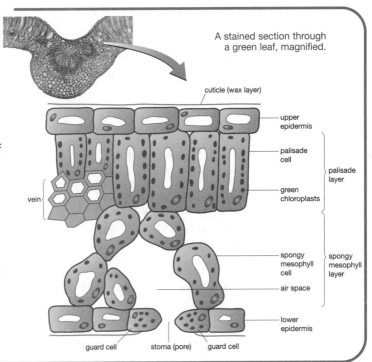

cuticle (wax layer)

upper epidermis

palisade cell

palisade layer

vein

green chloroplasts

spongy mesophyll cell

spongy mesophyll layer

air space

lower epidermis

guard cell   stoma (pore)   guard cell

Top Tip!

Exam questions often ask you to label a diagram of a leaf.

Questions

(Grades G-E)

1 Name the process that mainly takes place in the leaf of a plant.

2 How does water enter a plant?

(Grades D-C)

3 Explain why a plant leaf is broad.

4 Which type of leaf cell contains the most chloroplasts?

Water, water everywhere

Support in plants

- **Water** can move in and out of a plant cell through its **membrane** and **cell wall**. The presence of water in a plant cell and its cell wall give it **shape** and **support**. Without water the plant would wilt and die.

- To keep healthy, a plant balances its water loss with its water uptake.

G–E

Osmosis

- **Osmosis** is the **diffusion of water** across a **partially permeable membrane** from an area of high water concentration to an area of low water concentration.

- Water will move into cells by osmosis when they are placed in water. Cells will lose water by osmosis if they are placed in a strong sugar solution.

- Osmosis also happens in **animals cells**. They don't have a cell wall, so the cell swells and bursts (when water enters) or shrinks and collapses (when water leaves).

Top Tip!

Remember osmosis is about **water movement** not about salt or sugar molecules moving.

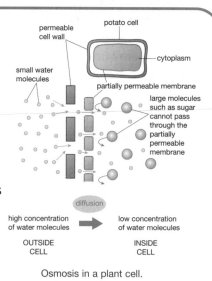

Osmosis in a plant cell.

D–C

Movement of water in plants

- The diagram shows the movement of water in a plant.

- **Root hairs** are long thin cells and have a large **surface area** to absorb lots of water from the soil by osmosis.

- The evaporation of water from leaves is called **transpiration**. It's useful because:
  – evaporation of water **cools** a plant
  – it brings water to the leaves for **photosynthesis**
  – a cell full of water gives **support**
  – the water moving up the stem carries useful **dissolved minerals**.

- To prevent too much water evaporating from the leaf it has a **waxy** covering called the **cuticle**, and **stomata** mainly on its shaded underside.

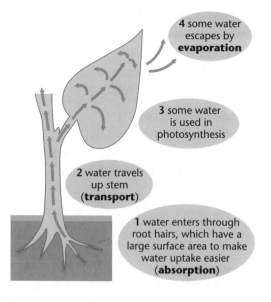

How water moves in a plant.

G–E

D–C

Questions

(Grades G-E)

1 What happens to plants if they aren't given water?

(Grades D-C)

2 What name is given to the movement of water in and out of cells?

3 What is meant by the term 'transpiration'?

4 Explain why stomata are mainly found on the underside of the leaf.

Transport in plants

Parts of a plant

G–E

- A green **flowering plant** has four main parts:
  - **flowers** to reproduce to make new plants
  - **leaves** to make food in photosynthesis
  - **stems** to hold up the leaves and flowers, and to carry food and water
  - **roots** to absorb water and minerals, and anchor the plant.

Transport in plants

D–C

- **Xylem** and **phloem** are specialised cells that form the **transport system** in a plant. They form continuous **vascular bundles** from the roots to the stems and leaves.

- **Xylem cells** carry **water** and **minerals from the roots** to the leaves for photosynthesis. Some water evaporates and escapes by **transpiration** from the leaves.

- **Phloem cells** carry dissolved **food** such as **sugars from the leaves** to other parts of the plant. This movement is called **translocation**. The sugars can be used for growth or stored as starch.

 Top Tip!

It's easy to get confused between xylem and phloem cells. Remember, phloem carries food.

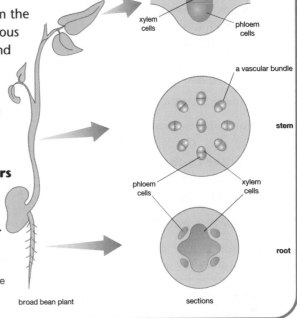

Horizontal cross-sections of a broad bean plant to show the arrangement of xylem and phloem.

broad bean plant

sections

Transpiration

G–E

- **Transpiration** is water loss from a plant leaf by **evaporation** from the leaf surface. Transpiration is affected by temperature, amount of light, wind and **humidity** (the amount of water in the air).

- Look at this **experiment** to show the **effect of light** on transpiration rate.
  - Similar sized leaves from the same type of plant are weighed and attached to string lines. Half of the lines are kept in the light and half are kept in the dark for one day. The leaves are re-weighed.
  - The average loss in weight of leaves in the light and dark conditions is compared. Loss of water in transpiration causes leaves to lose weight.

D–C

- A **high rate** of **transpiration** happens when:
  - light intensity increases
  - temperature increases
  - air movement (wind) increases
  - humidity (amount of water in the atmosphere) falls.

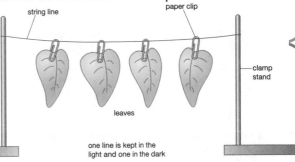

Experiment to show the effect of light on transpiration rate.

Questions

Grades G-E

1 Explain why plants have roots.

Grades D-C

2 Name the vessels that carry water and minerals up the stem.

Grades G-E

3 Look at the experiment in the third panel above (Transpiration). How would blowing the leaves with a hair dryer change the results?

Grades D-C

4 Name two things that increase the rate of transpiration.

Plants need minerals too

Fertilisers

- Farmers put **fertilisers** on their crop plants to help them grow in the same field for several years.

- A fertiliser contains **minerals** such as:
  - nitrates, containing **nitrogen** (chemical symbol, N)
  - phosphates, containing **phosphorus** (P)
  - **potassium** (K)
  - **magnesium** (Mg).

Top Tip!

Remember **K** is the symbol for **potassium**, not P.

- Fertilisers can be **natural** such as manure, or **manufactured**. In a manufactured fertiliser the amount of each mineral can be controlled. This is useful because different plants need different minerals at different stages of growth.

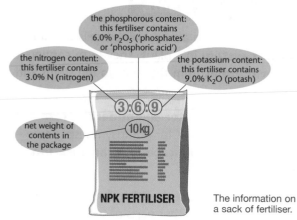

the phosphorous content: this fertiliser contains 6.0% P_2O_5 ('phosphates' or 'phosphoric acid')

the nitrogen content: this fertiliser contains 3.0% N (nitrogen)

the potassium content: this fertiliser contains 9.0% K_2O (potash)

3:6:9

net weight of contents in the package

10kg

- Plants must be **watered** to keep them alive. Gardeners **add fertiliser to the water** every week. The minerals in fertiliser **dissolve** in water.

NPK FERTILISER

The information on a sack of fertiliser.

- Minerals are essential for plants to **thrive**; if a plant is lacking in minerals it won't grow.

- The **soil** around a plant is **watered** (not the leaves) because it's the roots that absorb the water and the minerals.

Animal relationships

- Each mineral is used by a plant for different things.
  - **Nitrates** are needed to make **proteins** for growth.
  - **Phosphates** are used in **respiration** (releasing energy) and are needed for growth, especially in roots.
  - **Potassium** compounds are used in **respiration** and in **photosynthesis**.
  - **Magnesium** compounds are also needed in **photosynthesis**.

- A **mineral deficiency** in a plant is easy to detect and correct. A mineral is needed only in a very small amount.

no nitrates ⟶ • poor growth
• yellow leaves

no phosphate ⟶ • poor root growth
• discoloured leaves

no potassium ⟶ • poor fruits and flowers
• discoloured leaves

no magnesium ⟶ • yellow leaves

Symptoms of different mineral deficiencies in a plant.

Questions

Grades G-E

1 Name two minerals found in fertilisers.
2 Look at the diagram in the first panel. What is the percentage nitrogen content of 3:6:9 fertiliser?

Grades D-C

3 Name two minerals needed for photosynthesis.
4 Which mineral would you give a plant with poor root growth?

Energy flow

Food chains

G–E

- Each time an organism is eaten, **energy** is transferred from that organism. This **energy transfer** is shown in a **food chain**.

- **Sunlight** provides energy at the start of a food chain. Plants use this energy in **photosynthesis**.

- Plants are called **producers** because they produce food. All other organisms in a food chain are called **consumers** because they get their energy from other organisms by feeding.

- Food chains can be linked to form **food webs**.

Top Tip!

The direction of the **arrow** in a food chain shows the flow of energy.

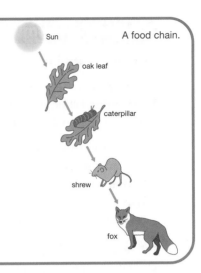

Sun   A food chain.

oak leaf

caterpillar

shrew

fox

Food pyramids

D–C

- The links in food chains and food webs show different **trophic levels**. Energy is passed from one organism to another and each organism is at a different trophic level.

- The numbers of organisms at different trophic levels can be counted and the information shown in a **pyramid of numbers**.

- An animal that eats plants is called a **herbivore** and an animal that eats other animals is a **carnivore**.

- A **pyramid of biomass** is a better way of showing trophic levels because the mass of the organisms is used.

- As energy flows along a food chain some is used up in growth. At each trophic level about 90% of the energy is transferred into other less useful forms, such as heat from respiration and egestion of waste.

a A woodland food chain doesn't show a pyramid shape because only one large tree supports all the other organisms **b** a pyramid of biomass of the same food chain.

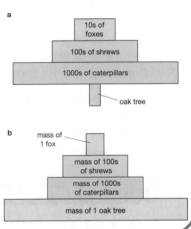

a

10s of foxes

100s of shrews

1000s of caterpillars

oak tree

b

mass of 1 fox

mass of 100s of shrews

mass of 1000s of caterpillars

mass of 1 oak tree

Biomass

G–E

- Green plants make **food** by **photosynthesis**. The plants use the energy in food to live and to grow. Some of the energy is passed up food chains and food webs.

- The mass of plants and animals is called **biomass**. The energy in biomass can also be used in **biofuels** such as wood, biogas and alcohol. When a **fuel** burns it releases energy.

Biofuels

D–C

- The energy from biomass can be used as **alternatives** to fossil fuels.
  - Fast-growing trees such as **willow** can be burnt in power stations. Because they are fast growing there's always a good supply.
  - Brazil produces a lot of **sugar cane**, which is **fermented** using yeast to make alcohol. The process uses **anaerobic respiration**. The alcohol is mixed with petrol to make 'Gasohol', a fuel for cars.

Questions

Grades G-E

1 Why are animals called consumers?

Grades D-C

2 Describe the difference between a pyramid of numbers and a pyramid of biomass.

Grades G-E

3 What name is given to the fuel made from plants.

Grades D-C

4 Explain how sugar cane can be used to fuel a car.

Farming

Intensive farming

- **Intensive farming** uses machines and chemicals to produce food **quickly** and **cheaply**.

- **Pesticides** are used to kill pests: **insecticides** kill insects; **fungicides** kill fungi; and **herbicides** kill unwanted plants. These chemicals can **damage** human and animal health as well as the environment.

- Some farmers use special methods to increase their production of food such as:
  - **greenhouses**, plants are given the best conditions for faster growth
  - **hydroponics**, growing plants without soil
  - **fish farms**, fish are kept in large tanks
  - **battery hens**, high numbers of hens in a small space.

- **Intensive farming** produces as much food as possible in the space available. Although it's an efficient method, it raises **ethical issues** such as cruelty to animals, and **environmental concerns** as the pesticides can pollute the land.

- Pesticides can build up to lethal doses in the food chain. For example, in Clear Lake, California, DDT was used to kill gnats on a lake.

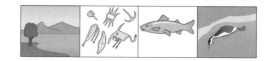

  - DDT got into the lake (0.02 parts per million).
  - Microscopic life absorbed small amounts of the pesticide (5 ppm).
  - Fish ate large amounts of microscopic life and the pesticides built up inside them (200 ppm).
  - Grebes ate the fish and the pesticide built up killing them.

- A **hydroponics system** can be used to grow lettuce and tomato plants. The system doesn't use soil, so there's less chance of disease or pests affecting the plants. The plant roots are specially treated in water that contains the required amounts of fertiliser and oxygen. This system is also useful in countries with poor soil or little water to irrigate fields.

Organic farming

- A farmer who doesn't use manufactured chemicals is called an **organic farmer**.

- Organic farmers don't use artificial fertilisers, pesticides or herbicides. They use other methods to control pests, such as using other animals. This is called **biological control**.

- **Ladybirds** are often used because they eat small flies called **aphids**. Aphids damage plants by sucking sap from them.

- Using other animals to kill pests saves on the use of harmful chemicals but it's often very slow to work. Also taking animals out of a food chain can result in other animals going hungry.

- Here are some other organic methods.
  - **Weeds** are removed to reduce competition for light and minerals.
  - **Seeds** are sown at **different times** so crops are ready at different times.
  - **Beans** are grown to put nitrogen back into the soil.
    They are called **nitrogen-fixing plants**.
  - **Manure** and **compost** are used in place of artificial fertilisers.
  - **Crop rotation** is used so the same crops don't grow in the same place each year.

Questions

1 Name the type of pesticide used to kill insects.

2 Suggest one way in which intensive farming is cruel to animals.

3 What is meant by the term 'biological control'?

4 Write down one way organic farmers can replace nitrogen lost from soil.

Decay

Decay

- When plants and animals die their bodies break down into simpler chemicals. This is called **decay**. These chemicals are **recycled** and used by living plants and animals.

- **Microorganisms** such as **bacteria** and **fungi** cause decay. They are called **decomposers**. A microorganism needs oxygen, water and a suitable temperature to survive.

- Microorganisms break down sewage (human waste) and dead plants into compost.

- An **experiment** to show that decomposers cause decay can be set up.
  - Two samples of soil are collected and one sample is heated (but not burned). Both samples are weighed and then put in sealed flasks containing limewater. After two days the soil samples are re-weighed.
  - Only the fresh soil sample loses mass. Limewater shows that carbon dioxide is produced by the decomposers.

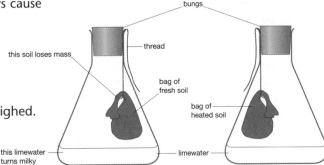

bungs

thread

this soil loses mass

bag of fresh soil

bag of heated soil

this limewater turns milky

limewater

- The remains of dead and decaying plants and animals are called **detritus**.

- Animals such as earthworms, maggots and woodlice depend on detritus for their food and are called **detritivores**.
  - Detritivores break down detritus into small pieces, which increases the surface area and so speeds up decay.
  - Detritivores are important as they **recycle** chemicals from dead plants and animals.

- Another method of using decay is for **compost**. These are the ideal conditions for speeding up the composting process:
  - **warmth**, such as placing a compost bin in the Sun
  - **moisture**
  - good **aeration**, such as regular mixing of the contents to allow oxygen in.

Preserving foods

- **Microbes** grow on decaying food producing the chemicals that cause **food poisoning**.

- **Preserving** food stops it from decaying. Food can be preserved by these methods.

- **Canning** involves heating food to kill bacteria, then sealing the food in a can to stop bacteria getting in.
- **Vinegar** is an acid. Very few bacteria can grow in acid conditions.
- **Drying** foods, such as cereals, works because bacteria and fungi can't grow without water.
- **Freezing** kills bacteria or slows their growth; **cooling** just slows down the growth.
- **Adding sugar** or **salt** kills some bacteria and fungi and stops the growth of others.

Top Tip!

Remember any preserving method stops microbes growing because it takes away warmth, moisture or oxygen.

Questions

(Grades G-E)

1 Name two types of decomposers.

(Grades D-C)

2 Name three detritivores.

3 Write down three examples of food preservation.

4 Explain why drying prevents food decay.

Recycling

Recycling

- Animals and plants take in food and digest it. The digested food molecules are used (**recycled**) to build up new chemicals for growth.

- When the animal or plant dies, they decay. Chemical elements released during decay, such as **carbon** and **nitrogen**, are **recycled**.

The carbon cycle

- **Carbon dioxide** is a compound that contains carbon.

- Carbon dioxide is **taken out** of the atmosphere by plants to use in **photosynthesis**. The carbon is then passed along the food chain when animals feed.

- Carbon dioxide is **put back** into the atmosphere by:
  – plants and animals **respiring**
  – bacteria and fungi in soil respiring when they **decompose** organism**s**
  – **burning** fossil fuels such as coal and oil
  – **erupting** volcanoes and forest fires.

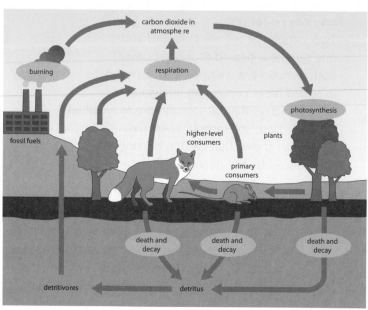

carbon dioxide in atmosphere

burning

respiration

photosynthesis

fossil fuels

higher-level consumers

plants

primary consumers

death and decay

death and decay

death and decay

detritivores

detritus

The carbon cycle.

The nitrogen cycle

- **Nitrogen** is another element that's recycled naturally.

- There's lots of nitrogen in the atmosphere (78%). Plants and animals need nitrogen for growth, but they can't directly use it because it's **unreactive**.

Top Tip!

Make sure you know which processes take carbon and nitrogen out of the atmosphere and which return them.

eaten

proteins in plants

plants and animals die and decay

proteins in animals

decomposers

nitrates in the soil

The nitrogen cycle.

Questions

Grades G-E

1 Give two elements that can be recycled.

Grades D-C

2 Name the process that removes carbon from the atmosphere.

3 Give one way in which carbon dioxide is returned to the atmosphere.

4 Name the type of organism that converts protein into nitrates.

B4 Summary

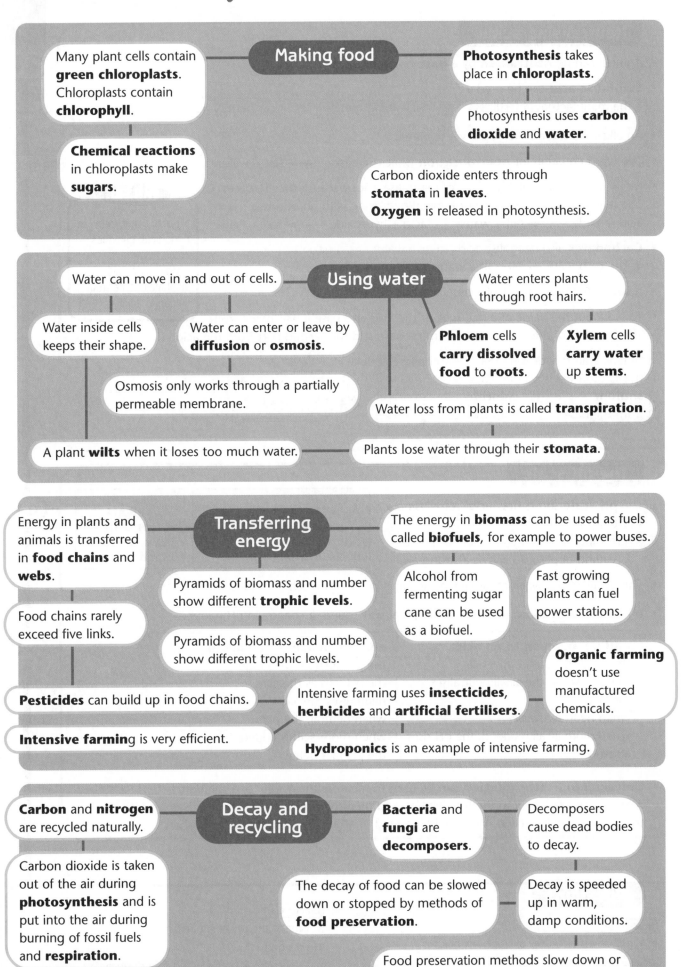

Making food

Many plant cells contain **green chloroplasts**. Chloroplasts contain **chlorophyll**.

Chemical reactions in chloroplasts make **sugars**.

Photosynthesis takes place in **chloroplasts**.

Photosynthesis uses **carbon dioxide** and **water**.

Carbon dioxide enters through **stomata** in **leaves**. **Oxygen** is released in photosynthesis.

Using water

Water can move in and out of cells.

Water inside cells keeps their shape.

Water can enter or leave by **diffusion** or **osmosis**.

Osmosis only works through a partially permeable membrane.

A plant **wilts** when it loses too much water.

Water enters plants through root hairs.

Phloem cells carry dissolved **food** to **roots**.

Xylem cells carry **water** up **stems**.

Water loss from plants is called **transpiration**.

Plants lose water through their **stomata**.

Transferring energy

Energy in plants and animals is transferred in **food chains** and **webs**.

Food chains rarely exceed five links.

Pyramids of biomass and number show different **trophic levels**.

Pyramids of biomass and number show different trophic levels.

Pesticides can build up in food chains.

Intensive farming is very efficient.

The energy in **biomass** can be used as fuels called **biofuels**, for example to power buses.

Alcohol from fermenting sugar cane can be used as a biofuel.

Fast growing plants can fuel power stations.

Organic farming doesn't use manufactured chemicals.

Intensive farming uses **insecticides, herbicides** and **artificial fertilisers**.

Hydroponics is an example of intensive farming.

Decay and recycling

Carbon and **nitrogen** are recycled naturally.

Carbon dioxide is taken out of the air during **photosynthesis** and is put into the air during burning of fossil fuels and **respiration**.

Bacteria and **fungi** are **decomposers**.

Decomposers cause dead bodies to decay.

The decay of food can be slowed down or stopped by methods of **food preservation**.

Decay is speeded up in warm, damp conditions.

Food preservation methods slow down or stop the growth of bacteria and fungi.

Acids and bases

Neutralising acids

- An acid can be **neutralised** by a **base** or **alkali**.

- **Sulphuric acid** can be used in:
  – the manufacture of fertilisers   – cleaning metals   – car battery acids.

- An alkali is a **base** which dissolves in water.

- The word equation for **neutralisation** is: acid + base ⟶ salt + water

- Metal oxides and metal hydroxides neutralise acids because they're bases.
  The reaction of a metal oxide or a metal hydroxide with an acid is:
  acid + oxide ⟶ salt + water   acid + hydroxide ⟶ salt + water

- **Carbonates** also neutralise acids to give water and a gas:
  acid + carbonate ⟶ salt + water + carbon dioxide

- A **salt** is made from part of a base and part of an acid.

- To work out the name of a salt, look at the acid and base it was made from.
  The first part of the salt name is from the base and the second part from the acid.

Top Tip!

Nitrates come from nitric acid, chlorides come from hydrochloric acid, sulphates come from sulphuric acid.

When sodium hydroxide reacts with hydrochloric acid,
the salt formed is sodium chloride:
sodium   **chloride**
from the base   from the acid

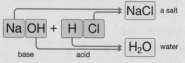

The pH scale

- The **pH scale** shows how acidic or alkaline a substance is.
  – A reading of pH = 1 shows a strong acid.
  – A reading of pH = 13 shows a strong alkali.

(low pH) **ACID** pH = 0	**NEUTRAL** pH = 7	(high pH) **ALKALI** pH = 14
acids have a pH of less than 7		Alkalis have a pH of more than 7

- The pH increases when an alkali is added and decreases when an acid is added.

- When an acid is added to alkali, or the other way round, a change in pH happens.

adding an alkali to an acid	adding an acid to an alkali
the pH at the start is low	the pH at the start is high
the pH rises as the alkali neutralises the acid	the pH falls as the acid neutralises the alkali
when neutral, the pH = 7	when neutral, the pH = 7
when more alkali is added, the pH rises above 7	when more acid is added, the pH falls below 7

- **Universal indicator solution** can be used to measure the acidity of a solution.
  A few drops are added to the test solution and then the colour of the solution is compared to a standard colour chart. When acid is added to alkali, they neutralise each other.

Questions

1 Write down two uses of sulphuric acid.

2 What's the base needed to make zinc sulphate?

3 What's the pH of an acid?

4 Which salt is made when magnesium hydroxide reacts with sulphuric acid?

Reacting masses

Grades

G–E

Relative atomic mass and relative formula mass

- Atoms of different elements 'weigh' different amounts. We compare their **masses** using the **relative atomic mass** scale. This can be found in the **periodic table**.

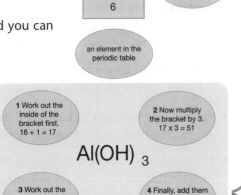

12
C
carbon
6

the relative atomic mass is always the larger of the two numbers by an element

an element in the periodic table

- If you add up all the masses in the formula of a compound you can work out the **relative formula mass** of the compound.

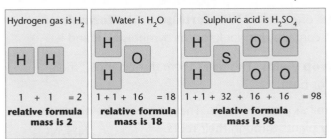

Hydrogen gas is H_2	Water is H_2O	Sulphuric acid is H_2SO_4
H H	H O H	H S O O H O O
1 + 1 = 2	1 + 1 + 16 = 18	1 + 1 + 32 + 16 + 16 = 98
relative formula mass is 2	**relative formula mass is 18**	**relative formula mass is 98**

1 Work out the inside of the bracket first. 16 + 1 = 17

2 Now multiply the bracket by 3. 17 x 3 = 51

$Al(OH)_3$

3 Work out the outside of the bracket. = 27

4 Finally, add them all together. 27 + 51 = 78

D–C

- Relative formula masses need to be added up in the right order if there are brackets in the formula.

Calculating mass and yield

G–E

- The total mass in a reaction never changes. The mass of the **products** (chemicals at the end) is exactly the same as the mass of the **reactants** (chemicals at the start).

- If the mass does seem to change, you need to look for a reason.
  – If the mass goes down, the reaction has given off a gas.
  – If the mass goes up, oxygen from the air has probably reacted with the chemical.

- The **yield** of a reaction is the amount of chemical that's produced in the reaction.
  – **100% yield** means that no product has been lost.
  – **0% yield** means that no product has been made.

- Sometimes a reaction doesn't give as much chemical as it should. Some chemicals always get left behind, so the amount of product that's collected is usually less than the amount that was expected. Some ways the product is lost include:
  – in **filtration** – small amounts stay on the filter paper
  – in **evaporation** – some chemicals evaporate into the room
  – in **transferring** liquids – tiny amounts of liquid stick to the sides of the beaker
  – because more than one reaction might be taking place, so the reactants are being used up in a different reaction.

- Calculations can be made of how much product is produced in a reaction without knowing the equations for the reactions.

D–C

- To calculate percentage yield, the following two things must be known:
  – the amount of product made, the 'actual yield'
  – the amount of product that should have been made, the 'predicted yield'.

$$\text{percentage yield} = \frac{\text{actual yield}}{\text{predicted yield}} \times 100$$

Questions

You may need to use the periodic table on page 238 to help you to answer the questions.

Grades G-E

1 Work out the relative formula mass of zinc carbonate, $ZnCO_3$.

Grades D-C

2 Write down the relative formula mass of calcium nitrate, $Ca(NO_3)_2$.

Grades G-E

3 Suggest two reasons why a yield is less than 100%.

Grades D-C

4 Tim made 24 g of crystals instead of 32 g. What's the percentage yield?

Fertilisers and crop yield

Fertilisers

- Carbon dioxide and water don't give a plant all the **elements** that it needs. It gets these essential elements by taking in **minerals** through its roots.

- **Fertilisers** are chemicals that provide plants with essential chemical elements to help plants grow bigger and faster. Examples are:
  – nitrogen, N   – phosphorus, P   – potassium, K.

- Fertilisers that contain these elements are often called **NPK fertilisers**. The **formula** of a fertiliser gives the essential elements it contains. Just look for the symbols N, P and K.

- Farmers use fertilisers to increase their **crop yields**. This gives them, for example, more grains of wheat, larger grains of wheat, or both.

- Fertilisers can't be put directly into the soil as pure elements. They must first be dissolved in water before they can be absorbed by plants through their roots.

- To calculate the yield when making a fertiliser, you need to calculate its **relative formula mass**. The relative formula mass of ammonium nitrate, NH_4NO_3, is 80.

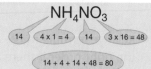

$$NH_4NO_3$$
14   $4 \times 1 = 4$ 14 $3 \times 16 = 48$
$14 + 4 + 14 + 48 = 80$

Making fertilisers

- Fertilisers can be made by **neutralising** alkalis with acids.

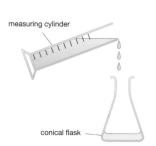

1   Use a measuring cylinder to pour alkali into a conical flask.

measuring cylinder

conical flask

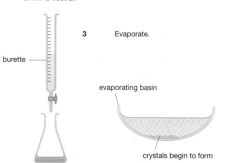

2   Add acid to the alkali until it is neutral.

burette

3   Evaporate.

evaporating basin

crystals begin to form

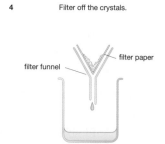

4   Filter off the crystals.

filter paper

filter funnel

- A fertiliser that contains nitrogen is called a **nitrogenous** fertiliser. Some examples are:
  – ammonium nitrate
  – ammonium phosphate
  – ammonium sulphate
  – urea.

Top Tip!

These nitrogenous fertilisers are all manufactured from ammonia.

- Many fertilisers are **salts**, so they can be made by reacting acids with bases.
  acid + base ⟶ salt + water

nitric acid + potassium hydroxide ⟶ potassium nitrate + water
nitric acid + ammonium hydroxide ⟶ ammonium nitrate + water
sulphuric acid + ammonium hydroxide ⟶ ammonium sulphate + water
phosphoric acid + ammonium hydroxide ⟶ ammonium phosphate + water

Questions

(Grades G-E)

1 What are the essential elements in potassium phosphate, K_3PO_4?

(Grades D-C)

2 What's the relative formula mass of ammonium phosphate, $(NH_4)_3PO_4$?

(Grades G-E)

3 Write down two nitrogenous fertilisers.

(Grades D-C)

4 Which acid and base react to make potassium phosphate?

The Haber process

Ammonia

- Ammonia is made by joining **nitrogen** and **hydrogen** in the **Haber process**.
  - Nitrogen comes from air.
  - Hydrogen is made from natural gas or by **cracking** oil fractions.

- The Haber process has two reactions.

  | nitrogen + hydrogen | ⟶ | ammonia | A forward reaction. |
  | nitrogen + hydrogen | ⟵ | ammonia | A backward reaction. |

- The reaction goes in both directions – at the same time. Reactions that go in both directions are called **reversible reactions**.

- To write an equation for a reversible reaction a special arrow is used: ⇌ .

  nitrogen + hydrogen ⇌ ammonia

- Eighty per cent of all ammonia goes into fertilisers. Ammonia is also used to make nitric acid, most of which goes into more fertilisers. Some ammonia is used to make household cleaners.

The Haber process

- The Haber process uses:
  - an iron catalyst
  - high pressure
  - a temperature of 450 °C
  - a recycling system for unreacted nitrogen and hydrogen.

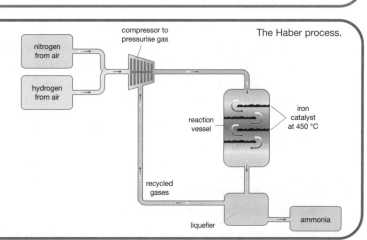

The Haber process.

The costs of ammonia production

- The cost of making the ammonia is affected by:
  - the cost of building the plant
  - people's wages
  - the cost of the raw materials
  - nitrogen and hydrogen and the energy costs
  - how quickly the new substance can be made (cost of a catalyst).

- Different factors affect the cost of making a new substance:
  - **labour** – chemical plants are heavily automated and need few people to operate them
  - **reactants** – hydrogen is made from natural gas or by cracking oil, which costs money; nitrogen has to be cleaned, dried and compressed
  - **recycling** of unreacted materials – means that money isn't wasted
  - **high pressure** – this makes the reaction work better but costs more
  - **energy** – the higher the temperature, the more fuel is needed
  - **reaction rate** – the faster the reaction, the more product is made from the same equipment, so the cheaper it is
  - **pollution control** – reducing pollution is expensive.

Questions

1 What's ammonia made from?

2 At what temperature is the Haber process carried out?

3 Write down three costs of making ammonia.

4 Why is low pressure not used in the Haber process?

Detergents

Rusting and corrosion

- A **detergent** is a salt. The ingredients in washing powders include:
  - **active detergent**, which does the cleaning
  - **water softener** to soften hard water
  - **bleaches** to remove coloured stains
  - **optical brighteners** to give a whiter than white appearance
  - **enzymes** to remove food stains at low temperatures.

perfume
makes clothes
smell nice

detergent
lifts dirt off
clothes

bleach
'removes'
coloured stains

enzymes
remove food stains,
they only work at
low temperatures

Automatic
biological
SUNSHINE
soap powder
2.5kg   2.5kg

optical brightener
sticks to clothes and
makes them 'whiter
than white'

water softener
softens hard
water

Some of the things in
washing powder.

- A detergent can be made by **neutralising** an organic acid using an alkali.

  acid + alkali $\longrightarrow$ salt + water

  It's suitable for cleaning uses because:
  - it dissolves grease stains
  - it dissolves in water at the same time.

- New washing powders allow clothes to be washed at low temperatures. It's good for the environment to wash clothes at 40 °C instead of at high temperatures because washing machines have to heat up a lot of water. This needs energy, so the lower the temperature of the water, the less energy is used and the less greenhouse gases are put into the atmosphere.

- Washing clothes at low temperatures is also good for coloured clothes as many dyes are easily damaged by high temperatures. It also means that many more fabrics can be machine washed as their structure would be damaged at higher temperatures.

Solvents and solutes

- Fresh coffee stains dissolve in water but Biro marks don't. However, Biro marks will often dissolve in methylated spirit.
  - Methylated spirit and water are both **solvents** – they dissolve other substances.
  - The substance that dissolves, the Biro ink, is a **solute**.
  - Biro ink dissolved in a solvent makes a **solution**.

- Different solvents dissolve different substances. If a substance dissolves, it's **soluble**. If it doesn't dissolve, it's **insoluble**.

Dry cleaning

- Some fabrics will be damaged if they are washed in water, so they must be **dry-cleaned**. A dry-cleaning machine washes clothes in an organic solvent. The word 'dry' doesn't mean that no liquids are used, just that the liquid solvent isn't water.

- Most of the stains on clothing contain grease from the skin or from food. Grease-based stains won't dissolve in water, but they will dissolve easily in a dry-cleaning solvent.

Questions

Grades G-E

1 Why are enzymes used in washing powders?

Grades D-C

2 What are the two reactants used in making a detergent?

Grades G-E

3 What does a solute dissolve in to make a solution?

Grades D-C

4 Give two reasons why a dry-cleaning method may be used.

Batch or continuous?

Making chemicals

G–E

- If a chemical is needed in large amounts, it's usually made by a **continuous process**.

- A continuous process is one which doesn't stop and reactants are continually fed in.

- Ammonia is made by a continuous process.

- Speciality chemicals, such as medicines and pharmaceutical drugs, are often made on demand in a **batch process**.

D–C

- Drugs companies make medicines in small batches, which are then stored.
  - New batches are made when the stored medicine runs low. If a lot of one medicine is needed, several batches can be made at the same time.
  - Once they have made a batch of one drug, it's easy to switch to making a different drug.

- The large scale production of ammonia is different to the small scale production of pharmaceuticals as it's a continuous process.

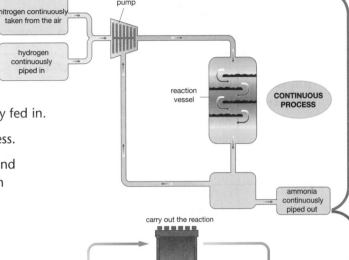

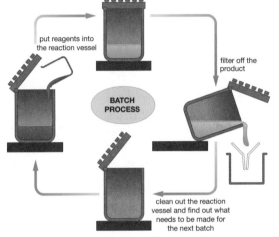

Raw materials

G–E

- The raw materials for a medicine can be made synthetically or extracted from plants.

D–C

- Chemical compounds in a plant are held in its cells. Plant cells have tough walls, so to extract the compound the plant is **crushed** to break the cell walls.
- Then the chemical must be **dissolved**. This only works if a suitable **solvent** is used.
- The solvent dissolves lots of different compounds, so the desired compound is then separated from the others. This can be done by **chromatography**.

Factors affecting the costs of medicines

G–E

- Factors affecting the cost of making and developing medicines and pharmaceutical drugs are shown here.

D–C

- The high costs of making and developing medicines and pharmaceutical drugs include:
  - **strict safety laws**
  - **research and development** – take years to develop
  - **raw materials** – may be rare and costly
  - **labour intensive** – because medicines are made by a batch process, less automation can be used.

Questions

(Grades G-E)
1 What's a continuous process?

(Grades D-C)
2 What's a batch process?

(Grades G-E)
3 Write down three costs involved in developing a medicine.

(Grades D-C)
4 Give two reasons why medicines are expensive to develop.

Nanochemistry

Forms of carbon

- There are three forms of **carbon** shown in the table.

G–E

	diamond	graphite	buckminster fullerene
physical properties	lustrous, colourless and clear hard high melting point insoluble in water doesn't conduct electricity	black, lustrous and opaque slippery insoluble in water conducts electricity	black solid deep red in solution in petrol
uses	cutting tools jewellery	electrodes pencil leads lubricants	can join together to make nanotubes that are very strong and can conduct electricity semiconductors in electrical circuits (nanotubes) industrial catalysts (nanotubes) reinforces graphite in tennis rackets (nanotubes)
reasons for use	cutting tools – very hard jewellery – lustrous and colourless	electrodes – conducts electricity and has high melting point pencil leads – slippery and black lubricants – slippery	
structure			

D–C

Nanochemistry

- Chemistry works with materials on a large scale.
- Nanochemistry works at the level of atoms – **nanoscale**.
- A **fullerene** changes at the **nanoscale**. The shape of the individual particles – balls or tubes, sieves or cages – is their nanostructure. This gives them their **nano properties**, which are different from **bulk properties**. Bulk chemical properties are the properties of large amounts of a material.

G–E
D–C

Questions

(Grades G-E)

1 Write down three different forms of carbon.

(Grades D-C)

2 Which properties of graphite make it useful as an electrode?

(Grades G-E)

3 What does 'nanochemistry' mean?

(Grades D-C)

4 What are bulk chemical properties?

How pure is our water?

Water

Water
Where water is found in the United Kingdom:
– lakes
– rivers
– aquifers
– reservoirs.

Water as a resource
Water is used by industry as:
– a cheap raw material
– a coolant
– a valuable solvent.

What's in water before it's purified?
– dissolved salts and minerals
– pollutants
– insoluble materials
– microbes (killed by chlorination).

Pollutants in drinking water
– nitrate residues
– lead compounds
– pesticide residues.

- Clean water saves more lives than medicines. That's why, after disasters and in developing countries, relief organisations concentrate on providing clean water supplies.

- Water is a **renewable resource**, but that doesn't mean the supply is endless. If there isn't enough rain in the winter, reservoirs don't fill up properly for the rest of the year.

- Producing tap water does incur costs. It takes energy to pump and to purify it – all of which increases climate change.

Water purification

- The water in a river is cloudy and often not fit to drink. It may also contain pollutants such as nitrates from fertiliser run off, lead compounds from lead pipes, and pesticides from spraying near to water resources. To make drinking water clean, it's passed through a **water purification** works.

- There are three main stages in water purification:
    - **sedimentation** of particles – larger bits drop to the bottom
    - **filtration** of very fine particles – sand is used to filter out finer particles
    - **chlorination** – kills microbes.

Precipitation reactions for testing water

- To test whether water contains sulphate or halide ions, we use a **precipitation reaction**.

- To test for **sulphate ions**, we add two drops of **barium chloride** solution to the water:
    - **sulphates** give a **white** precipitate

- To test for **chloride**, **bromide** and **iodide ions**, we add one or two drops of **silver nitrate** solution to the water in the test tube:
    - **chlorides** give a white precipitate
    - **bromides** give a cream precipitate
    - **iodides** give a yellow precipitate.

- In a precipitation reaction, two solutions react to form a solid that doesn't dissolve.

    lead nitrate + sodium **sulphate** ⟶ lead sulphate (**white** precipitate) + sodium nitrate
    silver nitrate + sodium **chloride** ⟶ silver chloride (**white** precipitate) + sodium nitrate
    silver nitrate + sodium **bromide** ⟶ silver bromide (**cream** precipitate) + sodium nitrate
    silver nitrate + sodium **iodide** ⟶ silver iodide (**yellow** precipitate) + sodium nitrate

Questions

Grades G-E
1 Write down three places that we get water from.

Grades D-C
2 Explain why filtration is used in the water purification process.

Grades G-E
3 What type of reaction takes place between barium chloride and sulphates?

4 What chemical is added to water to test for bromide ions?

C4 Summary

Ammonia is made all the time in a **continuous process**. Pharmaceutical drugs are made on a smaller scale by a **batch process**.

Nitrogen and hydrogen make ammonia in the **Haber process**.

We can change the **conditions** in the Haber process to give us the best **yield**.

Chemical industry

Ammonia reacts as a **base** to form fertilisers such as ammonium nitrate and ammonium phosphate.

If we know the mass of the reactants, we can work out what mass of products to expect.

Industry makes chemicals such as **fertilisers**. They must be cheap enough to use.

We can measure the **percentage yield** of a reaction.

$$\% \text{ yield} = \frac{\text{actual yield}}{\text{predicted yield}} \times 100$$

Different factors affect the **cost** of making new fertilisers or any new substance. High pressures mean higher energy costs.

Fertilisers make crops grow bigger as they provide plants with extra nitrogen, phosphorus and potassium. These are essential chemical elements for plant growth.

Water resources are found in lakes, rivers, aquifers and reservoirs.
Water needs testing and purifying before use. Purification includes:
– filtration
– sedimentation
– chlorination.

Detergents do the active cleaning in washing up liquid and washing powder. Detergents are molecules that combine with both grease and water. Washing powders have optical brighteners added to make clothes look whiter than white.

Nanochemistry

Diamonds are used in cutting tools and jewellery. They're **very hard** and have a **high melting point**.

Graphite is carbon. It's **slippery** so it can be used as a lubricant. It also **conducts electricity** so it can be used as electrodes.

The element carbon can exist in different forms. This is due to differences at the **nanoscale**.

Fullerenes were discovered fairly recently. Buckminster fullerene has the formula C_{60}.

Sparks!

Insulating materials

- Metals are good electrical **conductors**. They allow electric charges to move through them.

- Materials such as wood, glass and polythene are **insulators**. They do *not* allow electric charges to pass through them.

Positive and negative charges

- Charge can build up on an insulator. An insulator can be charged by friction.

- There are two kinds of electric charge, **positive** and **negative**. When rubbed with a duster:
  – acetate and perspex become positively charged
  – polythene becomes negatively charged.

- An **atom** consists of a small positively charged nucleus surrounded by an equal number of negatively charged electrons.

- In a stable, neutral atom, there are the same amounts of positive and negative charges.

- All **electrostatic** effects are due to the movement of electrons.

- The law of electric charge states that: like charges repel, unlike charges attract.

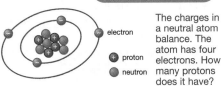

Top Tip!

It's only electrons that move in an atom.

electron

proton

neutron

The charges in a neutral atom balance. The atom has four electrons. How many protons does it have?

Electric shocks

- A person gets an electric shock if they become charged and then become earthed.

- A person can become charged if they walk on a nylon-carpeted or vinyl floor because:
  – the floor is an insulator
  – they become charged as they walk due to friction.

- The person can become earthed by touching water pipes or even another person.

- Synthetic clothing can also cause a person to become charged.

Dangers of static electricity

- When inflammable gases or vapours are present, or there is a high concentration of oxygen, a spark from static electricity could ignite the gases or vapours and cause an explosion.

- If a person touches something at a high **voltage**, large amounts of electric charge may flow through their body to earth.

- **Current** is the rate of flow of charge. Even small currents can be fatal.

- Static electricity can be a nuisance but not dangerous.
  – Dust and dirt are attracted to insulators, such as television screens.
  – Clothes made from synthetic materials often 'cling' to each other and to the body.

Questions

(Grades G-E)

1 Which of these materials are electrical insulators?
  a copper **b** paper **c** polythene **d** tin.

(Grades D-C)

2 What happens when **a** two acetate rods are brought near each other? **b** a polythene and an acetate rod are brought near each other?

(Grades G-E)

3 Suggest why synthetic clothes may become charged.

(Grades D-C)

4 Why must a mobile phone *not* be used on a petrol station forecourt?

Uses of electrostatics

Uses of static electricity

- A paint sprayer **charges** paint droplets to give an even coverage.
- A photocopier and laser printer use charged particles to produce an image.
- Charged plates inside factory chimneys are used to remove dust particles from smoke.
- A **defibrillator** delivers a controlled electric **shock** through a patient's chest to restart their heart.

G–E

Defibrillators

- Defibrillation is a procedure to restore a regular **heart rhythm** by delivering an electric shock through the chest wall to the heart.
  - Two **paddles** are charged from a high voltage supply.
  - They are then placed firmly on the patient's chest to ensure good electrical contact.
  - Electric charge is passed through the patient to make the heart contract.
  - Great care is taken to ensure that the operator does not receive an electric shock.

D–C

Paint sprayers

- Static electricity is used in paint spraying.
  - The **spray gun** is charged.
  - All the paint particles become charged with the same charge.
  - Like charges **repel**, so the paint particles spread out giving a fine spray.
  - The object to be painted is given the *opposite* charge to the paint.
  - Opposite charges **attract**, so the paint is attracted to the object and sticks to it.

- The advantages of electrostatic paint sprayers are:
  - less paint is wasted
  - the object gets an even coat of paint
  - paint gets into awkward corners well.

D–C

How an electrostatic paint sprayer works.

 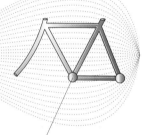

nozzle is charged up positively

object to be painted is negatively charged

Dust precipitators

- A dust precipitator removes harmful particles from the chimneys of factories and power stations that pollute the atmosphere.
  - A metal grid (or wires) is placed in the chimney.
  - The grid is connected to a high-voltage supply.
  - Dust particles are attracted to the metal grid.
  - The dust particles stick together to form larger particles.
  - When these particles get big enough they fall back down the chimney.

D–C

Questions

Grades D-C

1 Suggest why the paddles of a defibrillator must be placed firmly on the bare chest of the patient.

2 If the paint from an electrostatic paint spray is positively charged, what charge is given to the object to be painted?

Grades D-C

3 Why do the wires in an electrostatic dust precipitator need to be at a high voltage?

Safe electricals

Electric circuits

- A closed loop, with no gaps, is required for a **circuit** to work.

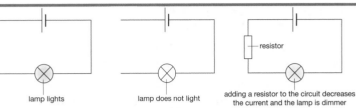

| lamp lights | lamp does not light | adding a resistor to the circuit decreases the current and the lamp is dimmer |

- An electric **current** is a flow of electric **charge**. Charge is carried by negatively charged **electrons**. The electrons flow in the *opposite* direction to the conventional current.

- The current is measured in **amperes** (A) using an **ammeter** connected in **series**.

Resistance and resistors

- A **resistor** is added to a circuit to change the amount of **current** in it.

- A **variable resistor** (or **rheostat**) changes the resistance.

- The **potential difference** (pd) between two points in a circuit is the difference in **voltage** between the two points.

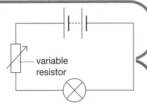

This circuit has a variable resistor and acts as a dimmer switch.

- Potential difference is measured in **volts** (V) using a **voltmeter** connected in **parallel**.
  - For a fixed resistor, as the potential difference across it **increases**, the **current increases**.
  - For a fixed power supply, as the **resistance increases**, the **current decreases**.

- The formula for resistance is: $\text{resistance} = \dfrac{\text{potential difference}}{\text{current}}$ $R = \dfrac{V}{I}$
  - Resistance is measured in **ohms** (Ω).

If the pd across a lamp is 5.0 V when the current is 0.2 A, the resistance of the lamp, $R = \dfrac{V}{I} = \dfrac{5.0}{0.2} = 25\ \Omega$

Top Tip!

Always remember to include the correct unit.

Live, neutral and earth wires

- The cable used to connect an appliance to the mains has three wires inside it. **Live**, **neutral** and **earth wires** can be seen in a plug. An earthed conductor can't become live.

live wire	neutral wire	earth wire
brown	blue	green/yellow striped
carries a high voltage around the house.	completes the circuit, providing a return path for the current	safety wire connected to the metal case of an appliance to prevent it becoming live

Wiring inside a plug.

Fuses and insulation

a Earth symbol
b double-insulation symbol.

- A **fuse** breaks a circuit if a fault occurs. A **circuit breaker** is a re-settable fuse.

- Double-insulated appliances don't need an earth wire. The case cannot become live.

- A fuse contains a length of wire which melts, breaking the circuit, if the current becomes too large. Fuse values of 5 A and 13 A are commonly available for use in three-pin plugs.

Questions

Grades G-E

1 What happens to the current in a circuit if the resistance increases?

Grades D-C

2 The pd across a resistor is 4.0 V when the current through it is 0.5 A. What is its resistance?

Grades G-E

3 Which mains wire only carries a current when a fault occurs?

Grades D-C

4 Explain how a fuse protects an appliance.

Ultrasound

Longitudinal waves

- All **sound**, including **ultrasound**, is produced by **vibrating** particles that form a **longitudinal wave**.
  - The vibrations of the particles are in the **same** direction as the wave.
  - This sets up a pressure wave with **compressions** and **rarefactions**.
  - The pressure wave makes a person's eardrums vibrate and signals are sent to the brain.

> **Top Tip!**
> With sound waves, **frequency** is linked to **pitch** and **amplitude** to **loudness**.

A sound wave showing rarefactions, compressions and wavelength.

vibrating cone emitting sound

λ

sound wave

compression (squashed together air particles)

direction of sound wave

rarefaction (spread out air particles)

- The features of a wave are:
  - **Amplitude** (*A*), which is the maximum distance a particle moves from its normal position.
  - **Wavelength** (λ), which is the distance occupied by one complete wave.
  - **Frequency** (*f*), which is the number of complete waves in a second. Frequency is measured in **hertz** (Hz). A frequency of 50 Hz means there are 50 complete waves in a second.

- The features of longitudinal sound waves are:
  - They can't travel through a vacuum. The denser the medium, the faster a wave travels.
  - The higher the frequency or pitch, the smaller the wavelength.
  - The louder the sound, or the more powerful the ultrasound, the more energy is carried by the wave.
- **Ultrasound** is sound of a higher **frequency** than humans can hear.
- Ultrasound travels as a pressure wave – compressions and rarefactions.

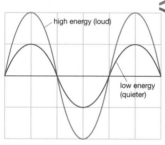

high energy (loud)

low energy (quieter)

Comparing a loud sound with a quieter sound. How does the amplitude change?

Uses of ultrasound

- **Ultrasound** can be used:
  - in body scans
  - to break down kidney stones
  - to measure the speed of blood flow in a vein or artery when a blockage is suspected.

- A body scan:
  - allows doctors to 'see' inside a patient without surgery
  - can investigate heart and liver problems
  - can check the condition of a foetus
  - can look for tumours in the body.

- A **pulse** of ultrasound is sent into the body:
  - at each boundary between different tissues or organs some ultrasound is **reflected** and the rest is transmitted
  - the returning **echoes** are recorded and used to build up an image of the internal structure.

- To break down kidney stones:
  - a high-powered ultrasound beam is directed at the kidney stones
  - the ultrasound energy breaks the stones down into smaller pieces
  - the tiny pieces are then excreted from the body in the normal way.

Questions

(Grades G-E)

1 Middle C has a frequency of 256 Hz. How many vibrations occur every second?

(Grades D-C)

2 Body fat is denser than air. In which medium will ultrasound travel faster?

(Grades G-E)

3 What is the advantage of using ultrasound to break down kidney stones?

(Grades D-C)

4 An ultrasound pulse travels 20 cm further when it is reflected from one side of the head of a foetus compared with the other side. How big is the head?

Treatment

Radiation

- X-rays and gamma rays are both **electromagnetic waves** with very short wavelengths. They are very penetrating so can pass into the body to treat internal organs.

- **X-rays** and **gamma** (γ) **rays** are used in medicine:
  – for diagnosis (finding out what is wrong)   – for therapy (treatment).

- **Gamma radiation** is emitted from the **nucleus** of an **atom**.

The electromagnetic spectrum.

increasing wavelength (in m)

| 10^{-15} | 10^{-13} | 10^{-11} | 10^{-9} | 10^{-7} | 10^{-5} | 10^{-3} | 10^{-1} | 10^{1} | 10^{3} |

gamma rays   ultraviolet   infrared

X-rays   microwaves   UHF VHF radio   long wave

- Radiation emitted from the nucleus of an unstable atom can be **alpha** (α), **beta** (β) or **gamma** (γ).
  – **Alpha radiation** is absorbed by the skin, so is of no use for diagnosis or therapy.
  – **Beta radiation** passes through skin but not bone. Its medical applications are limited but it's used, for example, to treat the eyes.
  – **Gamma radiation** is very penetrating and is used in medicine. **Cobalt-60** is a gamma-emitting radioactive material that is widely used to treat cancers.

- Gamma rays and X-rays have similar wavelengths but they're produced in different ways.

- When nuclear radiation passes through a material it causes **ionisation**. Ionising radiation damages living cells, increasing the risk of **cancer**.

- Cancer cells within the body can be destroyed by exposing the affected area to large amounts of radiation. This is called **radiotherapy**.

Gamma radiation

- Gamma radiation is used to treat **cancer**.
  – Large doses of high-energy radiation can be used in place of surgery. However, it's more common to use radiation after surgery, to make sure *all* the cancerous cells are removed or destroyed.
  – If any cancerous cells are left behind, they can multiply and cause **secondary cancers** at different sites in the body.

- Gamma radiation kills bacteria. It's used to **sterilise** hospital equipment to prevent the spread of disease. Each item is put in a sealed bag and exposed to intense gamma radiation.

used plastic tubing → tubing sealed in plastic pack, *unsterilised* → source of gamma radiation → tubing ready for use again, *sterilised*

- A **radiographer** carries out procedures using X-rays and nuclear radiation. Sterilising medical equipment.

Tracers

- A radioactive **tracer** is used to investigate inside a patient's body without surgery. Beta or gamma emitters are used.
  – Technetium-99m is a commonly used tracer. It emits only gamma radiation.
  – Iodine-123 emits gamma radiation and is used as a tracer to investigate the thyroid gland.
  – X-rays cannot be used as tracers as they're produced in an X-ray machine.

Questions

(Grades G-E)
1 Why do X-rays and gamma rays have many medical uses?

(Grades D-C)
2 What is 'radiotherapy'?

(Grades G-E)
3 Why is gamma radiation used to sterilise equipment?

(Grades D-C)
4 Why is iodine-123 used as a tracer in medicine?

What is radioactivity?

Radioactivity and radioactive decay

- A Geiger-Muller tube and ratemeter (together commonly called a Geiger counter) are used to detect the rate of **decay** of a radioactive substance.
  - Each 'click' or extra number on the display screen represents the decay of one **nucleus**.
  - A decaying nucleus emits **radiation**.

- The **activity** is measured by the average number of nuclei that decay every second.
  - This is also called the **count rate**.
  - Activity is measured in counts/second or **becquerels (Bq)**.
  - The formula for activity is:

$$\text{activity} = \frac{\text{number of nuclei which decay}}{\text{time taken in seconds}}$$

- The activity of a radioactive substance **decreases** with time – the count rate falls.

- Radioactive substances decay naturally, giving out **alpha**, **beta** and/or **gamma** radiation.

- Radioactive decay is a **random** process; it isn't possible to predict exactly when a nucleus will decay.
  - There are so many atoms in even the smallest amount of **radioisotope** that the average count rate will always be about the same.

- Radioisotopes have **unstable nuclei**. Their nuclear particles aren't held together strongly enough.

> **Top Tip!**
>
> Remember! Alpha, beta and gamma radiation are not radioactive; it's the source that emits them that is radioactive.

What are alpha and beta particles?

An **alpha (α) particle**
  - is positively charged
  - has quite a large mass
  - has helium gas around it
  - is a helium nucleus
  - consists of two **protons** and two **neutrons**.

A **beta (β) particle**
  - is negatively charged
  - has a *very* small mass
  - travels *very* fast (at about one-tenth of the speed of light)
  - is a fast-moving **electron**.

> **Top Tip!**
>
> Know the difference between alpha, beta and gamma radiation.

- When an **alpha** or a **beta** particle is emitted from the nucleus of an atom, the remaining nucleus is a **different** element. But **gamma** radiation it is not a particle, so does *not* change the composition of the nucleus; it remains the **same** element.

Alpha particles emitted from radiation

Questions

1 Ali records a count of 6000 in 10 seconds from a radioactive source. What is its activity?

2 Three successive measurements of the activity of a radioactive source are 510 Bq, 495 Bq and 523 Bq. Why are they different?

3 What is **a** an alpha particle **b** a beta particle?

4 Why does the emission of a gamma ray not change the composition of the nucleus?

Uses of radioisotopes

Background radiation

- **Background radiation** is ionising radiation that is always present in the environment.
  – It varies from place to place and from day to day.
  – The level of background radiation is low and doesn't cause harm.

- **Background radiation** is caused by:
  – radioactive substances present in **rocks** (especially **granite**) and soil
  – **cosmic rays** from Space.

> **Top Tip!**
> Remember to allow for background radiation when measuring the activity of a source of radiation.

Tracers

- **Radioisotopes** are used as **tracers** in industry and in hospitals.

- In addition to medical applications (see page 107), **tracers** are used to:
  – track the dispersal of waste materials
  – find leaks or blockages in underground pipes
  – track the route of underground pipes.

Smoke alarms

- One type of **smoke detector** uses a source of **alpha particles** to detect smoke. It's sensitive to low levels of smoke.

- Many **smoke detectors** contain a radioisotope such as **americium-241** which emits alpha particles. It has a long half life so decays slowly.
  – The alpha particles ionise some of the oxygen and nitrogen atoms in the air.
  – The positive ions and negative electrons move towards the negative and positive plates respectively (opposite charges attract).
  – This creates a tiny current which is detected by electronic circuitry in the smoke alarm.
  – If smoke particles enter, they attach themselves to the ions, neutralising them.
  – The smoke detector senses the drop in current and sets off the alarm.

oppositely charged plates

americium-241 source of alpha particles

How a smoke alarm works.

Dating

Radiocarbon-dating has shown that the Turin shroud, thought to date from the time of Christ, is only about 500 years old.

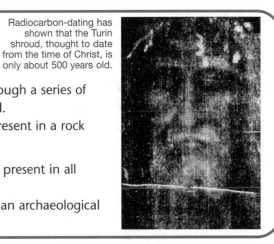

- Some **rock** types such as granite contain traces of **uranium**, a radioactive material.
  – The **uranium** isotopes present in the rocks go through a series of decays, eventually forming a stable isotope of **lead**.
  – By comparing the amounts of uranium and lead present in a rock sample, its approximate age can be found.

- **Carbon-14** is a radioactive isotope of carbon that is present in all living things.
  – By measuring the amount of carbon-14 present in an archaeological find, its approximate age can be found.

Questions

(Grades D-C)

1 Why might an oil company use a radioactive tracer?
2 Why is it important that the alpha source in a smoke detector has a long half-life?

3 Why would you expect a new rock to contain a bigger proportion of uranium to lead than an old rock?
4 Why can't carbon dating be used to find the age of an iron tool?

Fission

Nuclear power stations

- A **power station** produces **electricity**. It needs an **energy source** such as coal, oil, gas or nuclear:
  – to **heat water**
  – that **produces steam**
  – that **turns a turbine**
  – to **generate electricity**.

- A **nuclear** power station uses **uranium** as a fuel instead of burning coal, oil or gas to heat the water.

Diagram labels: hot gas, steam, source of energy, energy exchanger, cool gas, water, turbine, generator

- Natural uranium consists of two **isotopes**, uranium-235 and uranium-238.
  – The '**enriched uranium**' used as **fuel** in a nuclear power station contains a greater proportion of the uranium-235 isotope than occurs naturally.

- **Fission** occurs when a large unstable **nucleus** is split up and there is a release of energy in the form of **heat**.
  – The heat is used to boil water to produce steam.
  – The pressure of the steam acting on the turbine blades makes it turn.
  – The rotating turbine turns the generator, producing electricity.

Top Tip!
Learn the main stages in the production of electricity.

Chain reaction

- A **chain reaction** can carry on for as long as any uranium fuel remains.
  – This allows large amounts of energy to be produced.
  – In a **nuclear power station** the chain reaction is controlled to produce a steady supply of heat.
  – An **atomic bomb** is a chain reaction that has gone out of control.

Artificial radioactivity

- Materials can be made radioactive by putting them into a **nuclear reactor**. They are used:
  – in hospitals to diagnose and treat patients
  – in industry as tracers to detect leaks.

- **Artificial radioisotopes** can be produced by bombarding atoms with the neutrons present in a nuclear reactor.
  – Neutrons are uncharged so they're easily captured by **nuclei**, producing **unstable isotopes**.

Radioactive waste

- Nuclear fission produces **radioactive waste** that has to be handled carefully and disposed of safely.
  – **Very low-level waste**, such as that produced by medical applications, is placed in sealed plastic bags then buried or burned under strict controls.
  – Other **low-level waste** may be embedded in glass discs and buried in the sea.
  – **High-level waste**, such as spent fuel rods, is re-processed to make more radioactive materials.

Questions

(Grades G-E)
1 What fuel is used in a nuclear power station?

(Grades D-C)
2 What is meant by 'enriched uranium'?

(Grades G-E)
3 Where are artificial radioisotopes produced?

(Grades D-C)
4 Why is radioactive waste dangerous?

P4 Summary

Electrostatics

There are two kinds of electric charge, positive and negative:
- **like charges repel**
- **unlike charges attract**.

Electrostatic effects are caused by the **transfer of electrons.**

You can get an electric shock if you become charged and then become earthed.

Some uses of electrostatics are:
- defibrillators
- paint sprayers
- photocopiers.
- dust precipitators.

Using electricity safely

An electric current is a flow of electric charge. The **potential difference** (pd) between two points in a circuit is the difference in voltage between the two points.

$$\text{resistance } (\Omega) = \frac{\text{pd (V)}}{\text{current (A)}}$$

Electric circuits need a complete loop to work.
Resistors are used to change the current in a circuit.

In a plug:
L = live (brown)
N = neutral (blue)
E = earth (green and yellow stripe)
The **fuse** is connected in the live side. It melts if the current exceeds its stated value, breaking the circuit.

Ultrasound

Medical uses of ultrasound include:
- scans that allow a doctor to see inside you without surgery
- measuring the rate of blood flow in the body
- breaking up kidney or gall stones.

Ultrasound is sound of a higher frequency than we can hear (above 20 000 Hz).

Sound is a longitudinal wave; the particles vibrate in the same direction as the wave travels.
- **Wavelength** (λ) is the distance occupied by one complete wave.
- **Frequency** (f), measured in hertz (Hz), is the number of complete waves in 1 second.
- **Amplitude** is the maximum distance a particle moves from its normal position.

Nuclear radiation

Medical uses of radioactivity include:
- for diagnosis, as a tracer
- to sterilise equipment
- to treat cancers.
Only β- and γ-radiation can pass through skin. γ-radiation is the most widely used for medical purposes as it is the most penetrating. X-rays are similar to γ-rays but are produced in different ways.

Fission is the splitting of a large nucleus, such as uranium, releasing energy. This can set up a chain reaction producing a large amount of energy, as in a nuclear power station or an atomic bomb.

Nuclear radiation is emitted from the nuclei of radioactive materials:
- α-**particle** – helium nucleus
- β-**particle** – fast-moving electron
- γ-**radiation** – electromagnetic waves with very short wavelengths.

Background radiation is ionising radiation that is present in the atmosphere. It's caused by:
- radioactive substances in rocks (especially granite) and soil
- cosmic rays.

A power station uses a source of energy – coal, oil, gas or nuclear fuel:
- to heat water
- to produce steam
- to turn a turbine
- which turns a generator to produce electricity.
A nuclear power station uses uranium as a fuel.

Checklist – Science Unit 1

B1 Understanding ourselves

- I can explain why blood is under pressure in arteries.
- I can state the word equation for respiration.
- I can describe a balanced diet.
- I can calculate BMI and RDA.
- I can describe how the body defends against pathogens
- I can explain the difference between passive and active immunity.
- I can describe the functions of the main parts of the eye.
- I know the effects of the different types of drugs.
- I can interpret data on the effects of smoking.
- I can describe how heat can be lost or gained from the body.
- I know that sex hormones can be used as contraceptives and for fertility treatment.
- I know that chromosomes are made of DNA.
- I know that genes or the environment can cause different characteristics.
- I know that inherited characteristics can be dominant or recessive.

C1 Carbon chemistry

- I know that cooking food is a chemical change as a new substance is made and it's irreversible.
- I know that protein molecules in eggs and meat change shape when the food is cooked.
- I know that the main food additives are antioxidants, food colours, emulsifiers and flavour enhancers.
- I know that emulsifiers are molecules that have a water-loving part and an oil- or fat-loving part.
- I know that that alcohols react with acids to make an ester and water.
- I know that a solute is the substance dissolved in a solvent to make a solution.
- I know that crude oil is a non-renewable fossil fuel, which is a mixture of many hydrocarbons.
- I know that petrol is a crude oil fraction with a low boiling point, which exits at the top of the tower.
- I know that polymerisation is a process where many monomers react together to give a polymer.
- I know that a hydrocarbon is a compound formed between carbon atoms and hydrogen atoms only.
- I know that alkenes are hydrocarbons with one or more double bonds between carbon atoms.
- I know that complete combustion of a hydrocarbon fuel makes carbon dioxide and water only.
- I know that an exothermic reaction is one where energy is released into the surroundings.
- I know that energy of two fuels can be compared by the temperature rise in the same mass of water.

P1 Energy for the home

- I know the difference between temperature and heat.
- I can explain what is meant by specific heat capacity and specific latent heat.
- I can describe different forms of domestic insulation and explain how they work.
- I can calculate energy efficiency.
- I know the parts of the electromagnetic spectrum and their properties.
- I can describe how infrared radiation is used for cooking and for remote control devices.
- I can describe how microwaves are used for cooking and for communication.
- I know the difference between analogue and digital signals.
- I can describe total internal reflection and its use in optical fibres.
- I can describe the use of wireless signals for communication.
- I know why there is sometimes interference with radio signals.
- I know the properties of a transverse wave and that light is an example of a transverse wave.
- I can describe three types of earthquake wave and how they are detected.
- I know some of the effects of natural events and human activity on weather patterns.

Checklist – Science Unit 2

B2 Understanding our environment

- I know how to collect and use data to estimate a population.
- I know how to use a key to identify plants and animals.
- I know the characteristics of the different vertebrate groups.
- I can state the word equation for photosynthesis.
- I can describe the effect of increased light, temperature and carbon dioxide on photosynthesis rate.
- I can recognise organisms as predators or prey.
- I can explain how the size of a predator population will affect the prey population.
- I can describe how predators are adapted to hunt and how prey are adapted to escape.
- I can explain how camels and polar bears are adapted to their habitats.
- I can describe how organisms became fossilised.
- I know that the world population is increasing and causing more pollution.
- I can explain the effects of increased pollution on climate change, acid rain and the ozone layer.
- I can describe ways in which animals become extinct.
- I can explain the terms sustainable resource and sustainable development.

C2 Rocks and metals

- I know that paint is a colloid where solid particles are dispersed in a liquid, but aren't dissolved.
- I know that thermochromic pigments change colour when heated or cooled.
- I know that brick is made from clay, glass from sand, and aluminium and iron from ores.
- I know that the decomposition of limestone is: calcium carbonate → calcium oxide + carbon dioxide
- I know that the outer layer of the Earth is continental plates with oceanic plates under oceans.
- I know that igneous rock is made when molten rock cools down.
- I know that copper can be extracted by heating its ore with carbon, but purified by electrolysis.
- I know that alloys often have properties that are different from the metals they're made from.
- I know that aluminium doesn't corrode when wet as it has a protective layer of aluminium oxide.
- I know that iron is more dense than aluminium but both are malleable and electrical conductors.
- I know that respiration and combustion increase carbon dioxide levels and decrease oxygen levels.
- I know that toxic carbon monoxide comes from incomplete combustion of petrol or diesel in cars.
- I know that a temperature increase makes particles move faster, so increasing the rate of reaction.
- I know that a catalyst is a substance which changes the rate of reaction but is unchanged at the end.

P2 Living for the future

- I can describe how energy from the Sun can be used for heating and producing electricity.
- I can describe how generators produce electricity.
- I can describe how electricity is distributed via the National Grid.
- I know what fuels are used in power stations and some of their advantages and disadvantages.
- I can calculate power and the cost of using an electrical appliance for a certain time.
- I know how to measure radioactivity and why there is background radiation.
- I can list some uses of alpha, beta and gamma sources and relate their use to their properties.
- I can describe the Earth's magnetic field and its similarity to a bar magnet and a coil.
- I can describe how the Moon was formed.
- I know the names of the planets and their order from the Sun.
- I can describe how we are exploring space through manned and unmanned spacecraft.
- I know that there are bodies in space other than planets and moons.
- I can describe asteroids and comets and know the importance of constantly checking NEOs.
- I know that scientists believe the Universe started with a Big Bang and that it's still expanding.

Checklist – Additional Science Unit 1

B3 Living and growing

- I can label a diagram of an animal cell. ☐
- I can interpret data on DNA fingerprinting for identification. ☐
- I know that food and oxygen diffuse across the placenta. ☐
- I can describe diffusion as the movement of particles from a region of high to low concentration. ☐
- I know that arteries transport blood away from the heart. ☐
- I know that the patient can reject a heart transplant. ☐
- I know that at fertilisation haploid gametes join to form a diploid zygote. ☐
- I know that body cells are made by mitosis and gametes are made by meiosis. ☐
- I can identify the main stages of human growth. ☐
- I know that shoots are positively phototropic and negatively geotropic; roots are the opposite. ☐
- I can describe the stages in selective breeding. ☐
- I know that genetic engineering is used to make insulin. ☐
- I can describe some advantages and disadvantages of cloned plants. ☐
- I know that cloned animals could be used to produce organs for transplants. ☐

C3 The periodic table

- I know that the nucleus is made up of protons and neutrons, with each having a relative mass of 1. ☐
- I know that electrons surround the nucleus and occupy shells in order. They have almost no mass, 0. ☐
- I know that positive ions are formed by the loss of electrons from the outer shell. ☐
- I know that negative ions are formed by the gain of electrons into the outer shell. ☐
- I can work out the number of each different type of atom in a molecule or displayed formula. ☐
- I know that there are two types of bonding – ionic bonding and covalent bonding. ☐
- I know that lithium, sodium and potassium react vigorously with water and give off hydrogen. ☐
- I know that group 1 metals have one electron in their outer shell, which is why they are similar. ☐
- I know that chlorine is a green gas, bromine is an orange liquid and iodine is a grey solid. ☐
- I know that chlorine is more reactive than bromine, which is more reactive than iodine. ☐
- I know that in the electrolysis of dilute sulphuric acid, H_2 is made at the cathode and O_2 at the anode. ☐
- I know that when aluminium oxide is electrolysed, Al is formed at the cathode and O_2 at the anode. ☐
- I know that compounds of copper are blue, iron (II) are light green and iron (III) are orange/brown. ☐
- I know that metals have particles which are arranged close together in a regular arrangement. ☐

P3 Forces for transport

- I know that speed is measured in m/s and can use the formula: speed = distance ÷ time. ☐
- I can describe, draw and interpret distance-time graphs and speed-time graphs. ☐
- I know that acceleration is measured in m/s^2 and that: acceleration = change in speed ÷ time taken. ☐
- I can state and use the formula: force = mass x acceleration. ☐
- I can discuss the significance to road safety of thinking, braking and stopping distances. ☐
- I can state and use the formula: work done = force x distance. ☐
- I know that energy is needed to do work and that both work and energy are measured in joules (J). ☐
- I can state that power is measured in watts (W) and use the formula: power = work done ÷ time. ☐
- I can recognise objects that have kinetic energy (KE) and know the factors that increase it. ☐
- I can interpret data about fuel consumption. ☐
- I can describe typical safety features in modern cars. ☐
- I can describe how the motion of a falling object changes due to the effect of air resistance. ☐
- I can recognise objects that have gravitational potential energy (PE) ☐
- I can interpret a gravity ride (roller coaster) in terms of PE, KE and energy transfer. ☐

Checklist – Additional Science Unit 2

B4 It's a green world

- I can label a diagram showing the parts of the leaf. ☐
- I can explain how a leaf is adapted for photosynthesis. ☐
- I can describe how water travels through a plant. ☐
- I know that osmosis is the movement of water molecules across a partially-permeable membrane. ☐
- I can describe how transpiration rate can be increased. ☐
- I know that plants need nitrates, phosphates and potassium. ☐
- I can identify mineral deficiencies in plants. ☐
- I can construct pyramids of numbers and biomass. ☐
- I know that wood, alcohol and biogas are all fuels made from biomass. ☐
- I can describe the difference between intensive and organic farming. ☐
- I know that microorganisms need oxygen, moisture, and warmth for decay. ☐
- I can explain why the different preservation methods stop food decay. ☐
- I can describe the carbon cycle. ☐
- I can describe the nitrogen cycle. ☐

C4 Chemical economics

- I know that solutions with a pH of less than 7 are acids, more than 7 are alkali, but pH 7 is neutral. ☐
- I know that neutralisation is a reaction where: acid + base → salt + water. ☐
- I can work out the relative formula mass of a substance from its formula e.g. CO_2 is 12 + (2 × 16) = 44. ☐
- I can work out the percentage yield using the formula: % yield = actual yield × 100 ÷ predicted yield. ☐
- I know that fertilisers provide extra nitrogen, phosphorus and potassium, essential for plant growth. ☐
- I know that ammonia is made by the Haber process where N_2 and H_2 are put over an iron catalyst. ☐
- I know that the higher the pressure, the higher the energy bill for the industrial plant. ☐
- I know that a catalyst will reduce costs as the rate of reaction is increased. ☐
- I know that solutes are soluble and dissolve in solvents to make solutions. ☐
- I know that dry cleaning is a process used to clean clothes using a solvent that isn't water. ☐
- I know that a continuous process makes chemicals all the time but a batch process doesn't. ☐
- I can recognise the three structures of carbon: diamond, graphite and buckminster fullerene. ☐
- I can explain that graphite is slippery and is used as electrodes as it conducts electricity. ☐
- I know that water purification includes filtration, sedimentation and chlorination. ☐

P4 Radiation for life

- I know that there are two kinds of electric charge, positive and negative. ☐
- I can explain how static electricity can sometimes be dangerous and sometimes a nuisance. ☐
- I can describe some uses of static electricity. ☐
- I can explain the behaviour of simple circuits and how resistors are used in circuits. ☐
- I can state and use the formula: resistance = voltage ÷ current. ☐
- I know about live, neutral and earth wires, fuses, circuit breakers and double insulation. ☐
- I can describe the key features of longitudinal waves. ☐
- I know about ultrasound and can describe some medical uses of it. ☐
- I can describe how nuclear radiation is used in hospitals. ☐
- I can describe the properties of nuclear radiation. ☐
- I can state what alpha and beta particles are. ☐
- I can describe background radiation and state what causes it. ☐
- I can describe some non-medical uses of radioisotopes. ☐
- I can describe how domestic electricity is generated in a nuclear power station. ☐

Answers

B1 Understanding ourselves

Page 4
1 Respiration.
2 glucose → lactic acid + energy
3 Arteries.
4 It increases blood pressure.

Page 5
1 One from: carbohydrate, fat, protein.
2 80 x 0.75 = 60 g
3 One from: chewing, stomach squeezing.
4 Break down large food molecules into small soluble molecules.

Page 6
1 Bacteria, viruses, fungi, protozoa.
2 They carry pathogens from one host to another.
3 Immune system.
4 They lock onto antigens causing the bacteria to stick together.

Page 7
1 Tongue, eye, ears, skin, nose.
2 Iris.
3 We think about voluntary actions but reflex actions are done without thinking.
4 Stimulus, receptor, sensory neurone, CNS, motor neurone, effector, response.

Page 8
1 They speed up activity.
2 LSD.
3 A person loses their balance or finds it hard to talk clearly or finds it difficult to use their muscles.
4 Cigarette smoke stops the cilia from moving. Dust and particulates collect and irritate the cells. Smokers cough to move this mess upwards so it can be swallowed.

Page 9
1 Any two from: exercise, shivering, releasing energy from food, less blood flow near skin surface.
2 It is when body temperature falls too low.
3 Oestrogen and progesterone.
4 Hair growth in pubic area or under arms.

Page 10
1 DNA.
2 Four.
3 35.
4 Asexual reproduction.

Page 11
1 A change in the genes or chromosomes.
2 One from: radiation, chemicals, they occur spontaneously.
3 Blue.
4 One from: red-green colour blindness, cystic fibrosis, sickle-cell anaemia, haemophilia.

C1 Carbon chemistry

Page 13
1 Cannot change back.
2 They change shape.
3 Decomposes means that it breaks down. The three products are sodium carbonate, carbon dioxide and water.
4 It turns from colourless to cloudy (milky).

Page 14
1 An antioxidant.
2 Packaging that uses sensors to monitor the quality of the food.
3 Detergent.
4 The 'fat-loving' tail and 'water-loving' head act together to form emulsions.

Page 15
1 Esters.
2 One person may object to cosmetics being tested on animals, as the animals may be harmed and they have no control over what happens to them. The other may say that they feel safer if the cosmetics have been tested on animals.
3 Acid and alcohol.
4 Soluble.

Page 16
1 A fuel formed from the compression of dead animals and plants over millions of years.
2 At the top.
3 The breaking down of large hydrocarbon molecules to smaller, more useful ones such as petrol.
4 C_7H_{16}.

Page 17
1 Polystyrene.
2 High pressure and a catalyst.
3 Ethane.
4 Alkanes do not have a double C=C bond, alkenes do.

Page 18
1 Waterproof and rigid.
2 It makes people sweat as it is not breathable.
3 Is not decomposed by bacteria.
4 Toxic gases.

Page 19
1 Oxygen.
2 Blue.
3 Limewater.
4 Less soot is made, more heat is released and toxic carbon monoxide gas is not produced.

Page 20
1 Any two from: heat, light, sound, electricity.
2 A chemical reaction in which energy is transferred to the surroundings (energy is released).
3 Same mass of water, same mass of fuel.
4 Yellow flame.

P1 Energy for the home

Page 22
1 Temperature is a measure of hotness, heat is a form of energy.
2 Energy is transferred from your hand to the ice.
3 It changes into a liquid.
4 The specific heat capacity of the syrup is greater than the specific heat capacity of the sponge.

Page 23
1 Fibreglass contains trapped air.
2 It reflects radiation back into the room.
3 60 years.
4 £97.50.

Page 24
1 Air trapped in the fibres acts as an insulator.
2 Cooking and producing electricity.
3 A vacuum does not conduct heat.
4 Less energy is transferred through the ceiling into the roof.

Page 25
1 An electric fire.
2 For safety - microwaves could warm the water in human body.
3 Do not use mobile phones unless they have to or send text messages.
4 They are not in line of sight; they are in valleys, behind hills or tall buildings.

Page 26
1 Infrared.
2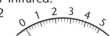
3 Any two from: visible light, infrared, laser.
4

Page 27
1 It can be used anywhere.
2 Less refraction of other waves that could interfere.

Page 28
1 300 000 km/s.
2 300 m/s.
3 It is quicker.
4 It uses a series of dots and dashes to represent letters of the alphabet.

Page 29
1 An instrument for detecting earthquakes.
2 The focus is the source of an earthquake. The epicentre is the point on the Earth's surface above the focus.
3 Burning fuels, cutting down trees.
4 150 minutes / 2.5 hours.

B2 Understanding our environment

Page 31
1 Natural: pond or lake. Artificial: aquarium or wheat field.
2 It suffocates.
3 A pitfall trap.
4 A group of animals or plants of the same species.

Page 32
1 Birds, reptiles, amphibians, fish and mammals.
2 To trap light or for photosynthesis or to make food.
3 One from: they give birth to live young, eat meat, produce milk.
4 Felidae.

Page 33

1 Carbon dioxide, water, sunlight and chlorophyll.
2 Any three from: respiration (energy), storage, make proteins, make cellulose.
3 It is colder and there is less light.
4 Keeping the plants warm, providing the plants with extra carbon dioxide, increasing the amount of light for the plant.

Page 34

1 Water.
2 So the species survives.
3 Lions, tigers, bears, alligators, etc.
4 A relationship where both organisms benefit.

Page 35

1 Bat, butterfly, etc.
2 To help it judge distance.
3 To stop sand getting in their eyes.
4 It would find it difficult to grip on the ice or compete with polar bear.

Page 36

1 The deepest rocks.
2 One from: some body parts decay quickly before they can be fossilised; fossilisation is rare, most living things will completely decay; there may still be fossils we have not found.
3 They swim faster.
4 In their genes.

Page 37

1 Carbon dioxide, sulphur dioxide.
2 Sulphur dioxide.
3 Polluted rivers have no fish for otters to eat and the pollution poisons them.
4 Any two from: bloodworm, water louse, sludge worm, rat-tailed maggot.

Page 38

1 There are very few left and they are close to extinction.
2 They may be unable to adapt to any change fast enough.
3 They follow the food supply.
4 The whales lose their freedom.

C2 Rocks and metals
Page 40

1 To thin the paint.

2 A **colloid** is when small solid particles are dispersed through the whole of a liquid, but are not dissolved in it.
3 A pigment that changes colour when it is heated.
4 The use of synthetic dyes has increased.

Page 41

1 Any three from: granite, marble, limestone, aluminium, iron (steel), brick, cement, concrete, glass.
2 Limestone and clay.
3 Calcium carbonate.
4 Calcium oxide and carbon dioxide.

Page 42

1 Iron core, mantle and crust.
2 They are less dense.
3 Igneous.
4 If the magma cools slowly, large crystals are made. Rapid cooling produces smaller crystals.

Page 43

1 To save resources and money.
2 The cathode.
3 An alloy is a mixture of a metal element with another element.
4 Copper and zinc.

Page 44

1 Water and oxygen.
2 The oxide of aluminium becomes a protective layer.
3 Iron.
4 Aluminium will corrode less and produce a lighter car than steel.

Page 45

1 It increases the level of carbon dioxide and decreases the level of oxygen.
2 Photosynthesis.
3 Sulphur dioxide.
4 Changes carbon monoxide to carbon dioxide, and oxides of nitrogen to nitrogen.

Page 46

1 Altering any three from: concentration of the reactants, temperature of the reactants, pressure of reactants that are gases, surface area of the reactants.

2 For a reaction to take place particles must collide often enough, with sufficient energy. If the particles move faster they will collide more successfully. If they are more crowded they will collide more often. In both cases the reaction will be faster.
3 Collecting the hydrogen given off with a gas syringe.
4 At a higher temperature the particles have more energy, so they collide more successfully, so the reaction is quicker. However, if the same mass of magnesium is used it will produce the same volume of hydrogen each time.

Page 47

1 Any two from: sulphur, flour, custard powder, wood dust.
2 Powdered reactants.
3 Half the mass of zinc will produce only half the volume of gas if the acid remains in excess both times.
4 A substance that is able to speed up a reaction but that is not used up in the reaction.

P2 Living for the future
Page 49

1 Photo cells use light and solar cells use light from the Sun.
2 No mains electrical supply is needed in remote areas.
3 So that it absorbs more radiation.
4 Sun over the equator - the equator is north of Australia but south of England.

Page 50

1 a dc b ac.
2 Coal, oil, natural gas.
3 Steam is pressurised.
4 There is less energy loss and lower distribution costs.

Page 51

1 An energy source which is being used up faster than it can be produced.
2 No carbon dioxide or smoke is produced.

3 Radiation causes ionisation, which changes the structure of atoms. DNA in the cell can change, so the cell behaves differently and divides in an uncontrolled way. This causes cancer.

Page 52

1 Radiation that is always present.
2 75%.
3 It increases the distance from the radioactive source and there is no skin contact.
4 Alpha radiation would not penetrate. Gamma radiation would give little change in the count rate when thickness changes slightly.

Page 53

1

2 They fluoresce.
3 A body in orbit around another body.
4 From a collision between two planets.

Page 54

1 Moon, planets, artificial satellites.
2 Mercury, Venus, Earth, Mars, Jupiter, Saturn, Uranus, Neptune, (Pluto).
3 20 000 years.
4 To keep the body at a suitable temperature, maintain suitable pressure, provide oxygen for breathing.

Page 55

1 Fires, tsunamis, dust clouds, falling temperature, extinction of life forms.
2 Large rocks or small planets orbiting the Sun.
3 Dust and rocks.
4 In case their orbit passes close to the orbit of Earth.

Page 56

1 Hydrogen and helium.
2 The galaxies furthest away.
3 Light cannot escape from it.
4 The remnants from a large star that has become a supernova can merge to form a new star.

B3 Living and growing
Page 58
1 The nucleus.
2 Amino acids are joined together.
3 To speed up the reaction.
4 An enzyme is a protein that acts as a biological catalyst.
Page 59
1 It goes into the body tissue.
2 In the alveoli.
3 Evaporation.
4 It diffuses through the stomata.
Page 60
1 Haemoglobin.
2 Cholesterol.
3 Advantage: no need for donor. Disadvantage: size or need for power supply.
4 Capillaries, arteries, veins.
Page 61
1 To grow, replace worn out cells, repair damaged tissue.
2 23 pairs or 46.
3 Fertilisation is when gametes join.
4 Meiosis.
Page 62
1 Chloroplast.
2 Any two from: cell wall, chloroplast, large vacuole.
3 Infancy, childhood, adolescence, adulthood, old age.
4 They are bigger so they need time to develop enough to survive outside the uterus.
Page 63
1 Hormones.
2 Stop fruit falling off tree.
3 It makes roots grow.
4 The root.
Page 64
1 Increased egg laying, grows big quickly.
2 Choose the characteristic; cross-breed; select the best offspring; repeat the selection and breeding process for a number of generations.
3 When humans change the genes or chromosomes of an organism.
4 The gene may have harmful effects on humans who eat the plants.
Page 65
1 Same DNA.
2 Embryo transplantation.

3 Strawberries grow stems called runners. The runners spread over the ground and have buds that grow into new strawberry plants.
4 One from: the plants are all genetically identical so if the environment changes or a new disease breaks out it is unlikely that any of the plants will survive; cloning plants over many years has resulted in little genetic variation.

C3 The periodic table
Page 67
1 Positive.
2 1.
3 11.
4 Copper and sulphur.
Page 68
1 An ion.
2 Electrons are gained.
3 A metal atom needs to lose electrons. The electrons transfer from the metal atom to a non-metal atom. A non-metal atom needs to gain electrons. The electrons transfer to the non-metal atom from the metal atom.
4 It is very high.
Page 69
1 Three.
2

3 Fluorine and chlorine.
4 Third.
Page 70
1 Because they react with air and water.
2 Because it is less dense than water.
3 They all have one electron in their outer shell.
4 Potassium.
Page 71
1 Halogens.
2 Chlorine.
3 Potassium + bromine → potassium bromide.
4 Iodine is less reactive than bromine, so does not displace it.
Page 72
1 The anode.
2 The formula of the compound breaking up is H_2O.
3 Bauxite.

4 They are worn away by oxidation.
Page 73
1 Cu and Ni.
2 Orange/brown.
3 A reaction between solutions that makes an insoluble solid.
4 In sodium hydroxide solution, Fe^{2+} ions form a grey/green solid and Fe^{3+} ions form an orange gelatinous solid.
Page 74
1 Any three from: lustrous, good conductors of heat and electricity, hard, high melting point, high boiling point, high density.
2 They have strong metallic bonds between the atoms that are very hard to break and a lot of energy is needed to separate them.
3 They become superconductors.
4 It levitates.

P3 Forces for transport
Page 76
1 m/s or km/h.
2 30 m/s.
3 a
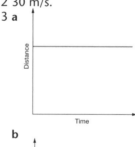
b
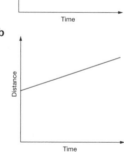
4 a It is constant b it is decreasing.
Page 77
1
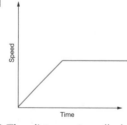
2 The distance travelled.
3 It is decelerating.
4 2.5 m/s^2.
Page 78
1 Car B.
2 6000 N.
3 Braking distance.
4 14 m.

Page 79
1 Ali.
2 1600 J.
3 Meera weighs more than Jan.
4 400 W.
Page 80
1 a Its food b coal or gas c falling water.
2 A larger mass means the car must gain more kinetic energy, so it uses more fuel.
3 The diesel-driven car.
4 One from: short range, slow speed, batteries take time to recharge, need a recharging facility, batteries take up a lot of space / are heavy, etc.
Page 81
1 Any two from: thermal energy, elastic energy, sound energy.
2 They open and close quickly at the push of a button so the driver is not distracted for too long and can concentrate on driving.
3 The seat belt and air bag.
4 This is less tiring on long motorway journeys. It helps a car keep to a steady speed so the driver does not have to use the pedals.
Page 82
1 A feather has a bigger surface area, so there is a bigger air resistance force; smaller weight.
2 Weight, air resistance / drag. a Weight constant, drag = 0 b weight = drag c drag greater than weight.
3 It increases the car's top speed.
4 There are more air molecules displaced each second.
Page 83
1 Jo's.
2 Gravitational PE → KE → gravitational PE, etc.
3 So less energy is needed to raise it /it needs to gain less gravitational PE.
4 It has very little KE at the top (mainly gravitational PE) but a lot of KE at the bottom.

B4 It's a green world
Page 85
1 Photosynthesis.
2 By the roots.

3 So it has a large surface area to absorb light.
4 Palisade cells.
Page 86
1 They wilt.
2 Osmosis.
3 Evaporation of water from leaf.
4 To reduce water loss.
Page 87
1 For anchorage and to absorb water and minerals.
2 Xylem.
3 More mass would be lost.
4 Any two from: increased light intensity, increased temperature, increased air movement (wind), a fall in humidity (amount of water in the atmosphere).
Page 88
1 Any two from: nitrogen, phosphorus, potassium, magnesium.
2 3%.
3 Potassium and magnesium.
4 Phosphorus.
Page 89
1 Because they get their energy from other organisms by feeding.
2 A pyramid of numbers shows the number of organisms, a pyramid of biomass shows the mass of the organisms.
3. Biofuel.
4 Sugar cane is fermented using yeast to make alcohol.The alcohol is mixed with petrol to make Gasohol, a fuel for cars.
Page 90
1 Insecticide.
2 Suggestion such as: enclosed in very small spaces, given harmful drugs, etc.
3 Using other animals to control pests.
4 One from: grow nitrogen-fixing plants, manure, compost.
Page 91
1 Bacteria and fungi.
2 Earthworms, maggots and woodlice.

3 Any three from: canning, adding vinegar, drying, freezing, cooling, adding sugar, adding salt.
4 Drying removes the moisture bacteria need for growth.
Page 92
1 Carbon and nitrogen.
2 Photosynthesis.
3 One from: burning, respiration, decay, volcanoes.
4 A decomposer.

C4 Chemical economics
Page 94
1 Any two from: making fertilisers, cleaning materials, car battery acids.
2 Zinc oxide, zinc hydroxide or zinc carbonate.
3 pH 1-6.
4 Magnesium sulphate.
Page 95
1 $65 + 12 + (3 \times 16) = 65 + 12 + 48 = 125$
2 $40 + 2(14 + (3 \times 16)) = 40 + 2(14 + 48) = 40 + 2(62) = 40 + 124 = 164$
3 Any two from: filtration losses, evaporation losses, losses when transferring liquids, more than one reaction taking place.
4 75%.
Page 96
1 Potassium and phosphorus.
2 149.
3 Any two from: ammonium nitrate, ammonium phosphate, ammonium sulphate, urea.
4 Potassium hydroxide and phosphoric acid.
Page 97
1 Nitrogen and hydrogen.
2 About 450 °C.
3 Any three from: building the plant, people's wages, raw materials, energy, catalyst.
4. The yield would be too low.
Page 98
1 To allow clothes to be washed at low temperatures.
2 An organic acid and an alkali.

3 A solvent.
4 Fabrics may be damaged by washing in water, grease stains do not dissolve in water but do in dry-cleaning solvent.
Page 99
1 Where the process does not stop and reactants are continually fed in.
2 A batch process is where the whole process takes a limited time then stops and can be changed if necessary.
3 Any three from: research and testing, labour, energy, raw materials, time taken for development, marketing costs.
4 Any two from: there are legal requirements, investment costs of its research and development, raw materials, expensive extraction from plants, it is labour intensive.
Page 100
1 Diamond, graphite and buckminster fullerene.
2 Conducts electricity and has a high melting point.
3 Working at the level of atoms.
4 The properties of large amounts of a material.
Page 101
1 Any three from: lakes, rivers, aquifers, reservoirs.
2 To filter out fine particles that do not sediment out.
3 A precipitation reaction.
3 Silver nitrate.

P4 Radiation for life
Page 103
1 b Paper c polythene.
2 a They repel b they attract.
3 Clothes are insulators and rub against each other, becoming charged by friction.
4 They could cause a spark which may lead to an explosion as fuel is highly inflammable.
Page 104
1 To ensure good electrical contact.
2 Negative.

3 To charge the soot particles when they come near the wires.
Page 105
1 It decreases.
2 8 Ω.
3 The earth wire.
4 The wire in the fuse melts if the current becomes too large, breaking the circuit and preventing overheating.
Page 106
1 256
2 Body fat.
3 It avoids major surgery.
4 10 cm.
Page 107
1 Both are very penetrating and can pass into the body.
2 Using radiation to treat diseases such as cancer.
3 It kills bacteria.
4 It emits only gamma radiation or iodine is taken up by the thyroid gland.
Page 108
1 600 Bq.
2 Radioactive decay is a random process.
3 a A helium nucleus b an electron.
4 It is radiation, not a particle.
Page 109
1 To locate a leak or blockage in a buried pipeline.
2 So that a decrease in ionisation current is due to the presence of smoke and not to the decay of the source reducing the number of ions present.
3 Less uranium has decayed to lead (i.e. more uranium and less lead than an old rock).
4 Iron was never living so does not contain carbon-14.
Page 110
1 Uranium.
2 It is uranium containing a greater proportion of the uranium-235 isotope than occurs naturally.
3 In a nuclear reactor.
4 It emits harmful ionising radiation for a long time.

Glossary/index

Term	Definition	Pages
breed	To produce young.	11, 32, 34, 64
buckminster fullerene	A very stable ball of 60 carbon atoms joined by covalent bonds; the whole structure looks like a geodesic dome.	100, 102
bulk properties	A bulk property of a substance is one that is independent of the amount of that substance being measured, e.g. density or refractive index.	100
cancer	A dangerous illness caused by radiation, smoking and some types of chemicals.	29, 30, 51, 52, 107
capillary	The narrowest type of blood vessel	9, 60, 66
carbohydrate	Carbohydrates are chemicals found in all living things. They contain the elements carbon, hydrogen and oxygen.	5, 13
carbon	A very important element, carbon is present in all living things and forms a huge range of compounds with other elements.	17, 43, 69, 92, 93, 100, 102
carbon dioxide	A gas containing only carbon and oxygen. Its chemical formula is CO_2.	4, 13, 19, 29, 33, 37, 41, 45, 51, 59, 66, 68, 69, 73, 79, 85, 92, 93
carbon monoxide	A poisonous gas containing only carbon and oxygen.	19, 45
carbon-14	A radioactive isotope of carbon used in carbon-dating calculations.	109
carbonate	Compounds containing the carbonate group of atoms; the carbonate group formula is CO_3.	13, 47, 94
carnivore	An animal that eats other animals.	89
carrier wave	An electromagnetic wave that can carry speech, music, images, or other signals.	26
catalyst	A chemical that speeds up a reaction but is not changed or used up by the reaction.	17, 47, 58, 66, 73, 97
catalytic converter	Boxes fitted to vehicle exhausts which reduce the level of nitrogen oxides and unburnt hydrocarbons in the exhaust fumes.	45
cathode	The negative electrode in a circuit or a battery.	43, 72
cation	A positively-charged ion, it moves towards the cathode in an electrolytic cell.	72
cell differentiation	The change of an unspecialised cell into a particular type of cell.	61
cell division	The multiplication of cells.	61, 62, 65, 66
cell membrane	The thin layer around the outside of a cell.	59, 62, 86
cell wall	A thick wall consisting of cellulose and starch found around plant cells.	62, 86, 99
cellulose	An insoluble carbohydrate molecule formed of spirals of glucose joined together. Cell walls in plants are made of cellulose.	33, 62
central nervous system	The brain and spinal cord.	7
chain reaction	A reaction where the products cause the reaction to go further or faster.	110
characteristic	Things that are true about something, e.g. it is a characteristic of mammals that they have fur.	11, 19, 64
charge	A property of matter, charge exists in two forms (negative and positive) which attract each other.	52, 67, 103, 104, 105
chemical change	A change that occurs when a number of substances react together to produce new substances.	13, 21
chemical property	The characteristic reactions of a substance.	69
chlorination	Adding chlorine to a molecule or substance.	101
chlorophyll	A green chemical found in photosynthetic plants that allows them to use energy from sunlight to make sugar from carbon dioxide and water.	33, 85, 93
cholesterol	A chemical found particularly in animal fats and foods made from them; the body uses cholesterol to make nerve tissue and some hormones but high levels of cholesterol may make heart attacks more likely.	60
chromatography	The science of producing chromatograms, chromatography can use paper or jelly-like films for the soluble substances to move along.	99
chromosome	A thread-like body made of DNA and protein found in the nucleus, it only becomes visible during cell division.	10, 11, 12, 58, 61, 66
cilia	Tiny hairs found on the surface of cells and some microorganisms.	8
circuit	The complete path around an electrical circuit that electricity can flow along.	105, 111
circuit-breaker	A device which breaks a circuit to switch off the power when a danger is detected, it behaves similarly to a fuse.	105
cirrhosis	A disease of the liver often caused by excessive alcohol intake. Cirrhotic livers have a lot of fibrous tissues and cannot break down toxins as well as healthy livers.	8
classification	Arranging things into sets according to the features that they have in common. Biologists classify living things into groups like animals, vertebrates and mammals.	39
clone	Two living thing are clones if they have exactly the same genes.	10, 65, 66
collision frequency	The number of collisions in a particular area in a particular time.	46, 47
colloid	A mixture in which small particles of one substance are suspended in another.	40
combustion	Combustion is the reaction between a fuel and oxygen to form carbon dioxide and water, and release energy as light and heat.	19, 20, 21, 45, 48
comet	A small body that moves through space and reflects light. Comets often show a tail caused by particles of dust and ice that trail behind it as it moves.	54, 55
compost	Organic material being rotted down to make fertiliser for the soil.	90, 91
compound	Groups of atoms bound together, in fixed proportions, by chemical bonds. Compounds have different chemical and physical properties to the elements that they contain.	43, 67, 73
compression	To push something together, to squeeze it and make it smaller.	16, 106

gestation	The time between conception and birth in humans, gestation is called pregnancy and lasts for roughly 42 weeks.	62
gland	An organ in the body that produces a secretion, for example the sweat gland. Endocrine glands pass their secretions, called hormones, directly into the bloodstream.	9
glucose	A type of sugar. Glucose is sometimes called dextrose.	4, 9, 33, 58
gradient	A slope or difference in measurements between two areas, for example there is a concentration gradient between water molecules inside and outside a cell.	46, 47, 76, 77
graphite	A type of carbon often used in pencils as the 'lead'.	100, 102
gravity	The force of attraction between two bodies caused by their mass; the force of gravity produced by a body depends on its mass – the larger the mass the larger the force.	56, 63, 82, 84
greenhouse gas	Gases like carbon dioxide and water vapour that increase the greenhouse effect.	29, 79
Haber process	The industrial process developed by Fritz Haber to make ammonia from nitrogen and hydrogen.	73, 97, 102
haemoglobin	A complex chemical found in red blood cells that can combine with oxygen to help transport it around the body.	5, 60
hallucinogen	A drug, like LSD, that gives the user hallucinations.	8
halogen	A group of reactive non-metals with only one electron missing from their outer electron shell, e.g. chlorine and iodine.	71, 75
haploid number	The number of chromosomes present in the sperm or egg of a species.	61, 66
herbicide	A chemical that can kill plants, usually used to mean a chemical that kills weeds.	64, 90, 93
herbivore	An animal that eats plants.	89
hertz	A unit of frequency equal to one cycle per second (Hz).	106
homeostasis	All living organisms attempt to maintain the conditions in their cells within certain limits. This is known as homeostasis.	9
homologous	A matched pair of chromosomes; humans have 22 homologous pairs of chromosomes and a pair of sex chromosomes.	61
hormone	A chemical produced by an endocrine gland which changes the way other parts of the body work; hormones pass around the body in the blood.	9, 63, 66
host	An organism that is carrying another one inside its body.	6, 34
hydrocarbon	Hydrocarbon molecules are molecules that contain only carbon and hydrogen atoms. Many fuels are hydrocarbons, e.g. natural gas (methane) and petrol (a complex mixture).	16, 17, 19
hydrogen	A colourless, odourless gas that burns easily in oxygen to form water; hydrogen is the lightest element.	17, 56, 69, 72, 75, 97, 102
hydroponics	Growing plants in mineral solutions without the need for soil.	90, 93
hydroxide	Chemicals containing an 'OH' group; hydroxides are often alkaline.	70, 94
hypothermia	A condition caused by the body getting too cold. Hypothermia can lead to death if untreated.	9
igneous	Rocks formed from solidified molten magma.	42
immune system	The parts of the body that protect against illnesses. The lymph glands are particularly important in the immune system.	6, 12
indicator species	A species that is particularly sensitive to an environmental pollution. The presence or absence of an indicator species is often used to assess the degree of pollution in an environment.	37
infrared	Radiation beyond the red end of the visible spectrum. Infrared radiation is efficient at transferring heat.	24, 25, 26, 30
inherit	To receive something from your parents, usually used to describe characteristics that can be passed down through sperm and eggs.	11, 12
insecticide	A chemical that can kill an insect.	90, 93
insoluble	A substance that will not dissolve. Something that is insoluble in water may be soluble in other liquids.	15, 33, 98
insulation	A substance that slows down the movement of energy. Heat insulation in the loft of a house slows down the movement of warmth to the cooler outside. Sound insulation cuts down the movement of sound in recording studios. Electrical insulation prevents the flow of electricity.	23, 24, 30, 35, 103
intensive farming	Farming that uses a lot of artificial fertilisers and energy to produce a high yield per farm worker.	90, 93
interference	Waves interfere with each other when two waves of different frequencies occupy the same space. Interference occurs in light and sound and can produce changes in intensity of the waves.	27
invertebrate	An animal without a backbone.	32, 39
ion	Charged particle made when an atom, or group of atoms, gains or loses electrons.	68, 75
ionisation	The formation of ions (charged particles).	51, 52, 107
isotope	One of two or more atoms having the same atomic number but different mass numbers.	67, 109, 110
joule	A unit of energy (J).	20, 22, 79, 84
kilowatt	1000 watts.	51, 79
kinetic energy	Energy due to movement.	46, 49, 57, 80, 81, 83, 84
kwashiorkor	An illness caused by protein deficiency due to lack of food.	5
lactic acid	A toxic chemical produced by anaerobic respiration in animals.	4
laser	A special kind of light beam that can carry a lot of energy and can be focused very accurately. Lasers are often used to judge the speed of moving objects or the distance to them.	28
latent heat	The energy needed to change the state of a substance.	22

lava	Molten rock thrown up by a volcano.	42
limestone	A kind of rock made from the remains of shells and skeletons; it is mainly calcium carbonate.	41, 48
lithosphere	The outer part of the Earth, consisting of the crust and upper mantle, approximately 100 km thick.	42
longitudinal	In longitudinal waves, the vibration is along the direction in which the wave travels.	29, 106
lustrous	Having a sheen or glow; highly polished metals like gold are often described as lustrous.	74, 100
magma	Molten rock inside the Earth.	42
magnet	An object that is magnetic is attracted by a magnet.	50, 53
malleable	Can be beaten into flat sheets. Metals are malleable.	44, 73, 74
mass	Mass describes the amount of something, it is measured in kilograms (kg).	20, 22, 78, 80, 83, 84, 95, 102
mass number	The mass of an atom compared with hydrogen.	67
meiosis	A specialised form of cell division that produces cells carrying half the usual number of chromosomes, these cells are called gametes and are used in sexual reproduction.	61, 66
melanin	The group of naturally occurring dark pigments, especially the pigment found in skin, hair, fur, and feathers.	29
melting point	The temperature at which a solid changes to a liquid.	22, 43, 68, 74, 100, 102
membrane	A flat sheet.	18, 86
metal halide	A compound containing only a metal and a halogen atom, e.g. sodium chloride.	71
methane	A colourless, odourless gas that burns easily to give water and carbon dioxide.	17, 51
micro-organism	An organism that is only visible under a microscope.	6, 91
migration	The movement of populations of animals or birds at certain times of the year.	38
mineral	Natural solid materials with a fixed chemical composition and structure, rocks are made of collections of minerals; mineral nutrients in our diet are things like calcium and iron, they are simple chemicals needed for health.	5, 37, 86, 87, 88, 96
mineral deficiency	Lack of essential minerals in the diet of animals or soil of plants.	88
mitochondria	Cell structures that carry out aerobic respiration.	58, 61
mitosis	The process of cell division that ensures that new cells have a complete copy of inherited information.	61, 66
mmHg	The height of mercury in a barometer that measures air pressure. It stands for millimetres of mercury.	4
molecular formula	A chemical formula that shows the number and kinds of atoms in a molecule.	69
molecule	A group of atoms joined together by chemical links.	5, 16, 17, 21, 58, 59, 68, 69, 75, 102
molten	Something is molten if it has been heated to change it from a solid to a liquid.	53, 68
monocular	Having only one eye or eyepiece. Many microscopes and telescopes are monocular.	7
Morse code	A code consisting of dots and dashes that code for each letter of the alphabet.	28
multi-cellular	Having more than one cell.	61
mutation	A random change in the genotype of an organism, mutations are almost always disadvantageous.	11, 51, 64
mutualism	Two different species live together but both benefiting, for example root nodule bacteria and certain leguminous plants.	34, 39
nano properties	The properties of materials at the nanoscale, often different to the same material's properties at the visible scale.	100
nanoscale	Objects and events occurring at distances of fewer than 100 nanometres.	100, 102
nanotube	A molecule consisting of carbon atoms joined in a cylinder one to two nanometres in diameter and about a millimetre in length.	100
National Grid	The network of electricity cables that distribute electricity across the country.	50, 57
natural selection	Factors in the environment affect animals and plants so that some survive to reproduce successfully and pass on their good combinations of genes. Others survive less well and do not pass on their poor combinations of genes as often.	36
negative ion	An ion with a negative charge.	68, 72
neurone	A nerve cell.	7, 12
neutral	A neutral solution has a pH of 7 and is neither acid nor alkaline.	67
neutralise	A reaction between an acid and an alkali to produce a neutral solution.	94, 96, 98
neutron	A particle found in the nucleus of an atom, it has no electrical charge and a mass of 1 atomic mass unit.	56, 67, 108, 110
Newton	The unit of force (N).	78
nitrate	A salt of nitric acid.	88, 94, 101
nitrogen	A non-reactive gas that makes up most of the atmosphere.	45, 88, 92, 93, 97, 102
non-biodegradable	Living organisms cannot breakdown non-biodegradable objects.	18, 44
non-renewable	Non-renewable fuels are not being made fast enough at the moment and so will run out at some point in the future.	16, 51, 80
nuclear	To do with the nucleus.	51, 52, 56, 57, 107, 110, 111
nucleus	(Biol) The control centre of the cell, the nucleus is surrounded by a membrane that separates it from the rest of the cell. (Chem) The central part of an atom containing the protons and neutrons.	58, 60, 62, 66, 67, 107, 108, 110
oestrogen	A female hormone produced by the ovary.	9
ohm	The unit used to measure electrical resistance (Ω).	105
optical fibre	A flexible, optically transparent fibre, usually made of glass or plastic, through which light passes by successive internal reflections.	26

Term	Definition	Pages
optimum temperature	The temperature range that produces the best reaction rate.	12
orbit	A path, usually circular, of a smaller object around a larger object, for example a planet orbits the Sun and electrons orbit the nucleus in an atom.	53, 54, 55, 57
organic farmer	A farmer who avoids artificial fertilisers, pesticides and energy inputs and concentrates on natural cycles and materials to increase yield.	90
oscilloscope	A device that displays a line on a screen showing regular changes (oscillations) in something. An oscilloscope is often used to look at sound waves collected by a microphone.	50
osmosis	When solutions of different concentrations are separated by a semi-permeable membrane, water molecules pass through the membrane moving from the dilute solution to the more concentrated one to reduce the difference.	86, 93
ozone layer	A layer of the upper atmosphere that is particularly rich in the gas ozone.	29, 37
palisade	A cell found on the upper side of a leaf, palisade cells are tightly packed together and contain lots of chloroplasts so that they can carry out photosynthesis very effectively.	85
pancreas	An organ in the abdomen that produces enzymes to break down food.	9
parasite	An organism that gets its food from another organism, called the host, without killing it.	6, 34
pathogen	An organism that causes a disease.	6, 12
performance enhancer	A drug used to improve performance in a sporting event.	8
period	A horizontal row of the periodic table.	69
periodic table	A way of grouping elements according to their similarities, first devised by Dimitri Mendeleev.	67, 75, 95
peripheral nervous system	The nerves leading from the brain and spinal cord.	7
pesticide	A chemical designed to kill a pest. Different types of pesticides kill rats, rabbits, worms or insects.	90, 93, 101
pH scale	The range of levels of acidity or alkalinity, a pH of 7 is neutral, a pH below 7 is acid, a pH above 7 is alkaline.	94
phloem	Specialised transporting cells which form tubules in plants to carry sugars from leaves to other parts of the plant.	87, 93
phosphorescent	Phosphorescent materials glow gently even after the original light source has been removed.	40, 48
phosphorus	A non-metallic element that bursts into flame in air.	88
photocell	A device which converts light into electricity.	49, 57
photosynthesis	The production, in green plants, of sugar and oxygen from carbon dioxide and water using light as an external energy source.	33, 39, 45, 48, 49, 59, 85, 86, 88, 89, 92, 93
phototropism	Growth of plants towards a source of light.	63, 66
pigment	Chemicals which absorb certain wavelengths of light and so look coloured.	29, 40
pitfall trap	A beaker or pot buried in the ground. The rim is level with the ground. Ground-dwelling insects fall into the pot and can be identified later.	31
placenta	The organ which allows materials to be exchanged between a mother and a foetus in the uterus.	59, 66
plasma	The liquid part of the blood.	5, 60
platelet	Platelets are found in the blood and are involved in clotting.	60
pollutant	A chemical that causes pollution.	45, 101
polymer	A molecule made of many repeating subunits, for example polythene or starch.	17, 18, 21
polymerisation	The process of forming large polymers from smaller monomer molecules.	17
pooter	A device used to transfer small insects safely between containers in a laboratory.	31
positive ion	An ion with a positive charge.	68, 72, 109
potassium	A soft group 1 metal.	70, 88
potential difference	The difference between two points which will cause current to flow in a closed circuit, it is measured in volts (V).	105, 111
power	The rate that a system transfers energy, power is usually measured in watts (W).	51, 79, 84
precipitate	To fall out of solution.	73, 101
predator	Animals that hunt and kill other animals.	34, 35, 36, 39
preserve	To prevent something decaying.	14, 91
pressure	The force acting on a surface divided by the area of the surface, measured in newtons per square metre (N/m^2).	17
prey	Animals that are hunted by other animals.	34, 35, 39
producer	An organism that makes organic material, green plants are sometimes called primary producers because they use energy in sunlight to make sugar.	89
product	Something made by a chemical reaction.	13, 20, 46, 58, 95
protein	A group of complex molecules that contain carbon, hydrogen, oxygen, nitrogen, and usually sulphur, they are made of one or more chains of amino acids.	5, 13, 21, 33, 58, 66, 88
protein synthesis	To make protein in a cell.	58
proton	A particle found in the nucleus of an atom with a charge of plus one and a mass of one atomic mass unit.	56, 67, 108
pyramid of biomass	A diagram to show the masses of living organisms present at each trophic level in an ecosystem.	89, 93
pyramid of numbers	A diagram to show the number of living organisms present at each trophic level in an ecosystem.	89, 93

synthetic auxin	A chemical made by chemists with auxin-like properties.	63
systolic pressure	The pressure of the blood when the ventricles of the heart contract. It is generally higher than diastolic pressure.	4, 12
tectonic plate	Sections of the Earth's crust that float on top of the mantle. Plates are hundreds of miles across and move relative to each other by a few inches a year.	42, 48
terminal speed	The speed at which the force of gravity and the force due to air resistance are equal and the object is falling as fast as possible.	82, 84
testosterone	A male hormone made by the testes.	9
thermal	To do with heat.	74
thermal decomposition	Breaking down a chemical using heat.	41, 73
thermal energy	Energy that can raise the temperature of an object, sometimes called 'heat'.	83
thermochromic	A pigment that changes colour when it gets hotter or colder.	40, 48
tissue	A group of cells of the same type, so nervous tissue contains only nerve cells.	62
toxin	A poison. Usually used to mean a poison produced by a living organism.	6
tracer	A radioactive, or radiation-emitting, substance used in a nuclear medicine scan or other research where movement of a particular chemical is to be followed.	52, 107, 109
transition element	A metal belonging to the transition group in the periodic table.	73
transpiration	The release of water vapour from a plant through the leaves.	86, 87, 93
transverse	In transverse waves, the vibration is at right angles to the direction in which the wave travels.	28, 29
trophic	The level at which an organism gets its food, primary producers are level one, primary consumers are level two and secondary consumers are level three.	89, 93
turbine	A device that converts movement in a fluid into circular movement, usually to drive a generator. Turbines are essential parts of a windmill and a hydroelectric power plant.	49, 50, 110
ultrasound	Sounds which have too high a frequency for humans to hear (above 20 khz).	106, 111
ultraviolet	Radiation just beyond the blue end of the spectrum of visible light. UV light is important in tanning and some sorts of skin cancer.	29, 30
Universe	Everything, everywhere.	54, 56, 57
uranium	A radioactive metal used in nuclear power stations and bombs.	51, 109, 110
uterus	The organ in the female where the baby grows during pregnancy, also known as the womb.	62
vacuole	A sac in a cell filled with a watery solution, plant cells tend to have large vacuoles but animal cells have small ones.	62
valve	Something that only lets liquids pass one way.	60
variable	This is something that can vary if you were in an investigation.	26
variable resistor	A resistor whose resistance can change.	105
variation	The existence of a range of individuals of the same group with different characteristics.	11, 61
vascular bundle	A collection of xylem and phloem vessels in a plant, they can be seen in leaves as the veins.	87
vein	In animals: a blood vessel carrying blood towards the heart. In plants: a collection of xylem and phloem vessels clearly seen on the surface of a leaf.	60, 66
ventricle	Large muscular chamber in the heart.	60
vertebrate	An animal with a boney backbone or spine.	32, 39
volt	The international unit of electrical potential (V).	105
voltage	The potential difference across a component or circuit.	50, 57, 103, 105, 111
voltmeter	A meter that measures the voltage between two points.	105
watt	A unit of power (W), 1 watt equals 1 joule of energy being transferred per second.	51, 79
wavelength	The distance between two identical points on a wave.	25, 26, 28, 106, 111
weight	The force of gravity acting on a body on Earth; weight is a force and is measured in newtons.	82, 84
withdrawal symptoms	The combination of physical and psychological symptoms produced when an addictive drug is withheld for a period of time. The symptoms of withdrawal sickness fade after a while as the body adjusts to the absence of the drug.	8
work	Work is done when a force moves, the greater the force or the larger the distance the more work is done.	79, 84
X-ray	Electromagnetic radiation used by doctors to look inside a patient's body or to destroy some types of cancer cells.	107, 111
XX chromosomes	The sex chromosomes present in a human female.	11
XY chromosomes	The sex chromosomes present in a human male.	11
xylem	Cells specialised for transporting water through a plant; xylem cells have thick walls, no cytoplasm and are dead, their end walls break down and they form a continuous tube.	87, 93
yeast	A unicellular fungus used extensively in the brewing and baking industries.	89
yield	The ratio of product to starting materials, a high yield means that most of the starting material is converted to useful products.	64, 95, 102
zygote	A cell produced when a male and female gamete join.	61, 66

Collins Revision

GCSE Foundation Science

Exam Practice Workbook

FOR OCR GATEWAY B

Fit for life

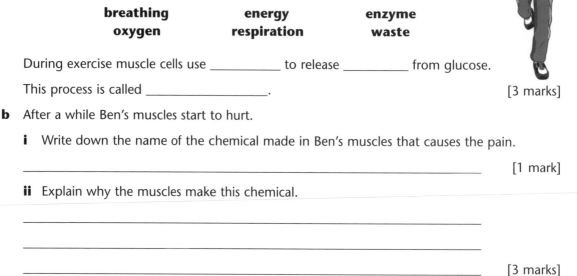

1 a Ben goes running to get fit. Describe what happens to Ben's muscles. Finish the sentences by choosing the **best** words from this list.

breathing	**energy**	**enzyme**
oxygen	**respiration**	**waste**

During exercise muscle cells use _____ to release _____ from glucose.

This process is called _____.   [3 marks]

b After a while Ben's muscles start to hurt.

i Write down the name of the chemical made in Ben's muscles that causes the pain.

_____   [1 mark]

ii Explain why the muscles make this chemical.

_____

_____

_____   [3 marks]

G–E

D–C

2 a Ben measures how fit he is. Here are four sentences (**A–D**) about how he measures his fitness. They are in the wrong order. Fill in the boxes to show the right order. The first one has been done for you.

A Ben ran on the spot for 2 minutes.

B Ben measured his resting pulse 3 times to get an average.

C Ben kept taking his pulse until it returned to normal.

D Ben sat down and measured his pulse.

B			

                    [2 marks]

b Ben finds out he is very fit. A week later Ben catches a cold. He is not in good health. Explain why being fit may not keep you healthy.

_____

_____   [2 marks]

G–E

D–C

3 Rashid has his blood pressure checked by a nurse.

a Write down the name of the body organ which contracts to put the blood under pressure.

_____   [1 mark]

b The nurse tells Rashid his blood pressure is too high. He fills in a questionnaire for the nurse.
Suggest **two** changes Rashid should make to lower his blood pressure.

Blood pressure questionnaire			
Questions	Notes	Answers Yes	No
1 Do you take regular exercise?	Strong heart muscles will lower blood pressure		✓
2 Do you eat a healthy balanced diet?	Reducing salt intake will lower blood pressure		✓
3 Are you overweight?	Being overweight by 5 kg raises blood pressure by 5 units	✓	
4 Do you regularly drink alcohol?	A high alcohol intake will damage liver and kidneys	✓	
5 Are you under stress?	Relaxation will lower blood pressure	✓	

_____

_____

_____

_____   [2 marks]

G–E

D–C

What's for lunch?

1 Look at the picture. It shows an African child with a swollen abdomen.
The child has a diet low in protein.

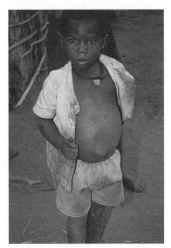

a **i** Why do we need protein in our diet?

_____ [1 mark]

ii The child has a mass of 40 kg. Calculate his recommended average protein
intake (RDA) in grams. Use this formula: RDA in g = 0.75 x body mass in kg
Show your working.

RDA = _____ g [2 marks]

b Simon is overweight.

i Which problem is he more likely to suffer from as he gets older?

Put a (ring) around the correct answer.

anaemia **diabetes** **lung cancer** **scurvy** [1 mark]

ii Simon would like to lose weight. He decides to change his diet.
Suggest **one** other way Simon could lose weight.

_____ [1 mark]

2 a Describe **one** type of mechanical digestion that takes place in the body.

_____
_____ [1 mark]

b Enzymes are used to digest food.

Finish the table to name the enzyme that digests each type of food and the product
of the digestion. The first one has been done for you.

food type	enzyme	product
starch	carbohydrase	glucose
protein		
fat		

[4 marks]

Keeping healthy

1 a Diseases are caused by different pathogens.

Put a tick (✓) in the box that shows the disease caused by a fungus.

athlete's foot ☐

flu ☐

cholera ☐

dysentery ☐

[1 mark]

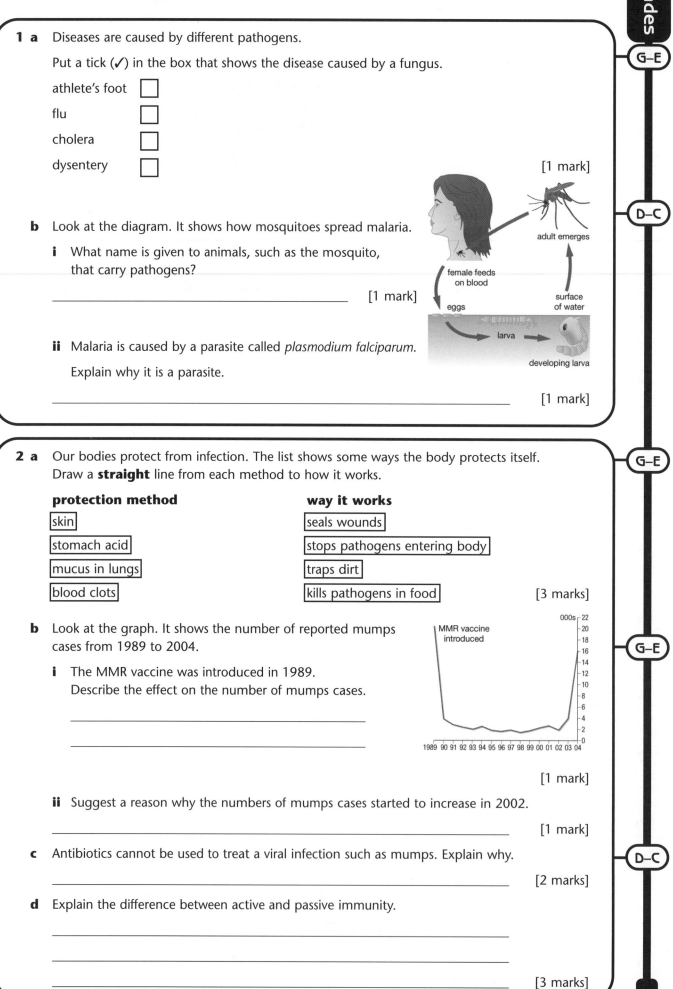

adult emerges

female feeds
on blood

eggs

surface
of water

larva →

developing larva

b Look at the diagram. It shows how mosquitoes spread malaria.

i What name is given to animals, such as the mosquito, that carry pathogens?

_____ [1 mark]

ii Malaria is caused by a parasite called *plasmodium falciparum*.

Explain why it is a parasite.

_____ [1 mark]

2 a Our bodies protect from infection. The list shows some ways the body protects itself. Draw a **straight** line from each method to how it works.

protection method	way it works
skin	seals wounds
stomach acid	stops pathogens entering body
mucus in lungs	traps dirt
blood clots	kills pathogens in food

[3 marks]

b Look at the graph. It shows the number of reported mumps cases from 1989 to 2004.

MMR vaccine
introduced

000s
22
20
18
16
14
12
10
8
6
4
2
0

1989 90 91 92 93 94 95 96 97 98 99 00 01 02 03 04

i The MMR vaccine was introduced in 1989.
Describe the effect on the number of mumps cases.

_____

_____

[1 mark]

ii Suggest a reason why the numbers of mumps cases started to increase in 2002.

_____ [1 mark]

c Antibiotics cannot be used to treat a viral infection such as mumps. Explain why.

_____ [2 marks]

d Explain the difference between active and passive immunity.

_____

_____

_____ [3 marks]

Keeping in touch

G–E

1 Write down the name of the sense organ that detects temperature.

_____ [1 mark]

G–E

2 a Look at the diagram of the eye. Choose words from this list to label the diagram.

cornea
iris
optic nerve
pupil
retina

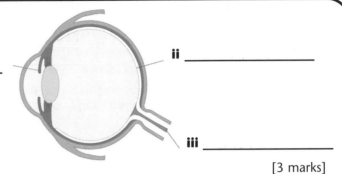

i _____

ii _____

iii _____

[3 marks]

D–C

b Finish the table to show which part of the eye does which job. The first one has been done for you.

part of the eye	job
iris	_controls the amount of light entering the eye_
retina	
optic nerve	
cornea	

[3 marks]

c Look at the picture of the owl. The owl uses both eyes to see the same image.

G–E

i Name the type of vision that uses both eyes.

_____

[1 mark]

D–C

ii Write down **one** advantage that this type of vision gives the owl when it hunts.

_____

_____ [1 mark]

G–E

3 When we touch something hot, we react by taking our hands away without thinking. Write down the name of this type of reaction.

_____ [1 mark]

D–C

4 The diagram shows the pathway taken by the impulse during an automatic reaction. Finish labelling the diagram to show the neurons involved.

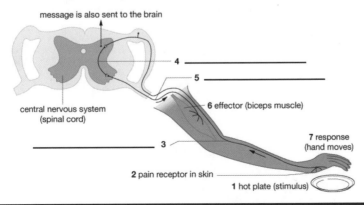

message is also sent to the brain

4 _____

5 _____

6 effector (biceps muscle)

central nervous system (spinal cord)

3 _____

7 response (hand moves)

2 pain receptor in skin

1 hot plate (stimulus)

[3 marks]

Drugs and you

1 a The list shows some different effects drugs have. Draw a **straight** line from each drug type to its effect on the body.

drug	effect
depressant	changes what you see and hear
hallucinogen	speeds up the working of the brain
stimulant	slows down the working of the brain

[2 marks]

b Finish the table by writing **one** example of each type of drug.
Choose words from this list.

alcohol   **anabolic**   **steroid**   **cannabis**   **caffeine**   **heroin**

type of drug	example
hallucinogen	
depressant	

[2 marks]

c Cannabis is a class C drug. Heroin is a class A drug.
Write down **one** way class C drugs are different from class A drugs.

_____

[1 mark]

2 a Carbon monoxide is a chemical found in tobacco smoke.
Write down the name of **two** other chemicals found in tobacco smoke.

1 _____   2 _____   [2 marks]

b Describe the effect of carbon monoxide on the body.

_____   [1 mark]

c i Finish the sentence about the diseases caused by smoking.

Smokers are more likely to get diseases such as _____

and cancer of the _____.   [2 marks]

ii Describe the effects of tobacco smoke on epithelial cells in the lining of the trachea.

_____

_____   [2 marks]

3 a Alcohol has long term effects on the body. Which of the following is a long term effect of alcohol? Put a (ring) around the correct answer.

blurred vision   **heat loss**   **liver damage**   **poor balance**   [1 mark]

b Look at the pictures. They show drinks that contain one unit of alcohol. Matthew drinks two pints of beer and a glass of whisky. Jo drinks three glasses of wine and a glass of whisky. Who drinks the most units? Explain your answer.

half pint beer   single whisky   glass of wine

_____

_____   [2 marks]

Staying in balance

Grades

1 a Chris is on holiday.
He is too hot and his body needs to lose heat.

    i How does the body lose heat?
Put a (ring) around the correct answer.

       exercising   **respiration**   **shivering**   **sweating**   [1 mark]

    ii The body needs to stay at a constant temperature.
What is normal body temperature?

    _____ [1 mark]

b If the body gets too hot you can suffer from dehydration. Explain why.

    _____

    _____ [2 marks]

c When the body gets too cold the pulse rate slows. Write down the name of the condition that the body suffers from when it gets too cold.

    _____ [1 mark]

d The body also controls other factors such as blood sugar level. Write down the name of the process that keeps these factors constant.

    _____ [1 mark]

---

2 Look at the flow chart. It shows the control of blood sugar by the hormone insulin.

Sugar enters blood from small intestine	→	Blood sugar level rises	→	Insulin released into blood	→	Blood sugar level falls

a **i** Write down the name of the organ that makes insulin.

    _____ [1 mark]

    ii Some people do not make enough insulin.
Write down the name of the condition they suffer from.

    _____ [1 mark]

    iii Suggest **one** way such people can control their blood sugar level.

    _____ [1 mark]

b Our bodies also make sex hormones.

    i Name the hormone made by the testes.

    _____ [1 mark]

    ii **Male** sex hormones cause changes that occur during puberty, such as the voice breaking. Describe **two other** changes caused by **male** sex hormones.

    1 _____

    2 _____ [2 marks]

Gene control

1 a Look at the picture. It shows human chromosomes. Finish the sentences about chromosomes. Choose the **best** words from this list.

codes
cytoplasm
DNA
genes
MRSA
nucleus

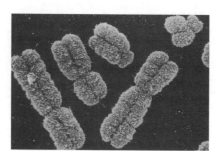

G–E

Chromosomes are found in the _____ of the cell. They carry instructions called

_____. The chromosomes are made of a chemical called _____. [3 marks]

b Chromosomes contain special chemicals called bases.
How many different bases are there in a chromosome?

_____ [1 mark]

D–C

2 Look at the picture of a squirrel. The squirrel developed from a fertilised egg. The fertilised egg has 20 chromosomes in it.

D–C

a How many chromosomes are in the egg before it is fertilised by a sperm?

_____ [1 mark]

b How many chromosomes are in one cell from the squirrel's ear?

_____ [1 mark]

c The nucleus of a human sperm is different from the nucleus of a squirrel sperm. Describe how they are different.

_____ [1 mark]

3 a Scientists can clone plants without using sexual reproduction. Write down the name of this type of reproduction.

G–E

_____ [1 mark]

b Describe **two** ways this type of reproduction is different from sexual reproduction.

1 _____

2 _____ [2 marks]

Who am I?

1 a Look at the diagram. It shows the characteristics of Darren's face.

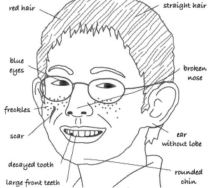

red hair

straight hair

blue eyes

broken nose

freckles

scar

ear without lobe

decayed tooth

large front teeth

rounded chin

G–E

i Write down **two** characteristics Darren inherited from his parents.

1 _____

2 _____ [2 marks]

ii Write down **two** of Darren's characteristics caused by the environment.

1 _____

2 _____ [2 marks]

D–C

b Darren inherited sex chromosomes from his parents.
Write down the type of sex chromosome he inherited from his father.

_____ [1 mark]

c Look at the diagram.
It shows a breeding experiment.

Parental generation

purple-stemmed   green-stemmed

F_1 generation

purple-stemmed

Which characteristic is dominant? Explain your answer.

_____

_____ [1 mark]

d Mutations are changes to genes. Mutations can occur spontaneously or they can be caused by some other factors. Write down **one** factor that can cause mutations.

_____ [1 mark]

G–E

2 People can inherit conditions from their parents. Put a tick (✓) in the box to show the condition inherited from parents.

chicken pox   ☐

cystic fibrosis ☐

dysentery   ☐

malaria   ☐   [1 mark]

B1 Revision checklist

- I can explain why blood is under pressure in arteries. ☐

- I can state the word equation for respiration. ☐

- I can describe a balanced diet. ☐

- I can calculate BMI and RDA. ☐

- I can describe how the body defends against pathogens. ☐

- I can explain the difference between passive and active immunity. ☐

- I can describe the functions of the main parts of the eye. ☐

- I know the effects of the different types of drugs. ☐

- I can interpret data on the effects of smoking. ☐

- I can describe how heat can be lost or gained from the body. ☐

- I know that sex hormones can be used as contraceptives and for fertility treatment. ☐

- I know that chromosomes are made of DNA. ☐

- I know that genes or the environment can cause different characteristics. ☐

- I know that inherited characteristics can be dominant or recessive. ☐

Cooking

G–E

1 a There are many different ways to cook food. Write down **three** ways.

_____

_____

_____ [3 marks]

D–C

b Some foods need to be cooked. Explain why.

_____

_____ [2 marks]

G–E

2 a Cooking food is an example of a chemical change. Finish the sentences to explain why. Choose the **best** words from this list.

energy   irreversible   reactant   reversible   substance

The change is _____ . An_____ change

takes place in the food. A new _____ is made.   [3 marks]

D–C

b What happens to protein molecules when they are cooked?

_____ [1 mark]

G–E

3 a This is a question about making cakes rise. Finish the sentences. Choose the **best** words from this list.

baking powder   carbon dioxide   dissolved   heated   nitrogen

_____ is added to make cakes rise. It gives off

_____ when it is _____ .   [3 marks]

D–C

b Baking powder is a chemical called **sodium hydrogencarbonate**. When it is heated it **decomposes** to give sodium carbonate, carbon dioxide and water.
i Write down the word equation for the reaction.

_____ [1 mark]

ii Write down the **reactant** of the reaction.

_____ [1 mark]

iii Write down the **product** of the reaction.

_____ [1 mark]

G–E

4 The chemical test for carbon dioxide is to pass it through limewater. It will turn the

limewater from _____

to _____ .

carbon dioxide ⟶

delivery tube

limewater

[2 marks]

Food additives

1 a What is all food made from? Put a (ring) around the correct answer.

        additives   **chemicals**   **emulsifiers**   **fibres**   **proteins**   [1 mark]   G–E

b What are the main types of food additives? Put a (ring) around the **four** correct answers.

    antioxidants   **carbohydrates**   **emulsifiers**   **fibres**   **flavour enhancers**

                food colours   **proteins**   **sugars**   [4 marks]

c Why are antioxidants added to tinned fruit?

    _____   [1 mark]

d Why was the yellow food colour, tartrazine, taken out of most sweets for children?

    _____   [1 mark]

e Ascorbic acid (vitamin C) is used as an antioxidant in which foods?   D–C

    _____

    _____   [2 marks]

f Write down **one** reason why additives are used.

    _____   [1 mark]

2 a Put these ingredients in order on the food label.   G–E
Sugar   6.0 g
Salt   0.2 g
Wheat 14.0 g

ingredient	typical value per 100g

[2 marks]

b Why is food packaging used?

    _____   [1 mark]   D–C

c What is active packaging?

    _____   [1 mark]

d What is intelligent packaging?

    _____   [1 mark]

3 a Oil and water do not mix. What needs to be added to clean oily plates?   G–E

    _____   [1 mark]

b Look at the diagram.   D–C
It is a detergent molecule made up of two parts,
a head and a tail. Describe how the detergent works
on removing grease in water. Use the word **emulsifier**
in your answer. Use the diagram to help you.

fat-loving part

water-loving part

grease spot

    _____

    _____

    _____

    _____   [5 marks]

c Write down **one** example of an **emulsion**.

    _____   [1 mark]

Smells

G–E

1 a Write down **two** sources of natural perfume.

_____

_____ [2 marks]

b How is the perfume extracted? Put a (ring) around the correct answer.

boiled   distilled   filtered   frozen   stirred   [1 mark]

D–C

c i Some people object to cosmetics being tested on animals. Explain why.

_____ [1 mark]

ii Some people say cosmetics should be tested on animals. Explain why.

_____ [1 mark]

G–E

2 a A good perfume needs to have several properties. These are listed in the boxes. Draw a **straight** line to match the **best** reason to the property needed.

evaporates easily	it can be put directly on the skin
non-toxic	its particles can reach the nose
insoluble in water	it does not poison people
does not irritate the skin	it cannot be washed off easily

[3 marks]

b What do perfumes stimulate to allow us to smell them?

_____ [1 mark]

D–C

3 a To make a perfume alcohol is mixed with an acid to make an ester.

i Write down a word equation for this reaction.

_____ [2 marks]

ii Look at the diagram. Label the alcohol and acid.   [1 mark]

iii Label the condenser.   [1 mark]

iv What is happening at X?

_____

_____ [1 mark]

v Why is the condenser used?

_____

_____

_____ [1 mark]

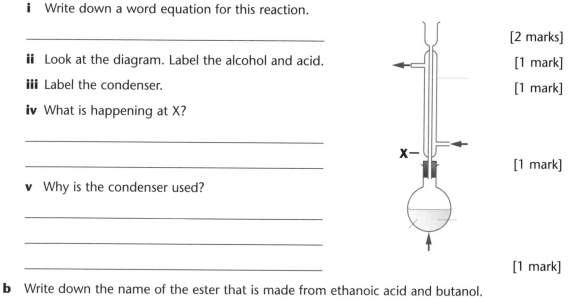

b Write down the name of the ester that is made from ethanoic acid and butanol.

_____ [1 mark]

G–E

4 a Finish these sentences by choosing the **best** words from this list.

insoluble   soluble   solute   solution   solvent

Nail varnish is _____ in water. Water cannot be used to remove

varnish from nails. Nail varnish is _____ in nail varnish remover.   [2 marks]

D–C

b A solute and a solvent that do not separate is a _____.   [1 mark]

Making crude oil useful

1 a Write down **three** fossil fuels.

_____ [3 marks]

b Write down how these fossil fuels were made.

_____

_____ [3 marks]

c Fossil fuels are called **non-renewable** sources. Explain why.

_____ [1 mark]

d Why are fossil fuels called **finite resources**?

_____ [1 mark]

2 a Crude oil is separated by heating it up and then cooling it down. The crude oil is separated into different **fractions** (parts). This is called **fractional distillation**.

The process works because each fraction has a different _____. [1 mark]

b All the oils of crude oil are **hydrocarbons**. What is a hydrocarbon?

_____ [2 marks]

c The hydrocarbons are separated by **fractional distillation**.
  i Label the diagram A where the crude oil is heated.
  ii Label the diagram B where the fraction bitumen exits from.
  iii Label the diagram C at the coldest part.
  iv Which fraction 'exits' from the coldest part?

_____ [4 marks]

3 a i How is crude oil taken out of the ground?

_____ [1 mark]

  ii Crude oil often has to be transported by tanker. Write down **one** problem if the tanker is damaged.

_____

_____ [2 marks]

b The demand for oil is enormous and increases each year. Explain why.

_____ [1 mark]

4 a Not enough petrol can be distilled from crude oil. Paraffin can be broken down or 'cracked' into petrol. Which **two** conditions are needed for this process?

_____

_____ [2 marks]

b Cracking breaks down long-chain molecules called **alkanes**. They have a general formula of C_nH_{2n+2}. What is the molecular formula of heptane which has 7 carbon atoms?

_____ [1 mark]

CI CARBON CHEMISTRY

Making polymers

1 a Finish the sentences by choosing the **best** words from this list.

chains   monomers   polymerisation   polymers

A plastic is made up of lots of _____ .

These are very big molecules made up of many small molecules joined together in

_____ . The small molecules are called

_____ . They join together. When lots of these are

joined to make a big molecule the reaction is called _____ .

[4 marks]

b Which molecule is a polymer? Put a (ring) around **A**, **B**, **C** or **D**.

A
$$H{-}\overset{\overset{\displaystyle H}{|}}{\underset{\underset{\displaystyle H}{|}}{C}}{-}\overset{\overset{\displaystyle H}{|}}{\underset{\underset{\displaystyle H}{|}}{C}}{-}OH$$

B
$$H{-}\overset{\overset{\displaystyle H}{|}}{\underset{\underset{\displaystyle H}{|}}{C}}{-}\overset{\overset{\displaystyle H}{|}}{\underset{\underset{\displaystyle H}{|}}{C}}{-}\overset{\overset{\displaystyle H}{|}}{\underset{\underset{\displaystyle H}{|}}{C}}{-}H$$

C
$$\left[{-}\overset{H}{\underset{H}{C}}{-}\overset{H}{\underset{H}{C}}{-}\overset{H}{\underset{H}{C}}{-}\overset{H}{\underset{H}{C}}{-}\overset{H}{\underset{H}{C}}{-}\overset{H}{\underset{H}{C}}{-}\right]_n$$

D
$$C{-}\overset{\overset{\displaystyle H}{|}}{C}{=}\overset{\overset{\displaystyle H}{|}}{C}{-}Cl$$

[1 mark]

c Write down **two** conditions needed for polymerisation.

_____

_____

[2 marks]

2 a Hydrocarbons are made up of _____ and _____ . [1 mark]

b Which molecule is not a hydrocarbon, **A**, **B**, **C** or **D**? Put a (ring) around the correct answer.

A
B
C   CH$_4$
D
$$H{-}\overset{\overset{\displaystyle H}{|}}{\underset{\underset{\displaystyle H}{|}}{C}}{-}\overset{\overset{\displaystyle H}{|}}{\underset{\underset{\displaystyle H}{|}}{C}}{-}\overset{\overset{\displaystyle H}{|}}{\underset{\underset{\displaystyle H}{|}}{C}}{-}Br$$

c i Look at the formula of propane. $H{-}C{-}C{-}C{-}H$ It is an alkane. How do you know?

_____

[1 mark]

ii What is the name of the alkene that has three carbon atoms?

_____

[1 mark]

d i Butanol, C$_4$H$_9$OH $\quad H{-}C{-}C{-}C{-}C{-}OH \quad$ is **not** a hydrocarbon. Explain why.

_____

[1 mark]

ii Butene is an alkene. $\quad H{-}C{-}C{-}C{=}C{-}H \quad$ Explain how you know.

_____

[1 mark]

iii Butene is a **monomer**. What is **polybutene**?

_____

[1 mark]

Designer polymers

1 a Write down **two uses** of polymers.

_____

_____ [2 marks]

b Write down the **names** of **two** polymers.

_____

_____ [2 marks]

c Each polymer is chosen carefully for the job that it does best. What kind of polymer do you need to cover electrical wires?

_____ [1 mark]

d There is a material used to make raincoats that is waterproof but 'breathable'. Why is this material better for raincoats than just a waterproof material?

_____ [1 mark]

e Nylon is tough, lightweight and keeps rainwater out but has a disadvantage. What is it?

_____ [1 mark]

f Suggest the properties that each polymer needs to have to be used for the purpose given. Finish the table.

polymer	property 1	property 2	use
PVC		flexible	raincoat
poly(ethene)	waterproof		plastic bags
poly(styrene)		absorbs shock	packaging
poly(propene)	strong		ropes

[4 marks]

2 a Most **addition polymers** are **non-biodegradable**. Explain what this means.

_____

_____ [2 marks]

b Disposing of non-biodegradable polymers causes problems. Explain the problems for each of the ways of disposing.

Landfill sites_____

_____

Burning waste plastic _____

_____

Recycling_____

_____

c i Scientists are developing addition polymers that are **biodegradable**. Explain why.

_____

_____ [2 marks]

ii Suggest a use for a biodegradable plastic.

_____ [1 mark]

Using carbon fuels

1 a Which is a good fuel for a car? Put a (ring) around the correct answer and then suggest why.

coal   petrol   wood

_____

_____ [2 marks]

characteristic	coal	petrol
energy value	high	high
availability	good	good
storage	bulky and dirty	volatile
toxicity	produces acid fumes	produces less acid fumes
pollution caused	acid rain, carbon dioxide and soot	carbon dioxide, nitrous oxides

b i Look at the table. Which fuel produces more acid fumes?

_____ [1 mark]

ii Give **two** advantages of using either coal or petrol for heating.

_____

_____ [2 marks]

2 a Which gas is needed for fuels to burn?

_____ [1 mark]

b Finish the sentence.

Combustion of a hydrocarbon fuel produces _____

and _____. [2 marks]

c Finish the sentences. Choose the **best** words from this list.

blue   less   monoxide   more   soot   toxic   water vapour   yellow

If a fuel burns in a shortage of oxygen it gives off unwanted gases. One of the gases

is carbon _____ which is a _____ gas and is very dangerous

if it is breathed in. A Bunsen burner flame produces energy from burning gas.

If the air hole is open a _____ flame is seen. If the air hole is closed a

_____ flame is seen. Carbon _____ , _____

and _____ are made and _____ energy is transferred.   [8 marks]

d i Write down a **word equation** for a hydrocarbon fuel burning in air.

_____ [1 mark]

ii Write down the names of **two** products made in the complete combustion of a fuel.

_____ [1 mark]

iii Describe how you would test for **one** of the products.

_____

_____ [2 marks]

Energy

1 a Finish the sentences. Choose the **best** words from this list.

electrical   **energy**   **heat**   **light**   **products**   **reactants**   **sound**

Chemical reactions can release energy such as _____ ,

_____ , _____ or

_____ .   [4 marks]

b Use the words **exothermic** and **endothermic** correctly in these sentences.

When energy is transferred **out** to the surroundings in a chemical reaction it is an

_____ reaction (energy is released).

When energy is taken in from the surroundings in a chemical reaction it is an

_____ reaction (absorbs energy).

An_____ reaction is shown by a temperature **increase**.

Burning magnesium is an example of an _____ reaction.   [4 marks]

2 a i Fuels need a gas to burn. Which gas?

_____   [1 mark]

ii Ethanol burns to make carbon dioxide and water. Write down the word
equation for this reaction.

_____   [2 marks]

iii Write down the names of the **two reactants**.

_____   [2 marks]

b i To compare the energy from two different fuels this apparatus is used twice.
Label the **spirit burner**, **fuel**, **water** and **thermometer**.   [4 marks]

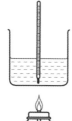

ii To compare the fuels, they are burned and the water is heated.
Write down **three** measurements that need to be made.

_____

_____   [3 marks]

iii Write down **one** way that the experiment is made fair.

_____   [1 mark]

C1 Revision checklist

- I know that cooking food is a chemical change as a new substance is made and it is an irreversible reaction. ☐

- I know that protein molecules in eggs and meat change shape when the food is cooked. ☐

- I know that the main food additives are antioxidants, food colours, emulsifiers and flavour enhancers. ☐

- I know that emulsifiers are molecules that have a water-loving part and an oil- or fat-loving part. ☐

- I know that alcohols react with acids to make an ester and water. ☐

- I know that a solute is the substance dissolved in a solvent to make a solution. ☐

- I know that crude oil is a non-renewable fossil fuel, which is a mixture of many hydrocarbons. ☐

- I know that petrol is a crude oil fraction with a low boiling point, which exits at the top of the fractional distillation tower. ☐

- I know that polymerisation is a process where many monomers react together to give a polymer. ☐

- I know that a hydrocarbon is a compound formed between carbon atoms and hydrogen atoms only. ☐

- I know that alkenes are hydrocarbons with one or more double bonds between carbon atoms. ☐

- I know that complete combustion of a hydrocarbon fuel makes carbon dioxide and water only. ☐

- I know that an exothermic reaction is one where energy is released into the surroundings. ☐

- I know that the energy of two fuels can be compared by the temperature rise in the same mass of water. ☐

Heating houses

1 a Finish the sentences by choosing the **best** words from this list.

degrees Celsius   **energy**   **joules**   **kilograms**   **power**   **watts**

Temperature is a measure of hotness and is measured in _____ .

Heat is a form of_____ and is measured in

_____ .   [3 marks]

G–E

b Kelly opens the front door on a very cold morning. Her mother complains that the house is getting cold. Use your ideas about energy flow to explain why the house gets cold.

_____

_____   [2 marks]

D–C

---

2 a A block of copper of mass 100 g is heated in a Bunsen flame. It takes 2 minutes to increase the temperature of the copper by 30 °C. How long will it take to increase the temperature of a 200 g block of copper by 60 °C? Put a (ring) around the correct answer.

30 seconds   **1 minute**   **2 minutes**   **4 minutes**   **8 minutes**   [1 mark]

G–E

b A block of iron of mass 100 g is heated in the same Bunsen flame. Why does it **not** take 2 minutes to increase the temperature of the iron by 30 °C?

_____   [1 mark]

D–C

c Finish the sentence.
The energy needed to raise the temperature of 1 kg of a material by 1 °C is known as the _____ .   [1 mark]

---

3 a What happens to a lead block at its melting point?

_____   [1 mark]

G–E

b What happens to water at its boiling point?

_____   [1 mark]

c Write down **one** example where energy is transferred but there is no change in temperature.

_____   [1 mark]

d What physical quantity is measured in units of J/kg?

_____   [1 mark]

D–C

Keeping homes warm

1 Dan wants to reduce the heating bills for his old house. He decides to insulate his loft and then replace his windows with double glazing.

a Loft insulation contains trapped air. Why does loft insulation reduce energy loss from the house?

_____ [1 mark]

b Write down **three** other ways Dan could insulate his house and reduce energy loss.

_____

_____

_____

_____ [3 marks]

c Dan spends £120 on loft insulation. He is told that this will reduce his heating bills by £40 per year. Calculate the payback time for loft insulation.
Show how you work out your answer.

_____ [2 marks]

d Why does Dan decide to insulate the loft before replacing his windows?

_____

_____ [1 mark]

e Dan heats his house with coal fires. He is told that his fires are **32% efficient**. Explain what is meant by 32% efficient.

_____

_____ [2 marks]

f Why are coal fires so inefficient?

_____

_____ [1 mark]

How insulation works

1 On a cold winter's day, Marc wears a thick waterproof coat and Daniel wears a thin hoody. Marc feels cold but Daniel stays warm. Finish the sentences to explain why Daniel stays warm.

The hoody contains _____ air. Air is a good_____ .

[2 marks]

2 The diagram represents the movement of air around a room. Show where the room heater is by writing the letter **F** on the diagram.   [1 mark]

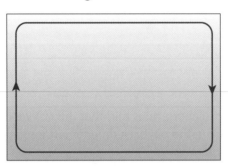

3 a The diagram shows a section through a double-glazed window. Michael says that it is just as effective to use a piece of glass twice the thickness. Use your ideas about energy transfer to explain why double glazing is better.

_____

_____

_____

_____

_____

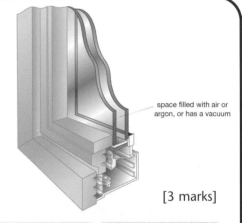

space filled with air or argon, or has a vacuum

[3 marks]

b New homes are built with insulation blocks in the cavity between the inner and outer walls. The blocks have shiny foil on both sides.

i Explain how the insulation blocks reduce energy transfer by conduction and convection.

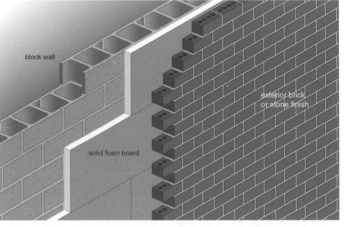

block wall

solid foam board

exterior brick or stone finish

_____

_____

_____

[4 marks]

ii Explain how the shiny foil helps to keep a home warmer in winter and cooler in summer.

_____

_____

[2 marks]

Cooking with waves

G–E

1 a Finish the sentences by choosing the **best** words from this list.

absorb	aluminium	induction	infrared
reflect	spectrum	ultraviolet	water

Warm and hot bodies emit _____ radiation.

Dark surfaces _____ more radiation than light surfaces.

Microwaves are part of the electromagnetic _____ .

_____ molecules absorb microwaves. [4 marks]

D–C

b Why do microwave ovens take less time to cook food than normal ovens?

_____ [1 mark]

G–E

2 a Young people are advised not to use mobiles phones too much. Texting is preferable to using them to make phone calls. Why is this advice given to young people?

_____
_____ [2 marks]

D–C

b Microwaves are suitable to communicate with spacecraft thousands of kilometres away while sometimes a mobile phone cannot receive a signal just a few kilometres from the nearest transmitter. Why do microwave signals seem to work better in space than they do on Earth?

_____
_____ [2 marks]

c Dave says that microwave signals 'bounce' off satellites. Jackie says Dave is wrong. What happens to a microwave signal when it is received by a satellite?

_____
_____ [2 marks]

Infrared signals

1 a Answer **true** or **false** to each of these statements.

Infrared radiation is part of the electromagnetic spectrum. _____

Passive infrared sensors emit infrared radiation to detect burglars. _____

A remote controller for a CD player emits infrared radiation. _____

[3 marks]

b The diagram shows a signal displayed on an oscilloscope. What type of signal is it? Put a (ring) around the correct answer.

background   digital   on/off   radial   square   [1 mark]

c Draw a diagram to represent an **analogue** signal.

[1 mark]

2 a A ray of laser light is shone into one end of an optical fibre.

Finish the path of the ray as it passes into, through and out of the optical fibre.   [2 marks]

b The diagrams show three rays of light travelling from water into air. The three angles of incidence are (i) smaller than the critical angle (ii) equal to the critical angle (iii) larger than the critical angle.

(i)   (ii)   (iii)

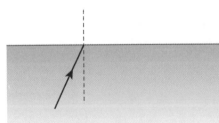

i Finish the diagrams to show what happens to the rays of light as they continue towards the water/air and after they meet the water/air boundary.   [5 marks]

ii Label the critical angle on the correct diagram with the letter **c**.   [1 mark]

Wireless signals

1 a Write down **one** advantage a mobile phone has over a land-line house phone.

_____ [1 mark]

b When Ruby is watching television, she notices that there is a feint second picture slightly offset to the main picture.

Finish the sentence to explain why there is this 'ghost' picture.
Choose the **best** word from this list.

| absorbed | dispersed | reflected | refracted |

The aerial has received a direct signal from the transmitter and a signal that
has been _____ . [1 mark]

c Ruby listens to her favourite radio station. Every so often, she notices that she can hear a foreign radio station as well.
Put ticks (✓) in the boxes next to the **two** statements that explain why this happens.

The foreign radio station is broadcasting on the same frequency.	
The foreign radio station is broadcasting with a more powerful transmitter.	
The radio waves travel further because of weather conditions.	
Ruby's radio needs new batteries.	

[2 marks]

d Finish the sentences by choosing the **best** words from this list.

| amplitude | atmosphere | frequency | wavelength |

Radio waves are refracted in the upper _____ .

There is less refraction if the _____ is higher.

[2 marks]

Light

1 a Light is a transverse wave that travels at a speed of 300 000 km/s.
Write down the names of **four other** types of transverse wave that travel
at 300 000 km/s.

G–E

_____

_____

_____

_____ [4 marks]

b The diagram represents a water wave. Water is a transverse wave.
The arrow shows the direction of motion of the **wave**.

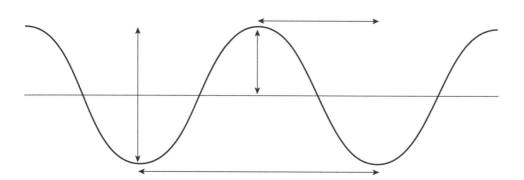

Add another arrow to the diagram to show the direction **water particles** move. [1 mark]

2 The diagram shows a transverse wave.

D–C

a Write the letter **A** next to the arrow which shows the amplitude of the wave. [1 mark]

b Write the letter **W** next to the arrow which shows the wavelength of the wave. [1 mark]

c What is meant by the **frequency** of a wave?

_____

_____ [1 mark]

3 a Write down **one** way of sending a message over a long distance without using
electricity or radio waves.

G–E

_____ [1 mark]

b Why was it necessary for Samuel Morse to devise a code of dots and dashes?

D–C

_____ [1 mark]

Stable Earth

1 a The diagram shows a device used to detect and measure the strength of earthquakes.

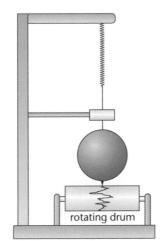

rotating drum

What is this device called? Put a (ring) around the correct answer.

joulemeter   **newtonmeter**   **seismometer**   **wattmeter**   [1 mark]

b Finish the sentences by choosing the **best** words from this list.

fault   plate   shock   ultraviolet   water

Earthquakes happen at a _____.

_____ waves travel through and round the Earth.   [2 marks]

c **P** waves and **S** waves are two of the waves which travel through the Earth after an earthquake. Put a tick (✓) in the box or boxes to correctly describe each wave. The first one has been done for you.

description	P wave	S wave
pressure wave	✓	
transverse wave		
longitudinal wave		
travels through solid		
travels through liquid		

[5 marks]

2 a What effect do greenhouse gases have on the Earth?

_____   [1 mark]

b When a fuel burns, a greenhouse gas is released. What is the name of this gas?

_____   [1 mark]

c Why does dust from factory chimneys cause warming of the Earth?

_____   [1 mark]

d Leah wants to sunbathe and get a good tan.

i Why must she be careful not to stay in the Sun for too long?

_____   [1 mark]

ii She uses a sun screen with **SPF 30**. What does SPF 30 mean?

_____

_____   [2 marks]

P1 Revision checklist

- I know the difference between temperature and heat. ☐

- I can explain what is meant by specific heat capacity and specific latent heat. ☐

- I can describe different forms of domestic insulation and explain how they work. ☐

- I can calculate energy efficiency. ☐

- I know the parts of the electromagnetic spectrum and their properties. ☐

- I can describe how infrared radiation is used for cooking and for remote control devices. ☐

- I can describe how microwaves are used for cooking and for communication. ☐

- I know the difference between analogue and digital signals. ☐

- I can describe total internal reflection and its use in optical fibres. ☐

- I can describe the use of wireless signals for communication. ☐

- I know why there is sometimes interference with radio signals. ☐

- I know the properties of a transverse wave and that light is an example of a transverse wave. ☐

- I can describe three types of earthquake wave and how they are detected. ☐

- I know some of the effects of natural events and human activity on weather patterns. ☐

Ecology in our school grounds

1 a Finish the sentences about an aquarium. Choose the **best** words from this list.

artificial   community   ecosystem   habitat   natural   population

An aquarium is an example of an _____ ecosystem. The fish and

the plants make up the _____ . Because the fish live in the aquarium,

the aquarium is the fish's _____ .   [3 marks]

b Clown fish are found in the coral reefs of the Pacific Ocean.
   i Suggest **one** reason why the clown fish are not found in British lakes.

   _____ [1 mark]

   ii Suggest **one** reason why there are many undiscovered species in the Pacific Ocean.

   _____ [1 mark]

2 a Jack uses a pooter and a net to collect certain animals.

What is a pooter and how it is used?

_____
_____ [2 marks]

b Jack uses a key to identify the animals he has collected. Use the key to describe
the butterfly Jack caught in his net.

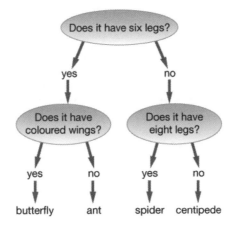

_____
_____ [2 marks]

3 The following formula is used to estimate a population.

$$\frac{\text{number of animals caught} \times \text{number of animals caught}}{\text{number of marked animals caught second time}} = \text{population}$$

number of animals caught first time × number of animals caught second time

Researchers want to know the number of voles living in a wood. They set traps and
catch 20 voles. They mark the voles and then release them. A week later they set
more traps and catch 10 voles. Five of them are marked. Estimate the population of
voles in the wood.

_____
_____ [2 marks]

Grouping organisms

1 a The picture shows a penguin.

  i Finish the sentence by choosing the **best** word from this list.

amphibians   **birds**   **mammals**   **reptiles**

The penguin belongs to the vertebrate group called

_____. [1 mark]

  ii Salmon belong to the vertebrate group called fish because they have scales. Write down **two** reasons why the penguin belongs to the group you have chosen.

_____

_____ [2 marks]

b Not all animals are vertebrates, some are invertebrates.

  i Put a (ring) around the animal that is an invertebrate.

         frog   **shark**   **snake**   **spider**   [1 mark]

  ii Why is this animal an invertebrate?

_____ [1 mark]

c This table compares animals and plants. Finish the table to describe animals.

	food	shape	movement
plants	make own	spread out	stay in one place
animals			

[3 marks]

2 The lion and tiger are different species.

a What is meant by the term **species**?

_____

_____ [2 marks]

b Lions and tigers belong to the same family of cats. This table shows the Latin names of different cats.

common name	latin name
bobcat	Felix rufus
cheetah	Acinonyx jubatus
lion	Panthera leo
ocelot	Felix pardalis

  i Two of these cats are more closely related than the others. Write down the **common** names of these **two** cats.

_____ and _____ [1 mark]

  ii What is the reason for your answer to part **b i**?

_____ [1 mark]

The food factory

G–E

1 Plants make their own food by a process called photosynthesis.

a Put a tick (✓) in the correct boxes to show which **two** of these substances are used in photosynthesis.

carbon dioxide ☐

fat ☐

nitrogen ☐

oxygen ☐

water ☐ [2 marks]

D–C

b The products of photosynthesis have many uses. Finish the table to describe these uses. The first one has been done for you.

product of photosynthesis	use in the plant
glucose	*energy*
cellulose	
protein	
oil	

[3 marks]

c Glucose is changed into starch for storage. Explain why.

_____

_____ [2 marks]

G–E

2 a In winter, plants get less light and this affects their growth. In what way is their growth affected? Put a ⬭ring⬭ around the correct answer.

grows faster   **grows slower**   **stays the same**   [1 mark]

D–C

b Light can change the rate of photosynthesis. Write down the names of **two other** factors that change the rate of photosynthesis.

1 _____

2 _____ [2 marks]

D–C

3 Glucose is a product of photosynthesis. The plant uses a process to release energy from glucose.

a Write down the name of this process.

_____ [1 mark]

b Plants carry out this process 24 hours a day. Explain why.

_____ [1 mark]

Compete or die

1 a The red and grey squirrel live in the same habitat so they compete for food. Write down **two other** things the squirrels compete for.

1 _____

2 _____ [2 marks]

b The red squirrel is native to Britain. The grey squirrel was introduced to Britain about 130 years ago. During the last 100 years grey squirrel numbers have increased and red squirrel numbers have decreased.

i Suggest **one** reason for the change in numbers.

_____ [1 mark]

ii Grey squirrels have been removed from the island of Anglesey. Suggest the effect this might have on the population of the red squirrel.

_____ [1 mark]

2 This is a diagram of a food chain.

a Write down the name of the predator shown here.

_____
[1 mark]

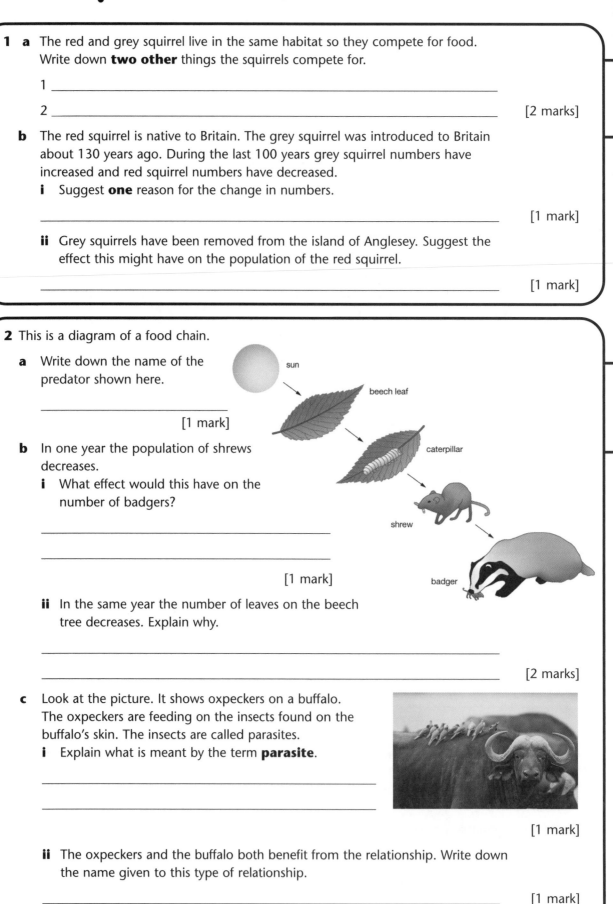

b In one year the population of shrews decreases.

i What effect would this have on the number of badgers?

_____

_____

[1 mark]

ii In the same year the number of leaves on the beech tree decreases. Explain why.

_____

_____ [2 marks]

c Look at the picture. It shows oxpeckers on a buffalo. The oxpeckers are feeding on the insects found on the buffalo's skin. The insects are called parasites.

i Explain what is meant by the term **parasite**.

_____

_____

[1 mark]

ii The oxpeckers and the buffalo both benefit from the relationship. Write down the name given to this type of relationship.

_____ [1 mark]

Adapt to fit

Grades

G–E

1 a Living things are adapted to live in different places. Draw a **straight** line from each living thing to the habitat it is adapted to live in. One has been done for you.

living thing	habitat
eagle	soil
earthworm	sea
shark	rainforest
rubber plant	air

[2 marks]

D–C

b Look at the picture of a camel. The table shows how the camel is adapted to help it live in the desert. Finish the table by writing how these adaptations help it to survive. The first one has been done for you.

adaptation	why it helps the camel survive
large feet	*stop sinking into sand*
no fat on body, except in hump	
hair-lined nostrils	
higher body temperatures do not harm camel	

[3 marks]

G–E

c Look at the picture of a polar bear.

Polar bears are adapted to hunt.
Put a tick (✓) in the box that indicates how polar bears are adapted to hunt.

eyes at front of head ☐

eyes at side of head ☐

streamlined ☐

thick fur ☐

[1 mark]

D–C

d Polar bears are adapted to live in the cold. They have thick fur for insulation as this stops them losing too much body heat.

i Write down **three other** ways that they are adapted to live in the cold.

_____

_____

_____ [3 marks]

ii Polar bears are not found in the same habitat as brown bears.
Explain why. Use ideas about competition in your answer.

_____

_____ [2 marks]

Survival of the fittest

1 a Finish the sentences about fossils by choosing the **best** words from this list.

change   deeper   evolution   lower   rocks   sand

Animals and plants have changed over time. This change is called _____.

Fossils found in _____ of different ages can show this change.

The oldest fossils are usually found _____ in the ground.   **[3 marks]**

b Here are four sentences (**A–D**) about how the fossil of a dinosaur is formed. They are in the wrong order. Fill in the boxes to show the right order. The first one has been done for you.

A The dinosaur's hard parts were replaced by minerals.

B The dinosaur died.

C The dinosaur's soft tissue rotted away.

D The dinosaur became covered by sediment.

B			

[2 marks]

c The fossil record shows how living things have changed over time. The fossil record is incomplete. Explain why.

_____

_____   **[2 marks]**

2 The following article gives information on the superbug MRSA. Read the article carefully and use it to help you answer the questions.

> **MRSA Where did it come from?**
> MRSA evolved because of natural selection. There are lots of different strains of the bacteria. Each strain has slightly different DNA. The DNA is also constantly mutating as the bacteria reproduce. Some of these mutations will be more resistant to antibiotics than others. When people take antibiotics, the less resistant strains die first, the more resistant strains are harder to destroy. If people stop taking the antibiotics too soon the resistant strains survive to reproduce and pass on their DNA. In this way, more and more strains evolve to be resistant to these new drugs.

a Explain what is meant by the term **natural selection**.

_____   **[1 mark]**

b It is important to complete a course of antibiotics. Explain what could happen if a course of antibiotics is not completed.

_____

_____   **[2 marks]**

Population out of control?

1 a Humans use many natural resources such as fossil fuels.

i Write down the name of **one** fossil fuel.

_____ [1 mark]

ii Carbon dioxide is a gas that comes from the burning of fossil fuels. Write down the name of **one other** gas that comes from the burning of fossil fuels.

_____ [1 mark]

b The rise in human population is causing an increase in the level of carbon dioxide in the air. Suggest **two** effects this increase may have on the environment.

1 _____

2 _____ [2 marks]

c The ozone layer in the Earth's atmosphere protects us from harmful ultraviolet rays. Chemicals are destroying the ozone layer.

i Write down the name of these chemicals.

_____ [1 mark]

ii The over-use of these chemicals has caused an increase in skin cancer. Write down **one** reason why.

_____ [1 mark]

2 The table shows the population of different species found in a small area of two different rivers.

species		water snail	carp	water vole	otter	kingfisher	heron
number	river A	25	20	6	5	2	1
of animals	river B	5	2	1	1	0	0

a Use this information to finish the bar chart for river A. The information for water snails and river B has been done for you.

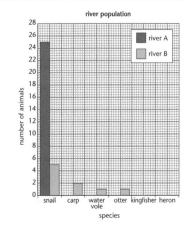

[3 marks]

b River B is polluted. Use the information in the table to explain how you know the river is polluted.

_____

_____

_____

_____ [2 marks]

c If the pollution in river B is cleaned up, what might happen to the number of snails in the river?

_____ [1 mark]

3 Scientists look for the water louse when they want to measure how polluted water is. Write down the name given to species that are used to measure levels of water pollution.

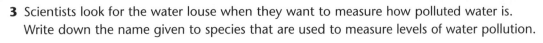

_____ [1 mark]

Sustainability

1 This is a picture of the dodo. The dodo no longer exists.

  a Write down the name given to an animal or plant that no longer exists.

_____ [1 mark]

  b Suggest **two** reasons why the dodo no longer exists.

    1 _____

    2 _____ [2 marks]

  c Some animals are close to no longer existing. They are called **endangered species**.
Put a (ring) around the animal that is an **endangered species**.

        badger   **fox**   **mammoth**   **osprey**   [1 mark]

  d The panda is an endangered species. Pandas only eat bamboo and bamboo forests are being rapidly destroyed. Scientists believe that it is important to save the bamboo forests.

    i Write down **one** reason why the forests should be saved.

_____ [1 mark]

    ii Pandas are kept in captivity. Suggest how this may help increase the panda population.

_____ [1 mark]

2 a Grey whales feed in the North Pacific Ocean near Alaska.
They migrate south to breed in sheltered bays on the warmer Japanese coast.

    i Suggest **one** reason why the grey whale does **not** breed near Canada.

_____ [1 mark]

    ii Suggest **one** reason why the grey whale cannot stay on the coast of the USA after breeding.

_____ [1 mark]

  b Some countries want to hunt whales for food. Suggest **one** argument for and **one** argument against hunting whales.

    For _____

_____

    Against _____

_____ [2 marks]

3 a Sustainable resources are resources that should not run out.

    i Put a (ring) around the resource that is **not** a sustainable resource.

        bamboo   **coal**   **trees**   **whales**   [1 mark]

    ii The government has set fish quotas. Fishermen can only catch so many fish at any one time. Fish quotas should help maintain the population of fish in the sea. Explain why.

_____

_____ [2 marks]

B2 Revision checklist

- I know how to collect and use data to estimate a population. ☐

- I know how to use a key to identify plants and animals. ☐

- I know the characteristics of the different vertebrate groups. ☐

- I can state the word equation for photosynthesis. ☐

- I can describe the effect of increased light, temperature and carbon dioxide on photosynthesis rate. ☐

- I can recognise organisms as predators or prey. ☐

- I can explain how the size of a predator population will affect the prey population. ☐

- I can describe how predators are adapted to hunt and how prey are adapted to escape. ☐

- I can explain how camels and polar bears are adapted to their habitats. ☐

- I can describe how organisms became fossilised. ☐

- I know that the world population is increasing and causing more pollution. ☐

- I can explain the effects of increased pollution on climate change, acid rain and the ozone layer. ☐

- I can describe ways in which animals become extinct. ☐

- I can explain the terms sustainable resource and sustainable development. ☐

Paints and pigments

1 a Write down **two** reasons why we use paints.

_____

_____ [2 marks]

b i Complete the sentence. Choose the **best** words from this list.

binding medium   **colloid**   **pigment**   **solute**   **solvent**

The three ingredients of paint are_____ ,

_____ and _____. [3 marks]

ii Oil paints are colloids. Explain why.

_____

_____ [2 marks]

c An **emulsion paint** is a water-based paint. Explain how it covers a surface.

_____

_____ [2 marks]

2 a Write down what happens to a thermochromic pigment when
i it gets hot _____

_____ [1 mark]

ii it cools down _____

_____ [1 mark]

b Another type of pigment takes in light energy during the day and gives out light energy at night. What is this pigment? Put a (ring) around the correct answer.

flammable   **luminescent**   **phosphorescent**   **radiant**

c A thermochromic pigment changes colour at 45 °C. Write down **two** examples it is used for.

_____

_____ [2 marks]

3 a Dyes are used to colour fabrics. Some dyes are **natural**. What are these made from?

_____ [1 mark]

b Write down **two** ways that dyes made from chemicals are better than natural dyes.

_____

_____ [2 marks]

c We can now buy clothes in a much wider range of colours than our great-grandparents could. Explain why.

_____

_____

_____ [3 marks]

Construction materials

1 a Write down **three** rocks that are used in construction.

_____

_____ [3 marks]

b Write down **two** metals that are used in construction.

_____ [2 marks]

c Put these materials into the order of hardness.

granite   **limestone**   **marble**

Least hard _____ _____ _____ Hardest   [3 marks]

d Brick, concrete, steel, aluminium and glass are manufactured.
Finish the table to show the raw materials they come from.

building material	brick	cement	glass	iron	aluminium
raw material					

[5 marks]

2 a There are environmental problems caused by taking rocks from the ground in a quarry.
Write down **three** problems.

_____

_____ [3 marks]

3 a Write down the names of **two** rocks that are forms of **calcium carbonate**.

_____

_____ [2 marks]

b Complete the sentence. Choose the **best** words from this list.

chemically electrolyses   **insolubly precipitates**   **thermally decomposes**

When calcium carbonate is heated, it _____ _____.   [1 mark]

c Write down how concrete is made.

_____

_____

_____ [4 marks]

d Why is concrete reinforced?

_____ [1 mark]

e Reinforced concrete is a **composite** material. Explain why.

_____ [2 marks]

f Calcium carbonate decomposes at a very high temperature. Write a word
equation to show this.

_____

_____ [3 marks]

Does the Earth move?

1 a This is a diagram of the Earth. Label the **iron core**, **mantle** and **crust**.

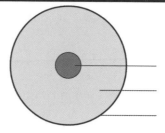

[3 marks]

b Sometimes the mantle comes through weaknesses in the Earth's crust. What is the mantle made of?

_____ [1 mark]

c Finish the sentences. Choose the **best** words from this list.

earthquakes	iron	rivers	tectonic plates	volcanoes

The outer layer of the Earth is made of_____, which

move very slowly over the molten rock. At the boundaries this movement causes

_____and_____. [3 marks]

d Are the tectonic plates that make up the Earth's crust less dense or more dense than the mantle?

_____ [1 mark]

e Write down the **two** kinds of tectonic plate.

_____ and _____ [2 marks]

G–E

D–C

2 a i Magma slowly moves up to the surface of the Earth, cools down and solidifies to make which type of rock?

_____ [1 mark]

ii Some molten rock reaches the surface of the Earth and goes through weaknesses.

This is called _____. [1 mark]

iii This molten rock comes out in a **volcano**. Volcanoes can have runny or sticky molten rock. Which one is fairly safe and which is more dangerous? Explain why.

_____

_____ [2 marks]

iv Why do most people think it is worth moving back to the area after a volcanic eruption?

_____ [2 marks]

b Magma can rise through the Earth's crust. Explain why.

_____ [1 mark]

c Magma cools and solidifies into igneous rock either after it comes out of a volcano as lava, or before it even gets to the surface. By looking at crystals of igneous rock, geologists can tell how quickly the rock cooled. Fill in the **two** boxes with an explanation and an example for each.

basalt	cools rapidly		cools slowly	granite

small crystals	large crystals

[4 marks]

G–E

D–C

Metals and alloys

1 a Finish the sentences. Choose the **best** words from this list.

| carbon | compound | element | oxygen | nitrogen |

Rocks containing copper ore are mined. An ore is a _____.

Copper is a metal _____. In the laboratory copper is

extracted from its ore by heating it with _____. [3 marks]

b More than a third of all copper is recycled. Write down **two** reasons why.

_____

_____ [2 marks]

c Copper used for recycling has to be sorted carefully so that valuable 'pure' copper scrap is not mixed with less pure scrap. When impure copper is used to make alloys what must happen first?

_____ [1 mark]

d If the scrap copper is very impure what must be done before it is used again?

_____ [1 mark]

2 Impure copper can be purified in the laboratory using an electrolysis cell.

a What is the **anode** made from?

_____ [1 mark]

b What happens at the **cathode**?

_____ [1 mark]

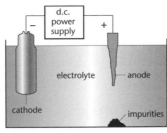

3 a What is an **alloy**? _____ [1 mark]

b Examples of alloys are: amalgam, brass, bronze, solder and steel. Draw a **straight** line to match the use to the alloy.

| amalgam | | used to join metals |
| solder | | used to make taps and door handles |
| brass | | used by dentists to fill cavities in teeth | [3 marks]

c Most metals form alloys. Draw a **straight** line to match the metals to the alloy.

| amalgam | | contains copper and zinc |
| solder | | contains mercury |
| brass | | contains lead and tin | [3 marks]

d Alloys are often more useful than the original metals, though nowadays pure copper is more important than bronze or brass. Why are vast amounts turned into electric wire?

_____ [1 mark]

Cars for scrap

1 a **Rust** is made when iron reacts with _____ and _____. [2 marks]

b In winter, icy roads are treated with salt. Why is this a problem for steel car bodies?

_____ [1 mark]

c Aluminium does not corrode in moist air. Explain why.

_____ [1 mark]

d Rust is an oxide layer but it does not protect the rest of the iron. Explain why.

_____ [1 mark]

2 a Label the parts of the car that are made from four different materials: **metals**, **plastics**, **glass** and **fibres**.

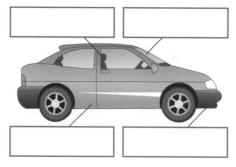

[4 marks]

b Draw a **straight** line to match the differences between iron and aluminium.

| magnetic |

| iron |

| less dense |

| aluminium |

| corrodes easily |

[2 marks]

c Finish the sentence. Steel is an alloy made of _____ and

_____. [2 marks]

i Write down **two** advantages of steel over iron.

_____ [2 marks]

ii Steel and aluminium can both be used to make car bodies but each material has its own advantages. Write down **two** advantages of cars made from aluminium and **one** disadvantage.

_____

_____

_____ [3 marks]

d Describe how the materials used in cars can be recycled at a scrap metal yard.

_____ [1 mark]

3 a Write down **three** benefits that recycling metals and the other materials of a car has on the environment.

_____

_____ [3 marks]

Clean air

G–E

1 a **Air** is a mixture of different gases. Write down the other **three** main gases.

| | | *Water vapour* | |

[3 marks]

b Three processes change the levels of gases in the air. Draw a **straight** line to match up the processes.

| increases the level of carbon dioxide and decreases the level of oxygen | combustion photosynthesis respiration | decreases the level of carbon dioxide and increases the level of oxygen |

[3 marks]

D–C

c i Label the pie chart with the **four** main gases of the air in the correct section.

[4 marks]

ii Mark in the percentages of the gases.

[4 marks]

iii Explain how the carbon cycle keeps the balance between the percentage of carbon dioxide and oxygen in the atmosphere. Use your answer to question **1 b** to help you.

_____

_____

_____

[4 marks]

D–C

2 a Scientists know that gases trapped in liquid rock under the surface of the Earth are always escaping. Where does this happen?

_____ [1 mark]

b Scientists guess about the original atmosphere of the Earth. It's known that at some point in the Earth's history, microbes developed that could photosynthesise. Why were these important?

_____ [2 marks]

G–E

3 a **Pollutants** are substances made by human activity that harm the environment. The atmosphere contains a large number of pollutants. Finish the table.

pollutant	carbon monoxide	oxides of nitrogen	sulphur dioxide
environmental problem	*a poisonous gas*		
origin of pollutant		*formed in the internal combustion engine*	*formed when sulphur impurities in fossil fuels burn*

[3 marks]

D–C

b A car can be fitted with a **catalytic converter**. What does this do?

_____

_____ [2 marks]

Faster or slower (1)

1 a Look at **Graph A** of results of the reaction between magnesium and hydrochloric acid.

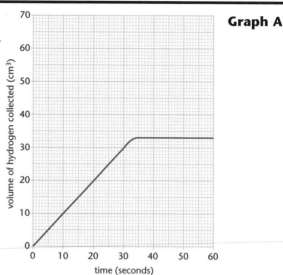

Graph A

i At what time does the reaction stop?

_____ [1 mark]

ii Why does the reaction stop?

_____ [1 mark]

iii How much hydrogen was made at the end?

_____ [1 mark]

2 Write down **two** ways that the speed of a reaction can be changed.

_____

_____ [2 marks]

3 Look at **Graph B**. It shows the reaction between magnesium and acid at 20 °C.

a i If the reaction takes place at a higher temperature mark the reaction line that you would expect on the graph.

[2 marks]

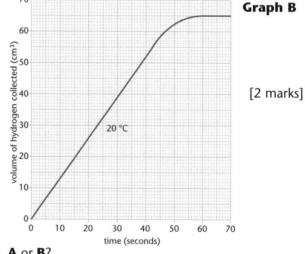

Graph B

20 °C

ii Which graph has the steeper gradient, **A** or **B**?

_____ [1 mark]

iii The reaction rate increases at higher temperatures. Explain why. Use ideas about particles in your answer.

_____

_____

_____ [4 marks]

Faster or slower (2)

1 a What is an explosion?

_____ [1 mark]

b Write down **two** examples.

_____

_____ [2 marks]

c What products are made during an explosion?

_____ [2 marks]

2 a If a reaction takes place with a powdered reactant or the same mass of a block of reactant, which will react faster? Use ideas about collisions between particles.

_____

_____ [3 marks]

b The reaction between calcium carbonate and hydrochloric acid is measured by the decrease in mass. Look at the equation. Why is there a decrease in mass?

$$CaCO_3 + 2HCl \rightarrow CaCl_2 + H_2O + CO_2$$

_____ [2 marks]

c The graph shows how the rate of reaction between calcium carbonate and dilute hydrochloric acid is measured.

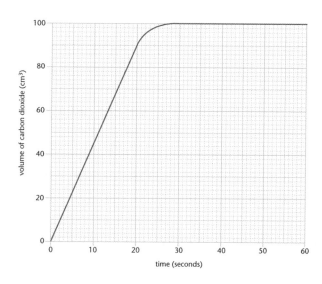

i At which time does the reaction stop? _____ [1 mark]

ii If this reaction used powdered calcium carbonate, sketch on the graph the line that would show the reaction of the same mass of calcium carbonate as lumps. [2 marks]

iii Why does the reaction slow down? Use ideas about collisions in your answer.

_____ [1 mark]

3 a What is a catalyst?

_____ [1 mark]

b A catalyst has two features. Describe them.

_____ [2 marks]

C2 Revision checklist

- I know that paint is a colloid where solid particles are dispersed in a liquid, but are not dissolved. ☐

- I know that thermochromic pigments change colour when heated or cooled. ☐

- I know that brick is made from clay, glass from sand, and aluminium and iron from ores. ☐

- I know that the decomposition of limestone is:
  calcium carbonate → calcium oxide + carbon dioxide ☐

- I know that the outer layer of the Earth is continental plates with oceanic plates under oceans. ☐

- I know that igneous rock is made when molten rock cools down. ☐

- I know that copper can be extracted by heating its ore with carbon, but purified by electrolysis. ☐

- I know that alloys often have properties that are different from the metals they are made from. ☐

- I know that aluminium does not corrode when wet as it has a protective layer of aluminium oxide. ☐

- I know that iron is more dense than aluminium, but both are malleable and electrical conductors. ☐

- I know that respiration and combustion increase carbon dioxide levels and decrease oxygen levels. ☐

- I know that toxic carbon monoxide comes from incomplete combustion of petrol or diesel in cars. ☐

- I know that a temperature increase makes particles move faster, so increasing the rate of reaction. ☐

- I know that a catalyst is a substance that changes the rate of reaction but is unchanged at the end. ☐

Collecting energy from the Sun

G–E

1 The Sun is the source of energy for the Earth.
Write down **two** ways in which the Sun provides plants with the energy they need.

_____

_____ [2 marks]

G–E

2 a Finish the sentence by choosing the **best** word from this list.

chemicals**electricity****heat****light**

A photocell uses _____ to produce electricity. [1 mark]

D–C

b Write down **four** advantages of using photocells.

_____

_____

_____

_____ [4 marks]

G–E

c What happens to the amount of electricity produced if part of the photocell is
covered over.

_____ [1 mark]

G–E

3 a Solar panels use energy from the Sun to heat water. The solar panel is black.
Water from the pipes in the solar panel is stored in a cylinder.

i Why is the solar panel black?

_____ [1 mark]

ii How is energy transferred from the water in the pipes to the storage cylinder?
Put a (ring) around the correct answer.

conduction**convection****radiation** [1 mark]

D–C

b During the day, energy from the Sun passes through the large window and
warms the room; this is called passive solar heating.
How is the room heated during the night?

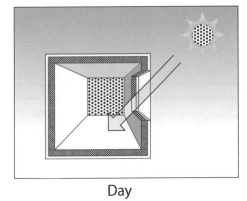

Day

_____

_____ [1 mark]

Generating electricity

1 a The diagram shows a wire connected to an ammeter moving upwards between the poles of a magnet. The needle on the ammeter moves to the right. What happens when the wire is moved **downwards** between the poles of the magnet?

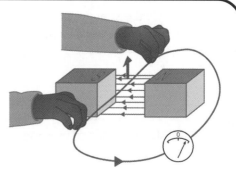

G–E

_____

_____

[1 mark]

b The diagram shows a model dynamo. When the coil is spun, a current is produced.
Write down **two** ways in which the size of the current can be increased.

D–C

_____

_____

_____

_____

[2 marks]

2 A model generator consists of a coil of wire rotating between the poles of a magnet.
How is the structure of a generator at a power station different from the model generator?

D–C

_____

[1 mark]

3 The flow diagram represents how fossil fuels at a power station provide electrical energy for distribution around the country.

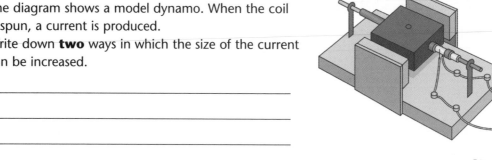

| fossil fuel burned | → | water heated to produce steam | → | steam turns turbine | → | A | → | generator produces electricity | → | electricity distributed |

a One step in the process has been missed out. What should be in box **A**?

D–C

_____

[1 mark]

b How is energy lost from the overhead power lines as electricity is distributed around the country?

G–E

_____

[1 mark]

4 a What is the job of a transformer? Put a tick (✓) in the box next to the correct answer.

G–E

change the size of an AC voltage	
change the size of a DC voltage	
change AC into DC	

[1 mark]

b High voltage transmission lines distribute electricity around the country at 400 kV.
We use electricity in our homes at 230 V. Why is electricity not distributed at 230 V?

D–C

_____

[1 mark]

Fuels for power

Grades

G–E

1 a Power stations use fuels. Some are **renewable** and some are **non-renewable**. Put ticks (✓) in the boxes next to the renewable fuels.

coal	
natural gas	
oil	
straw	
wood	

[2 marks]

D–C

b A nuclear power station uses uranium as its energy source. Uranium is not a fuel.

i What is a fuel?

_____ [2 marks]

ii How does uranium provide energy in the form of heat?

_____ [1 mark]

G–E

2 a A nuclear power station has two advantages over a fuelled power station. No smoke is produced and it does not produce carbon dioxide. Write down **one** disadvantage of using a nuclear power station.

_____ [1 mark]

D–C

b Finish the sentences by choosing the **best** words from this list.

calcium   cancer   DNA   kinetic   nuclear   mutate   react

Radiation from _____ energy sources causes ionisation.

This causes a change in the structure of atoms. One of the chemicals in

body cells is _____ and when this is exposed to radiation

it can _____. As a result, body cells may divide in an

uncontrolled way. This can lead to _____.   [4 marks]

D–C

3 a Each of the headlamp bulbs in Anna's car is connected to a 12 V battery. When she switches on the headlamps, a current of 2 A passes through the bulb. Calculate the power rating of the bulb.

_____ [4 marks]

b In her home, Anna uses a 2.5 kW kettle for $\frac{1}{2}$ hour each day. Electricity costs 12p per kWh. How much does it cost Anna to use her kettle each day?

_____ [4 marks]

Nuclear radiations

1 a The picture shows an instrument used to measure radioactivity. What is the name of this instrument?

_____

_____

[1 mark]

G–E

b Background radiation is always present. Write down **two naturally occurring** sources of background radiation.

_____

_____

[2 marks]

D–C

2 Answer **true** or **false** to each of the following statements about alpha, beta and gamma radiation.

Gamma radiation causes more ionisation than alpha radiation.	
Alpha radiation has a range of a few centimetres in air.	
Beta radiation comes from the nucleus of an atom.	
Beta radiation can be absorbed by a thin sheet of paper.	

[4 marks]

D–C

3 Max's teacher is showing the class an experiment using a source of gamma radiation. Write down **three** precautions the teacher should take to protect himself from the effects of the source.

_____

_____

_____

[3 marks]

G–E

4 a Gamma radiation is used to sterilise medical instruments. What property of gamma radiation makes it suitable?

_____

[1 mark]

G–E

b Gamma radiation has other medical uses.

i Write down **one other** medical use for gamma radiation.

_____

[1 mark]

D–C

ii What property of gamma radiation makes it suitable?

_____

[1 mark]

c A nuclear scientist is checking how much radiation there is outside a store containing radioactive material. In one particular position, the count rate is much higher. What happens to the thickness of the store wall at this position?

_____

[1 mark]

Our magnetic field

1 a The magnetic field around Earth is similar to the field around a bar magnet. The North pole of a compass points towards the North magnetic pole. The diagram shows a model of Earth's magnetic field with a bar magnet inside Earth.

Write the letter **N** on the bar magnet to show the position of the North pole of the **magnet**.

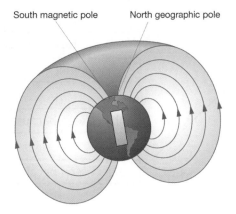

South magnetic pole   North geographic pole

[1 mark]

b Which statement **best** describes the magnetic field due to a coil of wire?
Put a tick (✓) in the box next to the correct answer.

The magnetic field is circular.	
The magnetic field is radial like the spokes of a bicycle wheel.	
The magnetic field is similar to the field due to a bar magnet.	

[1 mark]

2 There are many artificial satellites orbiting Earth. Some provide information about the weather.
Write down **two** other uses of artificial satellites.

_____

_____ [2 marks]

3 a Solar flares erupt from the surface of the Sun. What effect does this have on Earth?
Put a tick (✓) in the box next to the correct answer.

Communication signals are disrupted.	
Earth's average temperature increases by 10 ˚C.	
The Moon appears much brighter in the night sky.	

[1 mark]

b Finish the sentence by choosing the **best** words from this list.

charged particles   **gamma rays**   **hydrogen atoms**

Solar flares emit _____ that produce magnetic fields.

The magnetic fields interact with Earth's magnetic field. [1 mark]

4 Scientists believe that the Moon and Earth used to rotate much faster than they do now.
What do they think caused the rotation to slow down?

_____ [1 mark]

Exploring our Solar System

1 a When we look into the sky, there are some things we see because they produce their own light. Some things we see because they reflect light. Some things it is impossible to see at all.

The lists show some of the objects in the sky and a description of how the object may be see. Draw a **straight** line from each object to the correct way it may be seen. One has been done for you.

object
artificial satellite
black hole
comet
meteor
moon
star

how object may be seen
object cannot be seen at all
object seen because it produces its own light
object seen because it reflects light

[5 marks]

b On August 24 2006, the International Astronomical Union considered a proposal to redefine planets. There would be twelve planets in our Solar System. Ceres, the largest asteroid would become a planet. Charon, at the moment known as Pluto's moon, would become a 'twin planet' with Pluto. Recently, another planet has been discovered beyond Pluto. This proposal was rejected and the decision made that Pluto should no longer be called a planet.

The diagram shows the Sun, the eight planets, Pluto and the asteroid belt.

i Write the letter **C** on the diagram to show where Ceres orbits.

ii Write the letter **P** on the diagram to show Pluto.

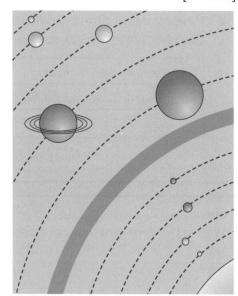

[2 marks]

2 Scientists are exploring space to find out if there are any other forms of life elsewhere in the Universe. Manned and unmanned spacecraft have been sent into space to investigate.

a How have scientists tried to find out if there are other life forms **without** sending a spacecraft into space?

_____ [1 mark]

b Helen Sharman was the first British astronaut. She spent eight days in the Mir Space Station doing science experiments. When she was in the Space Station she experienced **weightlessness** but was not **weightless**.
Why was Helen never weightless?

_____ [1 mark]

c When astronauts work outside a spacecraft, they have to wear special helmets with sun visors. Why do the helmets need special visors?

_____ [1 mark]

Threats to Earth

Grades

1 a An asteroid hit Earth about 65 million years ago making a very large crater.
What else happened when the asteroid hit Earth? Put ticks (✓) in the boxes next to the
three correct answers.

all life became extinct	
it got colder	
the first human appeared on Earth	
the Moon was formed	
there were a lot of fires	
tsunamis flooded large areas	

[3 marks]

b Most asteroids orbit the Sun in a belt between two planets. Which **two** planets?

_____ and _____

[2 marks]

c What are asteroids? Put a tick (✓) in the box next to the correct answer.

clouds of very dense gas	
cubes of ice	
rocks that have broken away from planets	
rocks left over when the Solar System formed	

[1 mark]

2 The diagram shows the orbits of two bodies orbiting the Sun.
One is a planet, the other is a comet.

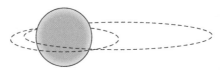

a Label the orbit of the comet with the letter **C**. [1 mark]

b When does the tail of a comet become visible?

_____

[1 mark]

c Why does a comet's tail always point away from the Sun?

_____

[1 mark]

3 Scientists are constantly updating information on the paths of **NEO**s.

a What are NEOs?

_____

[1 mark]

b Why is it important to constantly monitor the paths of NEOs?

_____

_____

[2 marks]

The Big Bang

1 Scientists think that 15 billion years ago there was a 'Big Bang'.

a What was the Universe like before the Big Bang?

_____ [1 mark]

G–E

b What were three of the first things formed after the Big Bang?
Put a (ring) around each of the **three** correct answers.

copper   helium   hydrogen   iron   protons   uranium

[3 marks]

D–C

c The Universe is expanding. Galaxies in the Universe are moving at different speeds.
Which galaxies are moving the fastest?

_____

_____ [1 mark]

2 a New stars are being formed all the time.
How do stars start to form?

_____

_____ [1 mark]

G–E

b A star's life is determined by its size.

i What happens to a medium-sized star, like our Sun, at the end of its life?

_____

_____

_____

_____

_____

_____

_____ [4 marks]

D–C

ii What happens to a very large star at the end of its life?

_____

_____

_____

_____

_____

_____

_____ [4 marks]

P2 Revision checklist

- I can describe how energy from the Sun can be used for heating and producing electricity. ☐

- I can describe how generators produce electricity. ☐

- I can describe how electricity is distributed via the National Grid. ☐

- I know what fuels are used in power stations and some of their advantages and disadvantages. ☐

- I can calculate power and the cost of using an electrical appliance for a certain time. ☐

- I know how to measure radioactivity and why there is background radiation. ☐

- I can list some uses of alpha, beta and gamma sources and relate their use to their properties. ☐

- I can describe the Earth's magnetic field and its similarity to a bar magnet and a coil. ☐

- I can describe how the Moon was formed. ☐

- I know the names of the planets and their order from the Sun. ☐

- I can describe how we are exploring space through manned and unmanned spacecraft. ☐

- I know that there are bodies in space other than planets and moons. ☐

- I can describe asteroids and comets and know the importance of constantly checking NEOs. ☐

- I know that scientists believe the Universe started with a Big Bang and that it is still expanding. ☐

Molecules of life

1 a Draw a **straight** line from the part of the cell to its function.

part of cell

cytoplasm

nucleus

cell membrane

function

carries genetic information

controls movement in and out

where chemical reactions take place

[2 marks]

b Respiration is a chemical reaction that takes place in the cell.
In which part of the cell does respiration takes place?

_____ [1 mark]

2 a Finish the sentences about DNA. Choose the **best** words from this list.

base   cytoplasm   fat   gene   nucleus   protein

DNA is a chemical found in the _____ of a cell. A section of DNA

is called a _____. Each section is a code for making _____.   [3 marks]

b This diagram shows DNA fingerprints of individuals connected to a robbery.
Who left blood at the crime scene? Explain your answer.

_____

_____

_____

_____

_____

DNA fingerprints from suspects' blood left at the broken
window of a jeweller's shop

Peter   Fred   Sue   James

blood from the scene of the crime

[2 marks]

3 This graph shows the effect of temperature on an enzyme.

a What is meant by the term **enzyme**?

_____

_____ [2 marks]

b Describe the pattern shown on the graph.

_____

_____ [2 marks]

c Write down the optimum temperature of this enzyme.

_____ [1 mark]

184

Diffusion

1 The diagram shows the movement of substances around the body.

a i Write down the name of **one** substance that moves **out** of body tissue into the blood.

_____

[1 mark]

ii Use the diagram to describe the movement of digested substances around the body.
In your answer include where they start and where they finish.

_____

_____

_____

_____

[2 marks]

b What is meant by the term **diffusion**?

_____

_____

[2 marks]

c Diffusion takes place in the placenta. Substances diffuse from the foetus into the mother's blood. Write down the name of **two** of these substances.

1 _____

2 _____

[2 marks]

d Diffusion of oxygen into the blood takes place in the lungs.
Name the part of the lungs where oxygen enters the blood.

_____

[1 mark]

2 a Water is lost from a plant into the air through its leaves.
Put a tick (✓) in the box that correctly indicates how the water is lost.

by evolution ☐

by evaporation ☐

by respiration ☐

by photosynthesis ☐

[1 mark]

b Describe how carbon dioxide moves into the leaf. Use the words **concentration**, **diffusion** and **photosynthesis** in your answer.

_____

_____

_____

[3 marks]

Keep it moving

1 a Look at this picture of blood flowing in a vein.
Label a white blood cell. [1 mark]

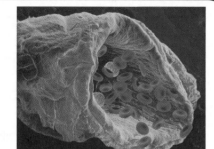

b Draw a **straight** line from each part of the blood to the job it carries out.

part of blood	job it does
white blood cell	transports oxygen
red blood cell	helps clot blood
platelet	defends against disease

[2 marks]

c Red blood cells are adapted to do their job because they are disc-shaped and have no nucleus.

i Explain how these adaptations help them do their job.

Disc-shaped _____

_____

No nucleus _____

_____ [2 marks]

ii Write down the name of the chemical that makes red blood cells red.

_____ [1 mark]

2 a What is the job of the heart?

_____ [1 mark]

b On the diagram of the heart

i put an **X** to show the part of the heart that receives blood from the lungs

ii label the bicuspid valve.

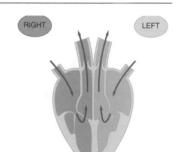

RIGHT   LEFT

[2 marks]

c The left ventricle has a thicker wall than the right ventricle. Explain why.

_____

_____ [2 marks]

d People with heart disease may need a heart transplant.
Describe **two** problems with heart transplants.

1 _____

2 _____ [2 marks]

3 Describe the role of blood vessels in circulating blood around the body.

_____

_____

_____ [3 marks]

Divide and rule

G–E

1 In order to make new cells the body carries out cell division.

a Suggest **two** reasons why the body needs to make new cells.

1 _____

2 _____ [2 marks]

D–C

b Write down the name of the type of cell division that makes new **body** cells.

_____ [1 mark]

c Amoebas are unicellular organisms. They only have one cell. Humans are multi-cellular; they are made of many cells. It may be a disadvantage to be unicellular rather than multi-cellular. Explain why.

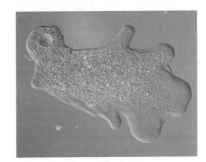

_____
_____
_____
_____ [2 marks]

G–E

2 a This is a picture of sperm cells.

i Write down **one** reason why the sperm cell has a tail.

_____
_____
_____

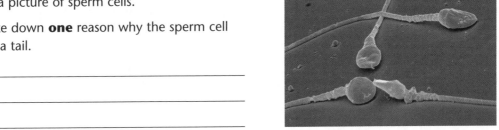

[1 mark]

ii Egg cells do not have a tail. Describe **one other** way egg cells are different from sperm cells.

_____ [1 mark]

D–C

b Sperm cells also have a structure called an acrosome. Why do sperm cells need an acrosome?

_____
_____ [2 marks]

c A special type of cell division makes sperm cells. What is the name of this type of cell division?

_____ [1 mark]

d Sperm cells are haploid. Explain what is meant by the term **haploid**.

_____ [1 mark]

Growing up

1 a Finish the sentences about the parts of a plant cell by choosing the **best** words from this list.

cell membrane **cell wall** **chloroplast** **nucleus** **vacuole**

i Two parts of the cell provide support. They are the _____ and

the _____. [2 marks]

ii The part of the cell needed for photosynthesis is _____. [1 mark]

b For a fertilised egg to grow into an embryo the cells need to divide and change.

i What name is given to the way simple cells change into specialised cells such as blood cells? Put a (ring) around the correct answer.

cell development **cell differentiation** **cell growth** **cell mutation** [1 mark]

ii Write down the name given to cells before they become specialised.

_____ [1 mark]

2 a Here are the five stages (**A**–**E**) of human growth. They are in the wrong order. Fill in the boxes to show the right order. The first one has been done for you.

A adolescence **B** infancy **C** old age **D** adulthood **E** childhood

				C

[3 marks]

b The table shows the change in weight of a baby from 0 to 30 months.

age in months	0	3	6	9	12	15	18	21	24	27	30
weight in kg	2.5	5.0	6.4	7.5	8.8	9.6	9.8	10.0	10.1	10.4	10.7

i Plot the points on the graph. The first two have been done for you.

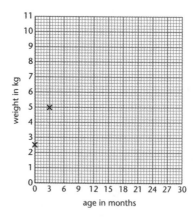

[3 marks]

ii Complete the graph by drawing the best curve. [1 mark]

iii Describe the pattern in the graph.

_____

_____ [2 marks]

iv Name the phase of human growth shown in the graph.

_____ [1 mark]

Controlling plant growth

G–E

1 a Plant hormones are chemicals that control different processes in the plant.
Ripening of fruit is one such process.
Write down the names of **two other** processes.

1 _____

2 _____ [2 marks]

b Ben grows apples. The apples ripen too quickly on the tree and fall off.
He decides to spray the tree with hormones.

i Explain how this will stop the apples falling off the tree.

_____ [1 mark]

D–C

ii Ben decides to take some shoot cuttings from his apple trees and uses
rooting powder to grow new trees.
What is the effect of the rooting powder on the shoot cuttings?

_____ [1 mark]

iii Ben also grows wheat and sprays the wheat with selective weedkiller.
The weedkiller destroys the weeds with broad leaves but not the crops.
Explain how the weedkiller destroys the weeds.

_____
_____ [2 marks]

iv Explain why the crops are not affected by the weedkiller.

_____
_____ [2 marks]

D–C

2 The diagram shows a germinating bean seed.

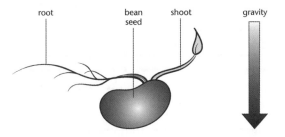

root   bean   shoot   gravity
        seed

a In which direction will the **shoot** grow?

i Put a (ring) around the correct answer.

down   **left**   **right**   **up** [1 mark]

ii On the diagram, continue the length of the **root** to show what happens
to its growth. [2 marks]

b i Write down the name of the response shown by the **root**.

_____ [1 mark]

ii The response of the **root** is a positive response. Explain why.

_____ [1 mark]

New genes for old

1 Richard grows apples. The table shows some information about different varieties of apples.

	variety		
	A	**B**	**C**
colour	green	red	green
resistant to disease	no	yes	no
large fruit	yes	no	no
sweet fruit	yes	no	no

Richard uses selective breeding to produce large apples that are resistant to disease and green in colour.

a Which **two** varieties should he use in his breeding programme?

_____

_____ [2 marks]

G–E

b Describe the process of selective breeding.

_____

_____

_____

_____ [3 marks]

D–C

2 Mutations are changes to genes.
Suggest **one** cause of gene mutations.

_____ [1 mark]

D–C

3 Beta-carotene is needed to produce vitamin A. Beta-carotene is found in carrots but not in rice.

a Describe how genetic engineering can be used to grow rice that provides beta-carotene.

_____

_____

_____

_____ [3 marks]

D–C

b Suggest **one** advantage and **one** disadvantage of genetic engineering.

Advantage _____

_____

Disadvantage _____

_____ [2 marks]

More of the same

1 This is a picture of a special sheep called Dolly. Dolly is a clone.

a What is a clone?

_____

_____

[1 mark]

b Some humans are **natural clones**. What name is given to two people that are natural clones of each other?

_____ [1 mark]

c Describe how cows can be cloned using **embryo transplants**.

_____

_____

_____

_____ [3 marks]

d Scientists are hoping to solve organ transplant problems by cloning pigs.

i Explain how the cloning of pigs could help solve organ transplant problems.

_____

_____ [2 marks]

ii Suggest **one** reason why people may object to this process.

_____ [1 mark]

2 a Gardeners can clone plants by taking cuttings.
Here are four sentences (**A–D**) about taking cuttings. They are in the wrong order.
Fill in the boxes to show the right order. One has been done for you.

A The cutting is put in a pot of sandy soil.
B The end of the stem is dipped in rooting powder.
C A polythene bag is put over the plant.
D A short stem is cut from the parent plant.

		A	

[2 marks]

b Suggest **one** advantage and **one** disadvantage of cloning plants.

Advantage _____

_____

Disadvantage _____

_____ [2 marks]

c Strawberries reproduce asexually by sending out runners. Describe how potatoes reproduce asexually.

_____

_____ [2 marks]

- I can label a diagram of an animal cell. ☐

- I can interpret data on DNA fingerprinting for identification. ☐

- I know that food and oxygen diffuse across the placenta. ☐

- I can describe diffusion as the movement of particles from a region of high to low concentration. ☐

- I know that arteries transport blood away from the heart. ☐

- I know that the patient can reject a heart transplant. ☐

- I know that at fertilisation haploid gametes join to form a diploid zygote. ☐

- I know that body cells are made by mitosis and gametes are made by meiosis. ☐

- I can identify the main stages of human growth. ☐

- I know that shoots are positively phototropic and negatively geotropic; roots are the opposite. ☐

- I can describe the stages in selective breeding. ☐

- I know that genetic engineering is used to make insulin. ☐

- I can describe some advantages and disadvantages of cloned plants. ☐

- I know that cloned animals could be used to produce organs for transplants. ☐

What are atoms like?

G–E

1 a i This is a diagram of an atom. Label the nucleus and the electrons.

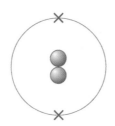

[3 marks]

ii Why is an atom neutral?

_____ [1 mark]

D–C

b What are the particles in the nucleus of an atom?

_____ [1 mark]

c Finish the table to show the relative mass and charge of the atomic particles.

	relative charge	relative mass
electron		0.0005 (zero)
proton	+1	
neutron		

[4 marks]

d What is the atomic number of an atom?

_____ [1 mark]

e What is the mass number?

_____ [1 mark]

G–E

2

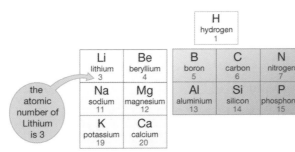

a What is the element of atomic number 15? _____ [1 mark]

b What is the atomic number of the element calcium? _____ [1 mark]

c What is an element?

_____ [1 mark]

d How many elements are there in the periodic table? _____ [1 mark]

e What is a compound?

_____ [1 mark]

D–C

f What is an isotope?

_____ [1 mark]

Ionic bonding

1 a Draw a **straight** line to match the word with the description.

atom	has more than one atom in its formula and no charge
molecule	is a charged atom or group of atoms
ion	is the smallest particle that can bond with another particle

[2 marks]

b Finish the table by writing these atoms, ions or molecules in the correct box.

O   Cl⁻   Mg   H₂   Na⁺   H   SO4²⁻   MgSO₄   NaOH

atom	ion	molecule

[3 marks]

---

2 a Put a tick (✓) in the box next to the sentence that describes a **metal** atom.

  i An **atom** has extra electrons in its outer shell and needs to **lose** them to be stable. ☐

  ii An atom has 'spaces' in its outer shell and needs to **gain** electrons to be stable. ☐

[1 mark]

b Draw a diagram to show how the electrons transfer from the metal atom to a non-metal atom to form a stable pair. **Outer shells only**.

[3 marks]

c Finish the sentences.

  i If an atom loses electrons a _____ **ion** is formed. [1 mark]

  ii An example of an atom which loses 1 electron is _____. [1 mark]

d Finish the sentences.

  i A **negative ion** is formed by an atom _____ electrons. [1 mark]

  ii An example of an atom gaining 1 electron is _____. [1 mark]

e Finish the sentences.
During **ionic bonding**, the metal atom becomes a _____

ion and the non-metal atom becomes a _____ ion.

The positive ion and the negative ion then attract one another. They attract to

a number of other ions to make a solid_____. [3 marks]

---

3 a Sodium chloride and magnesium oxide have similar properties. Describe their melting points.

_____ [1 mark]

b Put a tick (✓) in the boxes next to the substances that conduct electricity.

sodium chloride solution ☐   solid sodium chloride ☐

molten (melted) magnesium oxide ☐   solid magnesium oxide ☐

molten sodium chloride. ☐

[3 marks]

Covalent bonding

G–E

1 a A molecule has the formula **CO₂**.

    i How many atoms does it have altogether? _____ [1 mark]

    ii How many **different** atoms does it have? _____ [1 mark]

D–C

2 a Non-metals combine together by **sharing** electrons. What is this type of bonding?

_____ [1 mark]

b Look at the diagram.

Explain how a water molecule is formed from atoms of other elements.

_____

_____

_____ [4 marks]

c Carbon dioxide and water do not conduct electricity. Explain why.

_____ [1 mark]

G–E

3 Look at the section of the periodic table.

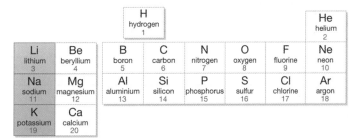

    a i Lithium is in a group. Which one?_____ [1 mark]

    ii Write down two other elements in this group.

_____ [2 marks]

b Three of these elements are in the same period. Put a (ring) around the correct answers.

    oxygen   **sodium**   **silicon**   **hydrogen**   **sulphur**   **potassium**   [3 marks]

D–C

c Sodium is in group 1. Explain why.

_____ [1 mark]

d Chlorine atoms have 7 electrons in the outer shell. In which group is chlorine?

_____ [1 mark]

    e i To which period does fluorine belong?

_____ [1 mark]

    ii Explain why.

_____ [1 mark]

The group 1 elements

1 a Sodium and potassium are stored under oil. Explain why?

_____

_____ [2 marks]

b Lithium, sodium and potassium react with water.

i They float on the surface. Explain why.

_____ [1 mark]

ii Which gas is given off?

_____ [1 mark]

c Sodium reacts very vigorously with water and forms sodium hydroxide.
Write down the word equation for the reaction of sodium with water.

_____ [2 marks]

d Finish the sentence about the order of reactivity of the alkali metals with water.

_____ is more reactive than _____

which is more reactive than _____. [2 marks]

e Reactivity of the alkali metals with water increases down group 1.

reactivity increases down		melting point in °C	boiling point in °C
	$_3$Li	179	1317
	$_{11}$Na	98	
	$_{19}$K		774

Estimate the melting point of potassium _____ and

the boiling point of sodium _____. [2 marks]

f Group 1 metals have similar properties. Explain why.

_____ [1 mark]

2 a Marie and Mitch have made some salts. They are salts of lithium, sodium and potassium. They have three labels to put on three bottles, but are not sure which one was the lithium salt. They decide to check with a flame test. Draw a **straight** line to match their results.

red   potassium

yellow   lithium

lilac   sodium   [2 marks]

b How did Marie and Mitch carry out their experiment?

_____

_____

_____

_____ [4 marks]

G–E

D–C

G–E

D–C

The group 7 elements

G–E

1 a Group 7 elements are called the halogens. Write down their uses.

    i Chlorine _____ [1 mark]

    ii Iodine _____ [1 mark]

b Write down **two** uses of sodium chloride.

_____

_____ [2 marks]

D–C

2 a There is a **trend** in the physical appearance of the halogens at room temperature. Finish the table.

chlorine	
bromine	*orange liquid*
iodine	

[2 marks]

b Group 7 elements have similar properties. Explain why.

_____ [1 mark]

c There is a trend in the reactivity of halogens.
Draw an arrow to show the trend of reactivity from the least reactive element towards the most reactive element.

Reactivity

$_9$F
$_{17}$Cl
$_{35}$Br
$_{53}$I

[1 mark]

d When a halogen reacts with an alkali metal a **metal halide** is made. Write down the word equation for the reaction between potassium and iodine.

_____ [2 marks]

D–C

3 a If halogens are bubbled through **solutions of metal halides** there are two possibilities: **no reaction**, or a **displacement reaction**.

    i If chlorine is bubbled through potassium bromide solution a red-brown colour is seen. Explain why.

_____ [1 mark]

    ii If bromine is bubbled through potassium chloride solution there is no reaction. Explain why.

_____ [1 mark]

b Bromine (Br_2) displaces iodine from potassium iodide solution (KI).

    i Write down a word equation for this reaction.

_____ [2 marks]

    ii Write down a balanced symbol equation for this reaction.

_____ [2 marks]

Electrolysis

1 a Finish the sentences by choosing the **best** words from this list. You may use any word more than once.

anode   cathode   electrolysis   electrolyte   negative   positive

The decomposition of a liquid by using electricity is called _____.

The _____ is a liquid that conducts electricity. There are two

electrodes called the _____ and the _____.

The _____ is the positive electrode and the _____

is the negative electrode.

During electrolysis the _____ ions are attracted to the anode

and the are _____ ions attracted to the cathode.   [8 marks]

2 a Explain the key features of the electrolysis of dilute sulphuric acid.

_____

_____

_____

_____

_____   [6 marks]

b Explain why the volume of hydrogen gas and the volume of oxygen gas given off in this process are different.

_____   [1 mark]

3 a The two gases given off during the electrolysis of sulphuric acid can be tested.

i Describe the test for hydrogen.

_____

_____   [2 marks]

ii Describe the test for oxygen.

_____

_____   [2 marks]

4 a Write about the key features of the production of aluminium by electrolytic decomposition.

_____

_____

_____

_____   [4 marks]

b Write down the word equation for the decomposition of aluminium oxide.

_____   [1 mark]

Transition elements

G–E

1 a Transition elements have typical metallic properties. Write down **six** properties.

_____

_____

_____

_____

_____

_____ [6 marks]

D–C

b A compound that contains a transition element is often coloured.

i What is the colour of copper compounds?

_____

ii What is the colour of iron(II) compounds?

_____

iii What is the colour of iron(III) compounds?

[3 marks]

_____

c A transition metal and its compounds are often catalysts.

i Which transition metal is used in the Haber process to produce ammonia?

[1 mark]

_____

ii If the metal used to harden margarine is number 28, suggest whether this is a transition metal or not. Use the periodic table on page 238 to help you.

[1 mark]

_____

G–E

2 a When a yellow solution of potassium chromate is added to a colourless solution of silver nitrate a yellow solid is formed. What is this type of reaction called?

_____ [1 mark]

D–C

3 a In a reaction a substance is broken down into at least **two** other substances by heat. What is this type of reaction?

[1 mark]

_____

b If a transition metal carbonate is heated it decomposes to form a metal oxide and carbon dioxide. Write down the word equation for the decomposition of copper carbonate.

[1 mark]

_____

D–C

4 a Sodium hydroxide solution is used to identify the presence of transition metal ions in solution. Finish the table.

ion	colour
Cu^{2+}	
Fe^{2+}	
Fe^{3+}	

[3 marks]

Metal structure and properties

1 a Look at the table.

property	lustre	hardness	density	heat conductor	electrical conductor	melting point	boiling point
A	yes	high	high	high	high	high	high
B	no	high	high	high	high	high	high
C	yes	low	high	high	high	lower	lower

   i   Which metal is not as hard as the others? _____ [1 mark]

   ii Which metal is not as shiny (lustrous) as the others? _____ [1 mark]

   iii Which metal has the lowest boiling point?_____ [1 mark]

 b The uses of a metal depend on its properties.
Which metal, **A**, **B** or **C** would be best to make a ring or other jewellery? _____ [1 mark]

 c Silver is often chosen to make a piece of jewellery. Which **two** properties does it have that are important for this? Choose words from this list.

       ductile   **good electrical conductor**   **high boiling point**

      high melting point   **lustrous**   **malleable**

              good thermal conductivity

    _____ [2 marks]

 d Copper is often used for the base or the whole of a saucepan. Use your knowledge about chemical properties to explain why.

    _____

    _____

    _____ [3 marks]

2 a In the box draw how the atoms of a metal form a structure.

    [box]
    [1 mark]

 b Write down **two** ways that you know this is the structure of a metal not a liquid.

    _____ [2 marks]

3 a What condition is needed for some metals to become **superconductors**?

    _____ [1 mark]

 b What are superconductors?

    _____ [1 mark]

 c What are **three** potential benefits of superconductors?

    _____

    _____

    _____ [3 marks]

C3 Revision checklist

- I know that the nucleus is made up of protons and neutrons, with each having a relative mass of 1. ☐

- I know that electrons surround the nucleus and occupy shells in order. They have almost no mass, 0. ☐

- I know that positive ions are formed by the loss of electrons from the outer shell. ☐

- I know that negative ions are formed by the gain of electrons into the outer shell. ☐

- I can work out the number of each different type of atom in a molecule or displayed formula. ☐

- I know that there are two types of bonding – ionic bonding and covalent bonding. ☐

- I know that lithium, sodium and potassium react vigorously with water and give off hydrogen. ☐

- I know that group 1 metals have one electron in their outer shell, which is why they are similar. ☐

- I know that chlorine is a green gas, bromine is an orange liquid and iodine is a grey solid. ☐

- I know that chlorine is more reactive than bromine, which is more reactive than iodine. ☐

- I know that in the electrolysis of dilute sulphuric acid, H_2 is made at the cathode and O_2 at the anode. ☐

- I know that when aluminium oxide is electrolysed, Al is formed at the cathode and O_2 at the anode. ☐

- I know that compounds of copper are blue, iron(II) are light green and iron(III) are orange/brown. ☐

- I know that metals have particles which are arranged close together in a regular arrangement. ☐

Speed

1 a Melissa and Eve are running in a 1500 m race. Melissa finishes in 300 s. Eve takes 250 s.

    i Who runs faster, Melissa or Eve? _____ [1 mark]

    ii How do you know?

    _____ [1 mark]

b Ivy is going to measure the average speed of a trolley across the laboratory floor.

    i What measurements will she need to take?

    _____

    _____ [2 marks]

    ii Suggest what instruments she could use to obtain her measurements.

    _____

    _____ [2 marks]

c Holly's father got a speeding ticket. His car was photographed twice as it crossed white lines in the road 1.5 m apart. He passed over eight lines in the 0.5 s between each photograph. How fast was he travelling?

    _____

    _____

    _____ [4 marks]

d Freddie is on holiday in France. He travels 390 km in 3 hours on a French motorway.

    i Calculate the average speed of his car on this journey in km/h.

    _____

    _____ [3 marks]

    ii Why is your answer the **average** speed of the car?

    _____ [1 mark]

    iii The speed limit on the motorway is 130 km/h. Did the car break the speed limit? Explain your answer.

    _____

    _____ [2 marks]

2 The graph shows Ashna's walk to her local shop and home again.

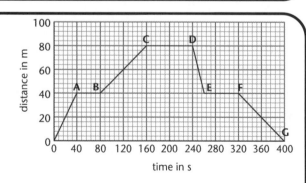

a Between which points did Ashna wait at traffic lights to cross the road?

    _____ [1 mark]

b How long did she spend in the shop? _____ [1 mark]

c How far is the shop from her home? _____ [1 mark]

d During which part of her journey did she walk fastest? _____ [1 mark]

Changing speed

1 a Darren is riding his bicycle along a road. The speed-time graph shows how his speed changed during the first minute of his journey.

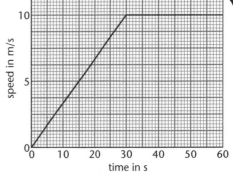
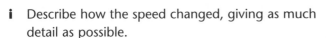

   i Describe how the speed changed, giving as much detail as possible.

_____

_____

_____

_____

_____ [4 marks]

   ii Darren makes the same journey the next day but:
     – increases his speed at a steady rate for the first 20 s, reaching a speed of 10 m/s
     – travels at a constant speed for 10 s
     – slows down at a steady rate for 15 s to a speed of 5 m/s
     – travels at a constant speed of 5 m/s.
     Plot the graph of this journey on the axes given. [4 marks]

   iii How could you calculate the distance Darren travelled in the first minute of his original journey?

_____ [1 mark]

b The way in which the speed of a car changes over a 60 s period is shown in the table.

   i Plot a speed-time graph for the car using the axes given.

time in s	speed in m/s
0	0
5	5
10	10
15	15
20	15
25	15
30	15
35	15
40	15
45	11
50	7.5
55	3.5
60	0

[5 marks]

   ii The car is in an area where the speed limit is 50 km/h.
     Does the driver exceed this limit? Show clearly how you decide.

_____

_____

_____

_____ [4 marks]

2 A car accelerates from 10 to 40 m/s in 6 s. Calculate its acceleration.

_____

_____

_____ [4 marks]

Forces and motion

1 The engine has just been switched on in the car shown in the diagram. P is the forward force on the car due to the pull of the engine.

G–E

a Put a (ring) around the word that **best** describes the motion of the car as it starts to move.

accelerate   **constant speed**   **decelerate**   [1 mark]

b **i** How will the size of force P change if the driver presses the accelerator pedal harder?

_____ [1 mark]

ii How will the motion of the car change?

_____ [1 mark]

c On another day the car carries four people and a fully loaded boot so its mass increases. How will its motion change if the value of P is the same as in **a**?

_____ [1 mark]

2 A car of mass 500 kg accelerates steadily from 0 to 40 m/s in 20 s.

D–C

a What is its acceleration?

_____
_____
_____ [4 marks]

b What resultant force produces this acceleration?

_____
_____ [3 marks]

c The actual force required will be greater than your answer to **b**. Why?

_____ [1 mark]

3 Helen is driving her car on a busy road when the car in front brakes suddenly. She puts her foot firmly on her brake pedal and just manages to stop without hitting the car in front.

a What is meant by 'braking distance'?

G–E

_____ [1 mark]

b What is meant by 'thinking distance'?

_____ [1 mark]

c How can Helen's stopping distance be calculated?

_____ [1 mark]

d Later that day Helen is driving at high speed on a motorway. How will Helen's thinking distance change?

D–C

_____ [1 mark]

Explain why.

_____ [2 marks]

e Write down **two** things, apart from speed, that could increase a driver's thinking distance.

_____
_____ [2 marks]

Work and power

G–E

1 Hilary lifts a parcel of weight 80 N onto a shelf 2 m above the ground.

    a Would she do more or less work if the parcel weighed 120 N? _____ [1 mark]

    b Would she do more or less work if she lifted the parcel onto a shelf 1.6 m high?

        _____ [1 mark]

    c Hilary tries to lift a parcel weighing 500 N but she cannot move it. How much work does she do?

        _____ [1 mark]

    d Where does Hilary get the energy she needs to do work to lift the parcels?

        _____ [1 mark]

D–C

    e Calculate the amount of work Hilary does when she lifts the parcel of weight 80 N onto a shelf 2 m above the ground.

        _____

        _____ [3 marks]

2 Chris and Abi both have a mass of 60 kg. They both run up a flight of stairs 3 m high. Chris takes 8 s and Abi takes 12 s.

G–E

    a What can you say about the amount of work that each does? _____ [1 mark]

    b What can you say about the power of Chris and Abi?

        _____ [1 mark]

D–C

    c Calculate Chris' weight. [Take g = 10 N/kg.]

        _____ [2 marks]

    d How much work does Chris do in running up the stairs?

        _____

        _____ [3 marks]

    e Calculate Chris' power.

        _____

        _____

        _____ [3 marks]

    f Calculate Abi's power.

        _____

        _____ [2 marks]

3 The table shows the fuel consumption of three cars in miles per gallon (mpg).

car	fuel consumption (mpg)
A	48
B	34
C	28

G–E

    a Which car has the best fuel consumption? _____ [1 mark]

    b Which car is likely to be most powerful? _____ [1 mark]

D–C

    c We should keep our fuel consumption to a minimum to protect the environment. Why?

        _____

        _____ [3 marks]

Energy on the move

1 a What is meant by **kinetic energy**?

_____ [1 mark]

b Which possesses more kinetic energy?

	mass in kg	speed in m/s		mass in kg	speed in m/s
A	2	5	B	2	7
C	20	2	D	15	2

A or B _____   C or D _____   [2 marks]

2 a Use the data about the fuel consumption of petrol and diesel cars to answer the following questions.

engine size in litres	fuel consumption in mpg	
	petrol	diesel
1.6	44	60
2.0	40	51

i Which car has the best fuel consumption? _____ [1 mark]

ii Which type of fuel, petrol or diesel, is more efficient? _____ [1 mark]

iii How did you decide?

_____ [1 mark]

b Use the data about fuel consumption to answer the following questions.

car	fuel	engine size in litres	miles per gallon	
			urban	non-urban
Renault Megane	petrol	2.0	25	32
Land Rover	petrol	4.2	14	24

i Suggest why fuel consumption is better in non-urban conditions.

_____

_____ [2 marks]

ii How many gallons of petrol would a Land Rover use on a non-urban journey of 96 miles?

_____ [2 marks]

iii Would a Renault Megane use more or less fuel for the same journey? _____ [1 mark]

iv Suggest a reason for the difference.

_____ [1 mark]

3 a How do battery-powered cars pollute the environment?

_____

_____ [2 marks]

b i Give **one** advantage of solar-powered cars compared to battery-powered cars.

_____ [1 mark]

ii Give **one** disadvantage of solar-powered cars compared to battery-powered cars.

_____ [1 mark]

Crumple zones

Grades

1 Kevin was involved in an accident on the M1 motorway. Luckily he was not seriously hurt but his car was badly damaged. Kevin was wearing a seat belt and his car had several safety features.

a Which safety feature

i badly damaged his car but helped to protect Kevin?

_____ [1 mark]

ii inflated and squashed to stop the steering wheel pushing into Kevin's chest?

_____ [1 mark]

iii stopped Kevin being thrown through the windscreen?

_____ [1 mark]

b How does each feature in the table help to reduce Kevin's injuries by absorbing energy?

safety feature	how it works
seatbelt	
crumple zones	
air bag	

[3 marks]

c **i** What is meant by an 'active safety feature' on a car?

_____ [2 marks]

ii What is meant by a 'passive safety feature' on a car?

_____

_____ [2 marks]

d **i** Give **two** examples of active safety features.

_____ [2 marks]

ii Give **two** examples of passive safety features.

_____

_____ [2 marks]

e **i** Why should all safety features in a car be checked regularly?

_____ [1 mark]

ii Why is it essential to do this after a car crash?

_____ [1 mark]

iii Why must seatbelts always be replaced after a car crash?

_____ [1 mark]

f **i** What does **ABS** stand for?

_____ [1 mark]

ii Why are ABS brakes safer when a driver has to slam his foot on the brakes to stop quickly?

_____

_____ [2 marks]

Falling safely

1 Charlie drops a golf ball and a ping pong ball from a height of 30 cm above a table.

a Why do the balls fall towards the table?

_____ [1 mark]

b How does the speed of the balls change as they fall?

_____ [1 mark]

c Both balls hit the table together although their masses are different.
Charlie now drops the two balls from a height of 130 cm above the table.
Explain why the golf ball hit the table before the ping pong ball.

_____

_____ [2 marks]

d Next Charlie drops the golf ball and a feather from a height of 50 cm above the
table. Which hits the table first? Put a (ring) around the correct answer.

golf ball   **feather**   **they arrive together**   [1 mark]

e Sarah is a sky diver. She has a mass of 60 kg.

i What is the value of her acceleration just
after leaving the aircraft?

_____

_____ [1 mark]

ii On the diagram mark and name the forces acting on Sarah as she falls.   [2 marks]

iii What can you say about the size of these forces?

_____ [1 mark]

iv Sarah's acceleration decreases as she falls. Explain why.

_____ [1 mark]

v Eventually she is travelling at a constant speed. What is this speed called?

_____ [1 mark]

vi What can you say about the size of the forces acting on her now?

_____ [2 marks]

2 Racing cyclists try to streamline their shape.

a Why do they do this?

_____

_____

[2 marks]

b Give **two** ways in which the cyclist shown has tried to streamline his shape.

_____

_____ [2 marks]

The energy of theme rides

1 Finish the sentences. Choose words from this list.

gravitational potential energy (GPE)   **kinetic energy (KE)**

more   **less**

Rob is about to dive into the swimming pool.

He has _____ . As he dives _____

changes to _____ . Rob climbs to the 10 m board.

He has more _____ than before.   [4 marks]

3 m

2 Kate is bouncing a ball. She drops it from **A** and it rises to **D** after the first bounce.

A

a What sort(s) of energy does the ball have at

A _____ [1 mark]

B _____ [1 mark]

C _____ [1 mark]

B

D

C

b Why is **D** much lower than **A**?

_____

_____   [2 marks]

3 The diagram shows a roller coaster. The carriages are pulled up to **B** by a motor and then released.

B

a At which point, **A**, **B**, **C**, **D** or **E**, do the carriages have the greatest gravitational potential energy?

_____ [1 mark]

Track

7.5 m

E

D

C

6.5 m

Carriages

A

b How does the gravitational potential energy at this point change when the carriages are full of people?

_____   [1 mark]

c At which point, **A**, **B**, **C**, **D** or **E** do the carriages have the greatest kinetic energy?

_____   [1 mark]

d Describe the main energy change as the carriages move from **B** towards **C**.

_____   [2 marks]

e Why must the height of the next peak at **D** be less than that at **B**?

_____

_____   [2 marks]

f The theme park decides to build a faster roller coaster. Suggest how they could modify the design to achieve this, using your knowledge of energy transfers.

_____

_____

_____   [3 marks]

P3 Revision checklist

- I know that speed is measured in m/s and can use the formula: speed = distance ÷ time. ☐

- I can describe, draw and interpret distance-time graphs and speed-time graphs. ☐

- I know that acceleration is measured in m/s^2 and that: acceleration = change in speed ÷ time taken. ☐

- I can state and use the formula: force = mass x acceleration. ☐

- I can discuss the significance to road safety of thinking, braking and stopping distances. ☐

- I can state and use the formula: work done = force x distance. ☐

- I know that energy is needed to do work and that both work and energy are measured in joules (J). ☐

- I can state that power is measured in watts (W) and use the formula: power = work done ÷ time. ☐

- I can recognise objects that have kinetic energy (KE) and know the factors that increase it. ☐

- I can interpret data about fuel consumption. ☐

- I can describe typical safety features in modern cars. ☐

- I can describe how the motion of a falling object changes due to the effect of air resistance. ☐

- I can recognise objects that have gravitational potential energy (GPE). ☐

- I can interpret a gravity ride (roller coaster) in terms of GPE, KE and energy transfer. ☐

Who planted that there?

G–E

1 a Choose **four** words from this list. Label the diagram of the plant cell.

cell membrane

chloroplast

cytoplasm

nucleus

vacuole

[4 marks]

b What is the name of the part of the cell that absorbs light energy?

[1 mark]

G–E

2 a Photosynthesis takes place in the leaf. Water is needed for photosynthesis.

i Describe how water gets into the leaf.

[2 marks]

ii Oxygen is made by photosynthesis. Describe how oxygen leaves the leaf.

[1 mark]

D–C

b The leaf is broad giving it a large surface area to absorb light. Write down **three other** ways leaves are adapted for photosynthesis.

[3 marks]

c Finish this sentence about gas exchange.
Carbon dioxide enters the leaf and oxygen leaves by ——————— . [1 mark]

D–C

3 The diagram shows the inside of a leaf.

a Label

i the upper epidermis

ii a palisade cell

iii a mesophyll cell

[3 marks]

b Put an **S** to show the position of a stoma.

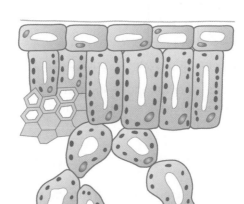

[1 mark]

Water, water everywhere

1 Look at the picture of the plant. The plant has wilted. Explain why.

_____

_____

_____

_____

[2 marks]

2 a Lauren investigates osmosis. She put some potato chips into pure water and some in salt water. She left them for two hours and the results are shown in the diagram.

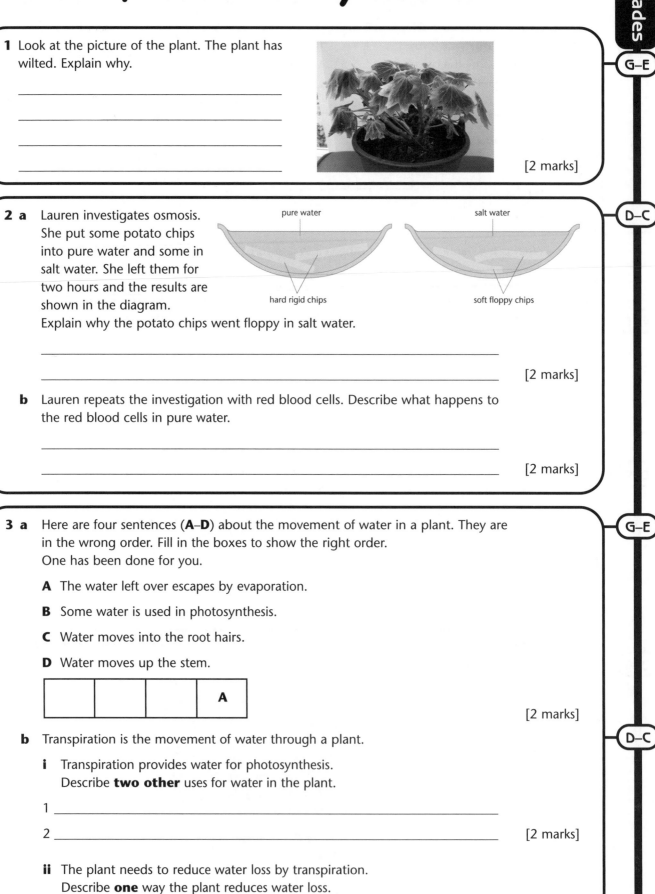

pure water

salt water

hard rigid chips

soft floppy chips

Explain why the potato chips went floppy in salt water.

_____

_____ [2 marks]

b Lauren repeats the investigation with red blood cells. Describe what happens to the red blood cells in pure water.

_____

_____ [2 marks]

3 a Here are four sentences (**A–D**) about the movement of water in a plant. They are in the wrong order. Fill in the boxes to show the right order.
One has been done for you.

A The water left over escapes by evaporation.

B Some water is used in photosynthesis.

C Water moves into the root hairs.

D Water moves up the stem.

			A

[2 marks]

b Transpiration is the movement of water through a plant.

i Transpiration provides water for photosynthesis.
Describe **two other** uses for water in the plant.

1 _____

2 _____ [2 marks]

ii The plant needs to reduce water loss by transpiration.
Describe **one** way the plant reduces water loss.

_____

_____ [1 mark]

Transport in plants

1 Draw a **straight** line from each part of the plant to the job it does.

part of the plant	job
root	support
stem	photosynthesis
leaf	reproduction
flower	anchorage

[3 marks]

2 The diagram shows the arrangement of cells in a cross section of the root.

    A   **B**

  a Write down the names of the **two** types of cells shown here.

    Cell **A** —————————————————————

    Cell **B** —————————————————————

    [2 marks]

  b Describe the job of cell **B**.

    _____

    _____ [2 marks]

3 Jasmine investigates transpiration in plants. She sets up two lines using the following apparatus.

string line   paper clip   clamp stand   leaves

  a One line is kept in the dark and one line is kept in the light. Indicate which variable Jasmine is investigating by putting a tick (✓) in the correct box.

    light intensity ☐

    temperature ☐

    air movement ☐

    humidity ☐ [1 mark]

  b The leaves in the **light** lost 7.4 g in mass. Suggest how much mass the leaves in the **dark** lost.

    _____ [1 mark]

  c Jasmine set up a third line and placed a clear plastic bag over the leaves. Describe how this will affect the rate of transpiration.

    _____ [1 mark]

Plants need minerals too

1 Jason is a farmer. He puts fertilisers on his crops.

  a   **i**   Suggest a reason why he uses fertilisers.

_____ [1 mark]

      ii   Fertilisers contain minerals such as nitrates and phosphates.
Write down the names of **two other** minerals found in fertilisers.

1 _____

2 _____ [2 marks]

  b   This is a picture of the bag of fertiliser that Jason uses on his crops.

      i   What is the percentage nitrogen content in the fertiliser?

_____ %

[1 mark]

3:6:9

10kg

NPK FERTILISER

      ii   What is the mass in kg of phosphates in the bag?

_____ kg

[1 mark]

2 a   Finish the table to show why a plant needs certain minerals.
The first one has been done for you.

mineral	why the mineral is needed
nitrate	for cell growth
phosphate	
potassium	
magnesium	

[3 marks]

  b   Mineral deficiency causes poor plant growth. A plant grown without nitrates will have poor growth and yellow leaves. Describe how a plant will look if it is grown without

    i   phosphate _____

_____ [2 marks]

    ii   potassium _____

_____ [2 marks]

    iii   magnesium _____

_____ [1 mark]

Energy flow

1 Look at the diagram of a food chain.

a i Write down the name of **one** producer from this food chain.

_____ [1 mark]

ii Explain why it is a producer.

_____ [1 mark]

b i Write down the name of **one** consumer from this food chain.

_____ [1 mark]

ii Explain why it is a consumer.

_____

[1 mark]

c What is the source of energy for the food chain?

_____ [1 mark]

Sun

oak leaf

caterpillar

shrew

fox

2 This is a pyramid of numbers.

a Explain what information is shown in a pyramid of numbers.

_____

_____

_____ [2 marks]

10s of foxes

100s of shrews

1000s of caterpillars

oak tree

b In the space below draw a pyramid of biomass for the same food chain.

[1 mark]

c Some energy is lost as it flows through the food chain.
Write down **one** way in which energy is lost.

_____ [1 mark]

3 Plants produce biomass.

a Write down the name of the process that produces biomass in plants.

_____ [1 mark]

b The energy in biomass can be used to make biofuels. Name a biofuel.
Put a (ring) around the correct answer.

alcohol   **plastic**   **rubber**   [1 mark]

4 Brazil produces a lot of sugar cane. The sugar cane is used to produce a biofuel.
Use the words **yeast**, **fermentation** and **petrol** to explain this.

_____

_____ [2 marks]

Farming

1 a Unwanted plants and animals can stop crops growing. Farmers use chemicals to get rid of them. Draw a **straight** line from the chemical to the unwanted plant or animal it kills.

chemical	unwanted plant or animal
herbicide	fungus
insecticide	insect
fungicide	weed

[2 marks]

b Some farmers use intensive farming methods to increase yields. Put a (ring) around the one that is **not** an intensive farming method.

greenhouse   **hydroponics**   **free range hens**   **fish farm**   [1 mark]

c DDT is a chemical that can be used to kill insects.
This is a food chain from a marine environment.

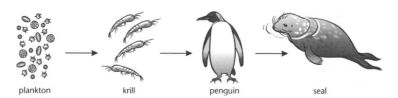

plankton   krill   penguin   seal

DDT contaminated the water in this marine environment. The plankton absorbed the DDT but did not die. The seals began to die from the DDT. Explain why.

_____

_____

_____ [3 marks]

d Describe how tomatoes can be grown without soil.

_____

_____ [2 marks]

2 a What is meant by the term **organic farmer**?

_____ [1 mark]

b Organic farmers use a method of farming called crop rotation to help the soil. Describe **two** other methods of farming used by organic farmers.

1 _____

2 _____ [2 marks]

c In 1935 large cane toads were introduced into Australia to control insects feeding on sugar cane. The toads did not eat the insects; they ate native toads instead. The cane toads have no predators in Australia.
i Write down the name given to this type of pest control.

_____ [1 mark]

ii Suggest **one** reason why the cane toads are now bigger pests than the insects they were sent to control.

_____ [1 mark]

Decay

1 a Look at the apparatus Shahid uses to investigate decay. Both samples are weighed, left for two days and then re-weighed. The table shows Shahid's results.

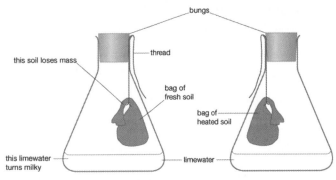

mass in g	bag of fresh soil	bag of heated soil
at start	6.2	6.5
at end	5.8	6.5
change		0

i Calculate the change in mass of the bag of fresh soil. Write your answer in the shaded box. [1 mark]

ii What is the name of the gas that turned the limewater milky? Put a ⃝ring around the correct answer

carbon dioxide   **carbon monoxide**   **nitrogen**   **oxygen**   [1 mark]

iii Microorganisms cause decay. They need factors such as oxygen to survive. Write down **one other** factor that microorganisms need to survive.

_____ [1 mark]

iv The heated soil did not change in mass. Explain why.

_____

_____ [2 marks]

b Earthworms feed on the remains of dead and decaying organisms.
i What is the name given to animals such as earthworms?

_____ [1 mark]

ii Earthworms help microorganisms to increase the rate of decay. Describe how.

_____

_____ [2 marks]

2 Jennifer grows strawberries but she has too many to eat before they decay. She decides to preserve some of the strawberries.

a Write down **two** methods that Jennifer can use to preserve the strawberries.

1 _____

2 _____ [2 marks]

b Explain how each method slows down the decay of the strawberries.

Method 1 _____

_____

Method 2 _____

_____ [2 marks]

Recycling

1 Look at the picture of the apples. Finish the sentences. Choose the **best** words from this list.

decay	digestion	nitrogen	oxygen
	preserved	recycled	

The apples are starting to break down. This is called

_____ . They are breaking down into simpler

chemicals such as carbon and _____ .

These chemicals are _____ and used by living

plants and animals.

[3 marks]

2 The diagram shows the carbon cycle.

a Finish labelling the carbon cycle. Choose **three** words from this list.

burning
digestion
feeding
photosynthesis
reproduction
respiration

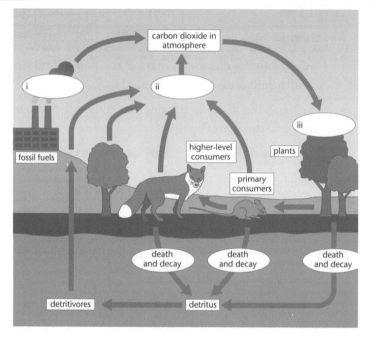

[3 marks]

b Write down the name of the process that removes carbon dioxide from the air.

_____ [1 mark]

c Decomposers return carbon dioxide to the air. Explain how.

_____

_____ [2 marks]

3 In the nitrogen cycle, plants take up nitrates from the soil.

a Explain why plants need nitrates.

_____ [1 mark]

b The nitrates are returned to the soil by decomposers. Explain how.

_____

_____ [2 marks]

c Nitrogen gas in the air cannot be used directly by the plants. Explain why.

_____ [1 mark]

B4 Revision checklist

- I can label a diagram showing the parts of the leaf. ☐

- I can explain how a leaf is adapted for photosynthesis. ☐

- I can describe how water travels through a plant. ☐

- I know that osmosis is the movement of water molecules across a partially-permeable membrane. ☐

- I can describe how transpiration rate can be increased. ☐

- I know that plants need nitrates, phosphates and potassium. ☐

- I can identify mineral deficiencies in plants. ☐

- I can construct pyramids of numbers and biomass. ☐

- I know that wood, alcohol and biogas are all fuels made from biomass. ☐

- I can describe the difference between intensive and organic farming. ☐

- I know that microorganisms need oxygen, moisture, and warmth for decay. ☐

- I can explain why the different preservation methods stop food decay. ☐

- I can describe the carbon cycle. ☐

- I can describe the nitrogen cycle. ☐

Acids and bases

1 a When an acid is added to an alkali or base a reaction takes place.

    i What is the name of this reaction?

_____ [1 mark]

    ii Write down **two** uses of sulphuric acid.

_____

_____ [2 marks]

b i What is an alkali?

_____ [1 mark]

    ii Finish the word equation for neutralisation.

_____ + base → salt + _____ [2 marks]

c Write down the word equation for the reaction between copper carbonate and sulphuric acid.

_____ + _____ → _____ + _____ + _____

[3 marks]

d Write down the name of the compound formed when sodium hydroxide reacts with nitric acid.

_____ [1 mark]

G–E

D–C

2 a The **pH scale** shows how acidic or alkaline a substance is. Write down if the pH numbers are acid or alkali.

    i A reading of pH = 2

_____ [1 mark]

    ii A reading of pH = 13.5

_____ [1 mark]

b How does the pH of an acid change when an alkali is added?

_____

_____ [2 marks]

c **Universal indicator solution** can be used to measure the acidity of a solution. A few drops are added to the test solution and then the colour of the solution is compared to a standard colour chart.

Describe how the colour changes when a strong acid is added to an alkali to neutralise it.

_____

_____

_____

_____

_____ [3 marks]

G–E

D–C

Reacting masses

G–E

1 a Look at the periodic table on page 238.

   i Find the relative atomic mass of iron, Fe. _____ [1 mark]

   ii Work out the relative formula mass of NaOH.

_____ [1 mark]

   iii Work out the relative formula mass of $CaCO_3$.

_____ [1 mark]

b Work out the relative formula mass of $Ca(OH)_2$.
Use the relative atomic masses.

        H 1   C 12   O 16   Na 23   Ca 40

_____ [1 mark]

c The total mass in a reaction never changes. The mass of the **products** is exactly the same as the mass of the reactants. However, if the mass of the reacting chemicals goes down there is a reason.

   i Write down a possible reason for the total mass in a reaction going down.

_____ [1 mark]

   ii Write down a possible reason for the mass of a burning reactant going up.

_____ [1 mark]

d Sometimes a reaction does not give as much chemical as it should. Some chemicals always get left behind, so the amount of product that is collected is usually less than the amount that was expected. Suggest **two** ways the product is lost.

_____

_____

_____ [2 marks]

D–C

2 a Leo and Lesley made some crystals of magnesium sulphate. They did not make as much as they hoped. They wanted to make 42 g. They only made 28 g.

   i What was their 'actual yield'?

_____ [1 mark]

   ii What was their 'predicted yield'?

_____ [1 mark]

   iii How will they calculate their percentage yield?

_____

_____ [1 mark]

   iv What was their percentage yield?

_____

_____ [2 marks]

Fertilisers and crop yield

1 a Plants need carbon dioxide and water. They also need essential elements.
How do they get these?

_____ [1 mark]

b What are the essential elements that help plants grow bigger and faster?

_____ [3 marks]

c These essential elements are found naturally in the ground. What can be added
to increase the amount needed for plants to grow bigger?

_____ [1 mark]

d Why do farmers add fertilisers?

_____ [1 mark]

e How do fertilisers get into the plants?

_____ [1 mark]

f To calculate the yield when making a fertiliser you need to calculate its **relative
formula mass**. What is the relative formula mass of ammonium sulphate $(NH_4)_2SO_4$?
Use the periodic table on page 238.

_____ [2 marks]

G–E

D–C

2 a This is the apparatus needed to make a fertiliser from an acid and an alkali.

A
evaporating basin
crystals begin to form

B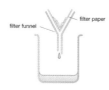
filter funnel
filter paper

C
measuring cylinder
conical flask

D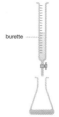
burette

The pictures are in the wrong order. Write the letters of the pictures in the right order.

_____ [1 mark]

b Describe what is happening at each stage.

A_____ [1 mark]

B_____ [1 mark]

C_____ [1 mark]

D_____ [1 mark]

c Many fertilisers are **salts**, so they can be made by reacting acids with bases.
What else is made?

acid + base → salt + _____ [1 mark]

d Don and Demi want to make some ammonium phosphate.

i Which acid will they need to use?_____ [1 mark]

ii Which alkali will they need to use? _____ [1 mark]

iii Write down a word equation to show this reaction.

_____ [2 marks]

G–E

D–C

The Haber process

G–E

1 a Write down the name of the chemical made by joining nitrogen and hydrogen in the Haber process.

_____ [1 mark]

b Where does the nitrogen for this process come from?

_____ [1 mark]

c What does the sign ⇌ mean?

_____ [1 mark]

D–C

2 Write about how ammonia is made. Include the conditions needed in your answer.

_____

_____

_____ [3 marks]

G–E

3 a Write down **three** things that affect the cost of making the ammonia.

_____

_____

_____ [3 marks]

D–C

b For the factors you have chosen above, explain why they affect the cost of making a new substance.

factor	explanation

[3 marks]

c Look at the graph. At which pressure is most ammonia made at 400 °C ?

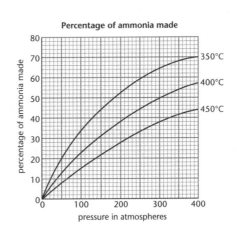

Percentage of ammonia made

350°C
400°C
450°C

percentage of ammonia made

pressure in atmospheres

_____ [1 mark]

d As the pressure increases what happens to the yield of ammonia?

_____ [1 mark]

e As the temperature increases what happens to the yield of ammonia?

_____ [1 mark]

Detergents

1 a Draw a **straight** line to match the ingredients in detergents with their action.

active detergent   to soften hard water

water softener   to give a whiter than white appearance

bleaches   to remove food stains at low temperatures

optical brighteners   to do the cleaning

enzymes   to remove coloured stains

[4 marks]

b A detergent can be made by **neutralising** an organic acid using an alkali.
Write a word equation for this reaction.

_____ [2 marks]

c Why are detergents used to clean greasy plates?

_____

_____ [2 marks]

d New washing powders allow clothes to be washed at low temperatures.
i This is good for the environment. Explain why.

_____

_____ [2 marks]

ii It is also good for coloured clothes to be washed at low temperatures.
Explain why.

_____

_____ [2 marks]

2 Finish the sentences. Choose the **best** words from this list.

solution   soluble   solute   insoluble   solvents

We need to dissolve blue ink. Methylated spirit and water are both _____.

They dissolve other substances. The blue ink is the substance that dissolves.

Blue ink is the _____. Blue ink dissolved in a solvent makes a

_____.

Different solvents dissolve different substances. If a substance dissolves,

it is _____.   If it does not dissolve, it is _____.   [5 marks]

3 a Some fabrics will be damaged if they are washed in water. How are they cleaned?

_____ [1 mark]

b Machines are used to wash clothes in an organic solvent. Why is the solvent used
called 'dry'?

_____ [1 mark]

Batch or continuous?

1 a There are two types of processes, **batch** and **continuous**.

   i Which type of chemical is made by a batch process?

_____ [1 mark]

   ii Which type of chemical is made by a continuous process?

_____ [1 mark]

  b Why are pharmaceuticals made in small batches?

_____ [1 mark]

  c How is the large scale production of ammonia different from the small scale production of pharmaceuticals?

_____ [1 mark]

2 a The raw materials for a medicine can be made synthetically. Write down another way these raw materials can be found.

_____ [1 mark]

  b Explain the steps needed.

_____

_____

_____

_____ [4 marks]

3 a Write down **three** factors that affect the cost of making and developing a medicine.

_____

_____

_____ [3 marks]

  b Draw **straight** lines to match the reasons for the high costs of making and developing medicine and pharmaceutical drugs to the **best** explanation.

strict safety laws	The medicines are made by a batch process so less automation can be used
research and development	They may be rare and costly
raw materials	They take years to develop
labour intensive	People need to be feel a benefit without too many side effects

[3 marks]

Nanochemistry

1 a Finish the table to show the properties and uses of these three forms of carbon.

	diamond	**graphite**	**buckminster fullerene**
appearance		*black solid*	
solubility	*insoluble in water*	*insoluble in water*	*deep red solution in petrol*
electrical conductivity	*does not conduct electricity*		
uses			*can join together to make nanotubes*
reasons for use			

[9 marks]

b Draw a **straight** line to match the carbon to its correct structure.

carbon
diamond
graphite
buckminster fullerene

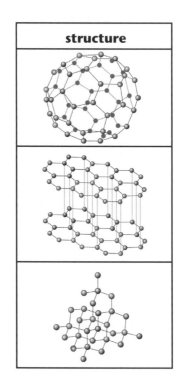

structure

[3 marks]

2 a Fullerenes are black solids that dissolve in petrol. What colour solution do they make?

_____ [1 mark]

b Fullerenes can join together to make nanotubes.

   i Write down **two** properties of nanotubes.

_____

_____ [2 marks]

   ii Write down **two** uses of nanotubes.

_____

_____ [2 marks]

How pure is our water?

1 a Write down **four** places where large amounts of water are found in the United Kingdom.

_____

_____

_____

_____ [4 marks]

b Write down **two** ways that water is used by industry.

_____ [2 marks]

c Write down **two** things that are in water before it is purified.

_____ [2 marks]

d Write down **two** pollutants found in drinking water.

_____ [2 marks]

e Explain why relief organisations concentrate on providing clean water supplies.

_____ [1 mark]

2 The water in a river is cloudy and often not fit to drink. To make clean drinking water it is passed through a **water purification** works.
Label the **three** main parts of this process. Explain what happens at each stage.

| _____ | → | _____ | → | _____ |

_____

_____

_____

_____

_____

_____ [6 marks]

3 a Water may contain sulphate ions or halide ions. Precipitation reactions are used for testing water. Martin and Mariella tested for **chloride**, **bromide** and **iodide ions**. They added two drops of **silver nitrate** solution to the water in a test tube. Finish their results table.

chlorides	
bromides	*cream precipitate*
iodides	

[2 marks]

b Which chemical do they add to test for sulphate ions? It gives a white precipitate.

_____ [1 mark]

c Write a word equation for the precipitation reaction between lead nitrate and potassium chloride.

_____ [2 marks]

C4 Revision checklist

- I know that solutions with a pH of less than 7 are acids, more than 7 are alkalis, but pH 7 is neutral. ☐

- I know that neutralisation is a reaction where: acid + base → salt + water. ☐

- I can work out the relative formula mass of a substance from its formula e.g. CO_2 is 12 + (2 × 16) = 44. ☐

- I can work out the percentage yield using the formula: % yield = actual yield × 100 ÷ predicted yield. ☐

- I know that fertilisers provide extra nitrogen, phosphorus and potassium, essential for plant growth. ☐

- I know that ammonia is made by the Haber process where N_2 and H_2 are put over an iron catalyst. ☐

- I know that the higher the pressure, the higher the energy bill for the industrial plant. ☐

- I know that a catalyst will reduce costs as the rate of reaction is increased. ☐

- I know that solutes are soluble and dissolve in solvents to make solutions. ☐

- I know that dry cleaning is a process used to clean clothes using a solvent that is not water. ☐

- I know that a continuous process makes chemicals all the time but a batch process does not. ☐

- I can recognise the three structures of carbon: diamond, graphite and buckminster fullerene. ☐

- I can explain that graphite is slippery and is used as electrodes as it conducts electricity. ☐

- I know that water purification includes filtration, sedimentation and chlorination. ☐

Sparks!

G–E

1 Sonya rubs a polythene strip with a cloth. The strip becomes charged. It can pick up small pieces of paper.

    a What charge does the polythene strip gain? _____ [1 mark]

    b   **i** What material could she rub to obtain a strip with a different charge?

        _____ [1 mark]

      ii What effect will this strip have on the small pieces of paper?

        _____ [1 mark]

    c Ed rubs a copper strip with a cloth. Explain why it has no effect on the small pieces of paper.

    _____

    _____ [2 marks]

D–C

2 Sally stands on an insulating mat. She puts her hands on the dome of an uncharged Van de Graaff generator. The Van de Graaff generator is switched on and Sally's hair starts to stand on end.

    a Why does Sally stand on an insulating mat?

    _____ [1 mark]

    b Why must the Van de Graaff generator be uncharged when Sally puts her hands on it?

    _____ [1 mark]

    c   **i** What happens to Sally when the Van de Graaff generator is switched on?

        _____ [1 mark]

      ii Why does this make Sally's hair stand on end?

        _____

        _____ [2 marks]

D–C

3 Use your knowledge of electrostatics to explain the following.

    a You sometimes get an electric shock on closing a car door after a journey.

    _____

    _____ [2 marks]

    b You should never shelter under a tree during a thunderstorm.

    _____ [1 mark]

    c Cling film often sticks to itself as it is unrolled.

    _____ [1 mark]

    d Priya becomes charged when she walks on a nylon carpet.

    _____

    _____ [2 marks]

    e Tom touched a bare wire at the back of his TV, when switched on, and got a serious shock.

    _____

    _____ [2 marks]

Uses of electrostatics

1 A defibrillator delivers an electric shock through the chest wall to the heart.

a What is the purpose of defibrillation? _____

[1 mark]

b What does the electric shock do to the heart?

_____

[1 mark]

c The paddles, charged from a high voltage supply, are placed on the patient's chest. How does the operator ensure that there is good electrical contact with the patient's chest?

_____

_____

[2 marks]

d A current of about 50 A passes through the patient for about 4 ms (0.004 s). In general, such a large current would be fatal. Why can it be used in this situation?

_____

[1 mark]

2 In a bicycle factory the frames are painted using an electrostatic sprayer. The paint is positively charged. The frames are given the opposite charge to the paint.

+   +

+   +

nozzle is
charged up
positively

object to be painted
is negatively charged

a A paint sprayer charges the paint droplets. Give **one** advantage of having charged paint droplets.

_____

[1 mark]

b Why does the paint spread out on leaving the sprayer?

_____

_____

[2 marks]

c Why are the bicycle frames given the opposite charge to the paint?

_____

[2 marks]

3 a Why is an electrostatic precipitator placed in power station and factory chimneys?

_____

[1 mark]

b What type(s) of power station need an electrostatic precipitator?

_____

[1 mark]

c An electrostatic precipitator contains some wires and plates which are connected to a high voltage supply.
If the wires are given a negative charge, what charge must be given to the plates?

_____

[1 mark]

Safe electricals

G–E

1 Lee sets up the circuit shown. The lamp does not light.

a i Why does the lamp not light? _____ [1 mark]

ii Change Lee's circuit so that the lamp will light. [1 mark]

D–C

b Meera sets up another circuit.
  i What effect will this have on the brightness of the lamp?

  _____ [1 mark]

variable resistor

ii Add an ammeter and voltmeter to Meera's circuit to allow her to measure the current through the lamp and the potential difference across the lamp. [2 marks]

iii If the voltmeter reads 6 V and the ammeter 0.25 A, calculate the resistance of the lamp.

_____

_____ [4 marks]

G–E

2 a Choose words from the list to complete the sentences describing mains electricity.

  earthed   **live**   **neutral**   **power station**

There are two wires connecting a house to a power station called live and neutral.

The _____ wire brings the supply into the house.

The _____ wire provides the return path and is _____

at the _____ _____. [4 marks]

D–C

b A battery has positive and negative terminals. Give **two** differences between the voltage from a battery and mains voltage.

_____

_____ [2 marks]

G–E

3 a Label the live (L), neutral (N) and earth (E) wires in the plug shown. [3 marks]

b Which wire, live, neutral or earth, carries a high voltage?

_____ [1 mark]

c i Label the fuse, F, on the diagram. [1 mark]

ii What does it do?

_____ [2 marks]

D–C

d i Which wire, live, neutral or earth, is a safety wire? _____ [1 mark]

ii How does it work?

_____

_____ [2 marks]

e An electric kettle passes a current of 10.5 A when working normally. Should the plug contain a 5 A or 13 A fuse?

_____ [1 mark]

Ultrasound

1 a What is meant by a **longitudinal** wave?

_____

_____ [2 marks]

b What is meant by the **frequency** of a wave?

[1 mark]
_____

c Sound is a longitudinal wave.

i Explain how sound travels through the air to reach your ear.

_____

_____ [2 marks]

ii How does the frequency of a note change if its pitch increases?

_____ [1 mark]

iii What is 'ultrasound'?

_____ [1 mark]

2 a Why does a pregnant woman usually have an ultrasound scan?

_____ [1 mark]

b The ultrasound waves used vibrate 1 000 000 times a second. What is the frequency of the ultrasound?

_____ [1 mark]

c Give **two other** uses of ultrasound.

_____

_____ [2 marks]

d Finish these sentences about an ultrasound scan. Choose words from this list.

echoes   **gel**   **image**   **probe**   **pulse**

reflected   **skin**   **tissues**   **ultrasound**

A _____ of ultrasound is sent into a patient's body. At each boundary between

different _____ some ultrasound is _____ and the rest is transmitted.

The returning _____ are used to build up an _____ of the internal structure.

A _____ is placed on the patient's body between the ultrasound _____ and

their _____. Without it nearly all the _____ would be _____ by the _____ .

[4 marks]

e **High-powered** ultrasound is used to treat a patient with kidney stones.

i How does ultrasound do this?

_____

_____ [3 marks]

ii Why must **high-powered** ultrasound be used?

_____ [2 marks]

Treatment

1 a In medicine, what is the difference between diagnosis and therapy?

_____

_____ [2 marks]

b Give **one** similarity and **one** difference between X-rays and gamma rays.

_____

_____ [2 marks]

c Why are X-rays and gamma rays suitable to treat cancer patients?

_____

_____ [2 marks]

d Why are alpha and beta particles **not** suitable to treat cancer patients?

_____

_____ [2 marks]

2 a Why is nuclear radiation suitable for treating cancer?

_____ [1 mark]

b What is 'radiotherapy'?

_____ [1 mark]

c Why is radiotherapy often used after surgery to remove a cancerous tumour?

_____

_____ [2 marks]

d Give another use of gamma radiation in hospitals.

_____ [1 mark]

3 a What is a radioactive tracer?

_____

_____ [2 marks]

b Why is it used?

_____

_____ [2 marks]

c What sort of radiation should a tracer emit?

_____ [1 mark]

d Which organ of the body is investigated using iodine-123 as a tracer?

_____ [1 mark]

e X-rays and gamma rays have similar properties.
Why are gamma rays suitable to use as tracers but X-rays are not?

_____

_____ [1 mark]

What is radioactivity?

RADIATION FOR LIFE

1 Jay is going to measure the activity of a radioactive source.

a What is meant by the 'activity' of a radioactive source?

_____

_____ [2 marks]

b i What will he use to detect the radiation emitted by the source?

_____ [1 mark]

ii What will he use to measure the rate at which radiation is emitted by the source?

_____ [1 mark]

c What does each count recorded represent?

_____ [1 mark]

d Jay records a count of 750 in 30 s.
i What is the activity of the source? Show how you work out your answer.

_____

_____

_____

_____ [4 marks]

ii Would you expect the activity of the source to increase or decrease as time passes?

_____ [1 mark]

iii Jay's teacher tells him he should repeat his readings several times to find an average value for the activity of the source. Why?

_____

_____ [2 marks]

2 a Finish the table about the **three** types of nuclear radiation.

type of radiation	charge (+, – or 0)	what it is	particle or wave
alpha			
beta			
gamma			

[5 marks]

b Name the type of nuclear radiation that

is the most penetrating_____

is stopped by several sheets of paper_____

has the greatest mass_____

does not change the composition of the nucleus_____

travels at about one-tenth the speed of light _____

[5 marks]

D–C

234

Uses of radioisotopes

G–E

1 a What is meant by background radiation?

_____

_____ [2 marks]

D–C

b Suggest **two natural** sources of background radiation.

_____

_____ [2 marks]

D–C

2 Write down **three** examples of the use of a radioisotope as a tracer.

_____

_____

_____ [3 marks]

D–C

3 Smoke alarms use a source of alpha radiation in a small chamber.

oppositely charged plates

americium-241 source of alpha particles

a Why is alpha radiation more suitable than either gamma or beta radiation for use in a smoke alarm?

_____ [1 mark]

b Explain how the smoke alarm works.

_____

_____

_____

_____ [4 marks]

D–C

4 Trees contain carbon-14 which is radioactive. The graph shows how the activity of 1 kg of wood changes after a tree has died. This can be used to estimate the age of objects that were once alive.

a This method cannot be used to date a wooden bowl made from a tree that died less than 200 years ago. Explain why.

_____

_____ [1 mark]

b The remains of an ancient civilisation were found. Put a (ring) around objects that could be dated using this method.

      animal bone   **bronze tool**   **seeds**   **stone** [2 marks]

c Why cannot carbon-14 be used to date rocks?

_____ [1 mark]

Fission

1 A power station makes electricity.

a Label the diagram.

**generator, source
of energy, steam,
water, turbine**

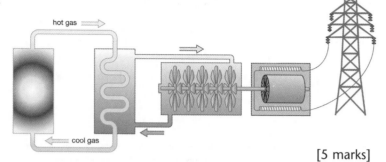

hot gas

cool gas

[5 marks]

b Finish the sentences to explain how a power station works. Choose words from the
list used to label the diagram.

The _____ provides heat to boil the _____ to produce

_____. The pressure of the _____ turns the _____

which turns the _____ making electricity. [6 marks]

2 a i What element is used as the fuel in a nuclear power station? _____ [1 mark]

ii What is meant by 'fission'?

_____

_____ [2 marks]

b i What do we call the process that allows fission to continue until all the fuel is
used up?

_____ [1 mark]

ii What is the difference between a nuclear reactor in a power station and a
nuclear bomb?

_____ [2 marks]

3 a i How can materials be made radioactive?

_____ [1 mark]

ii Give one use of a man-made radioisotope.

_____ [1 mark]

b i What is a neutron?

_____ [2 marks]

ii Radioisotopes can be produced by bombarding atoms with neutrons.
Why are neutrons good at doing this?

_____

_____ [3 marks]

4 Nuclear power stations produce radioactive waste.

a Suggest **one** method of disposing of low level radioactive waste.

_____ [1 mark]

b Suggest **one** method of disposing of high level radioactive waste such as spent
fuel rods from a nuclear reactor.

_____ [1 mark]

P4 Revision checklist

- I know that there are two kinds of electric charge, positive and negative. ☐

- I can explain how static electricity can sometimes be dangerous and sometimes a nuisance. ☐

- I can describe some uses of static electricity. ☐

- I can explain the behaviour of simple circuits and how resistors are used in circuits. ☐

- I can state and use the formula: resistance = voltage ÷ current. ☐

- I know about live, neutral and earth wires, fuses, circuit breakers and double insulation. ☐

- I can describe the key features of longitudinal waves. ☐

- I know about ultrasound and can describe some medical uses of it. ☐

- I can describe how nuclear radiation is used in hospitals. ☐

- I can describe the properties of nuclear radiation. ☐

- I can state what alpha and beta particles are. ☐

- I can describe background radiation and state what causes it. ☐

- I can describe some non-medical uses of radioisotopes. ☐

- I can describe how domestic electricity is generated in a nuclear power station. ☐

The periodic table

Key

relative atomic mass
atomic symbol
name
atomic (proton) number

Example:
1
H
hydrogen
1

1	2											3	4	5	6	7	8
																	4 **He** helium 2
7 **Li** lithium 3	9 **Be** beryllium 4											11 **B** boron 5	12 **C** carbon 6	14 **N** nitrogen 7	16 **O** oxygen 8	19 **F** fluorine 9	20 **Ne** neon 10
23 **Na** sodium 11	24 **Mg** magnesium 12											27 **Al** aluminium 13	28 **Si** silicon 14	31 **P** phosphorus 15	32 **S** sulfur 16	35.5 **Cl** chlorine 17	40 **Ar** argon 18
39 **K** potassium 19	40 **Ca** calcium 20	45 **Sc** scandium 21	48 **Ti** titanium 22	51 **V** vanadium 23	52 **Cr** chromium 24	55 **Mn** manganese 25	56 **Fe** iron 26	59 **Co** cobalt 27	59 **Ni** nickel 28	63.5 **Cu** copper 29	65 **Zn** zinc 30	70 **Ga** gallium 31	73 **Ge** germanium 32	75 **As** arsenic 33	79 **Se** selenium 34	80 **Br** bromine 35	84 **Kr** krypton 36
85 **Rb** rubidium 37	88 **Sr** strontium 38	89 **Y** yttrium 39	91 **Zr** zirconium 40	93 **Nb** niobium 41	96 **Mo** molybdenum 42	[98] **Tc** technetium 43	101 **Ru** ruthenium 44	103 **Rh** rhodium 45	106 **Pd** palladium 46	108 **Ag** silver 47	112 **Cd** cadmium 48	115 **In** indium 49	119 **Sn** tin 50	122 **Sb** antimony 51	128 **Te** tellurium 52	127 **I** iodine 53	131 **Xe** xenon 54
133 **Cs** caesium 55	137 **Ba** barium 56	139 **La*** lanthanum 57	178 **Hf** hafnium 72	181 **Ta** tantalum 73	184 **W** tungsten 74	186 **Re** rhenium 75	190 **Os** osmium 76	192 **Ir** iridium 77	195 **Pt** platinum 78	197 **Au** gold 79	201 **Hg** mercury 80	204 **Tl** thallium 81	207 **Pb** lead 82	209 **Bi** bismuth 83	[209] **Po** polonium 84	[210] **At** astatine 85	[222] **Rn** radon 86
[223] **Fr** francium 87	[226] **Ra** radium 88	[227] **Ac*** actinium 89	[261] **Rf** rutherfordium 104	[262] **Db** dubnium 105	[266] **Sg** seaborgium 106	[264] **Bh** bohrium 107	[277] **Hs** hassium 108	[268] **Mt** meitnerium 109	[271] **Ds** darmstadtium 110	[272] **Rg** roentgenium 111							

Elements with atomic numbers 112–116 have been reported but not fully authenticated.

* The Lanthanides (atomic numbers 58–71) and the Actinides (atomic numbers 90–103) have been omitted.
Cu and Cl have not been rounded to the nearest whole number.

Notes

Notes

Workbook answers

B1 Understanding ourselves

Page 130 Fit for life

1 a Oxygen; energy; respiration

  b i Lactic acid

    ii Body needs more energy; not enough oxygen to muscle; anaerobic respiration takes place

2 a (B) A D C *(A before D = 1 mark; D before C = 1 mark)*

  b Bacteria/viruses can still enter the body

3 a Heart

  b Take more exercise; eat a balanced diet; lose weight; drink less alcohol; relax more *(Any 2 = 1 mark each)*

Page 131 What's for lunch?

1 a i Growth/repair

    ii RDA = 40 x 0.75
          = 30 g

  b i Diabetes

    ii More exercise

2 a Chewing/squeezing stomach *(Any 1 = 1 mark)*

  b

food type	enzyme	product
protein	protease	amino acids
fat	lipase	fatty acids and glycerol

(1 mark for each correct box)

Page 132 Keeping healthy

1 a Athlete's foot

  b i Vector

    ii Feeds off living host

2 a skin — seals wounds
stomach acid — stops pathogens entering body
mucus in lungs — traps dirt
blood clots — kills pathogens in food

(4 correct = 3; 2 or 3 correct = 2; 1 correct = 1 mark)

  b i Number of cases went down

    ii People stopped having MMR jab

  c Antibiotics do not kill viruses; they only treat bacterial/fungal infections

  d Active: given pathogen; body makes antibodies; long lasting
Passive: given antibodies; body does not learn how to make antibodies; short lived
(Any 3 = 1 mark each)

Page 133 Keeping in touch

1 Skin

2 a i iris ii retina iii optic nerve

  b

part of the eye	job
retina	contains light receptors
optic nerve	carries impulses to brain
cornea	refracts light

  c i Binocular

    ii Advantage: allows it to judge distance

3 a Reflex

  b 3: sensory neurone; 4: relay neurone; 5: motor neurone

Page 134 Drugs and you

1 a

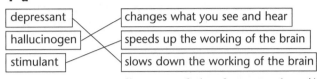

depressant — slows down the working of the brain
hallucinogen — changes what you see and hear
stimulant — speeds up the working of the brain

(3 correct = 2; 1 or 2 correct = 1 mark)

  b

type of drug	example
hallucinogen	cannabis
depressant	alcohol

  c Class C: less dangerous/they carry lighter penalties

2 a Nicotine; tars; particulates *(Any 2 = 1 mark each)*

  b Reduces oxygen in the blood/causes heart disease
(Any 1)

  c i Emphysema/bronchitis; *(Any 1)*
mouth/throat/oesophagus/lung *(Any 1)*

    ii Stops cilia moving; dust collects; leads to smokers' cough; produce more mucus
(Any 2 = 1 mark each)

3 a Liver damage

  b Matthew; because he drinks 5 units and Jo drinks only 4 units

Page 135 Staying in balance

1 a i Sweating

    ii 37 °C

  b Get too hot, start to sweat and lose too much water

  c Hypothermia

  d Homeostasis

2 a i Pancreas

    ii Diabetes

    iii Diet/insulin injections *(Any 1)*

  b i Testosterone

    ii Hair growth on face; hair growth on body; more muscular body; genitals develop; sperm production starts *(Any 2 = 1 mark each)*

Page 136 Gene control

1 a Nucleus; genes; DNA

  b 4

2 a 10

  b 20

  c Human sperm: 23 chromosomes; squirrel sperm: 10

3 a Asexual

  b Only one parent; offspring identical to parent

Page 137 Who am I?

1 a i Red hair; straight hair; blue eyes; freckles; large front teeth; rounded chin; ear without lobe
(Any 2 = 1 mark each)

    ii Scar; broken nose; decayed tooth
(Any 2 = 1 mark each)

  b Y

  c Purple; because F1 are all purple

  d Radiation/chemicals (e.g. tobacco smoke) *(Any 1)*

2 Cystic fibrosis

C1 Carbon chemistry

Page 139 Cooking

1 a Barbeque; in a grill; on an electric/gas ring (frying, boiling or steaming); in a microwave; in an oven
(Any 3 = 1 mark each)

b The food needs high temperature to kill harmful microbes in food; the texture of food is improved; the taste of food is improved; the flavour of food is enhanced; food is easier to digest
(Any 2 = 1 mark each)

2 a Irreversible; energy; substance

b They change shape

3 a Baking powder; carbon dioxide; heated

b i Sodium hydrogencarbonate $\xrightarrow{\text{(heat)}}$ sodium carbonate + carbon dioxide + water

ii Sodium hydrogencarbonate

iii Sodium carbonate/carbon dioxide/water *(Any 1)*

4 Colourless; milky (cloudy)

Page 140 Food additives

1 a Chemicals

b Antioxidants; food colours; emulsifiers; flavour enhancers

c Stop food from reacting with oxygen and turning bad

d It was found to be harmful to some children

e Tinned fruit and wine

f Preserve food from reacting with oxygen and preventing bacteria or mould; to give a different sensory experience such as enhancing the colou/flavour of food *(Any 1 = 1 mark)*

2 a

ingredient	typical value per 100g
wheat	14.0 g
sugar	6.0 g
salt	0.2 g

(Wheat before sugar = 1 mark; sugar before salt = 1 mark)

b To stop food spoiling

c Packaging that changes the condition of the food to extend its shelf life

d Packaging that uses sensors to monitor the quality of the food and lets the customer know when the food is no longer fresh

3 a Detergent

b A detergent in washing-up liquid provides 'hooks' between oil and wate; the oil is 'hooked' on to the water and pulled off a dirty plate; the detergent in washing-up liquid acts as an emulsifier; the tail is a 'fat-loving' part and the head is a 'water-loving' part; the fat-loving part of the molecule goes into the oil and attracts it towards this end; the water-loving part will not go in; the water-loving part stays out of the oil but is attracted to the water molecules; the oil is 'hooked-up' to the water

c Some paints; milk; mayonnaise
(Any 1 = 1 mark each)

Page 141 Smells

1 a Rose; lavender

b Distilled

c i Animals have no control over what is happening to them

ii They feel safer if the cosmetics have been tested

2 a

evaporate easily	it can be put directly on the skin
non-toxic	its particles can reach the nose
insoluble in water	it does not poison people
does not irritate the skin	it cannot be washed off easily

b Sense cells in the nose

3 a i Acid + alcohol $\longrightarrow$ ester + water
(reactants = 1 mark, products = 1 mark)

ii *(Alcohol and acid label = 1 mark)*

iii *(Label to upward condenser tube = 1 mark)*

iv At X the vapour is cooling down again and condensing back to a liquid

v So that the mixture can be boiled/react for longer (without drying out)

b Butyl ethanoate

4 a Insoluble; soluble

b Solution

Page 142 Making crude oil useful

1 a Coal; gas; crude oil

b Formed from dead animals and/or plants; trapped in the Earth and compressed over millions of years

c When these fossil fuels are used up there will be no more

d Because they are no longer being made

2 a Boiling point

b A molecule containing carbon and hydrogen only

c i *(A: at the bottom, left-hand side, of the tower = 1 mark)*

ii *(B: it 'exits' through the bottom of the tower = 1 mark)*

iii *(C: at the top of the tower = 1 mark)*

iv Fractions with lower boiling points such as petrol/LPG

3 a i It is pumped using oil rigs and goes through pipelines

ii The oil spills and forms an oil slick

b Increase in wealth in population and therefore an increase in number of cars on roads

4 a High temperature; a catalyst

b C_7H_{16}

Page 143 Making polymers

1 a Polymers; chains; monomers; polymerisation

b C

c High pressure; catalyst

2 a Carbon; hydrogen *(Both = 1 mark)*

b D

c i An alkane has a single bond, C–C

ii Propene

d i Contains an oxygen atom

ii It contains a double bond

iii A polymer (made from the monomer butene)

Page 144 Designer polymers

1 a Fabrics for clothes; paint for cars; cases for computers; packaging; insulating or any other reasonable use *(Any 2 = 2 marks)*

b Poly(ethene); nylon; polyester; polystyrene; poly(propene) *(Any 2 = 2 marks)*

c Flexible – to allow insulating/non-conducting or able to be coloured

d Keeps people dry not only from the rain but also from sweat

e It keeps water vapour from body sweat in, the water vapour from the sweat condenses and makes the wearer wet and cold inside their raincoat

f

polymer	property 1	property 2	use
PVC	waterproof	flexible	raincoat
poly(ethene)	waterproof	flexible	plastic bags
poly(styrene)	rigid	absorbs shock	packaging
poly(propene)	strong	flexible	ropes

2 a They do not decay and are not decomposed by bacteria

b Landfill sites: waste valuable land; burning: toxic gases; recycling: difficulty in sorting different polymers *(1 mark each = 3 marks)*

c i So that they do not have to be disposed of in landfill sites; burned but can decay by bacterial action

ii To make laundry bags for hospitals so that they degrade when washed leaving the laundry in the machine *(Or any other suitable use)*

Page 145 Using carbon fuels

1 a Petrol; it flows around an engine

b i Coal

ii High energy value; good availability

2 a Oxygen

b Oxygen; carbon dioxide; water.

c Monoxide; toxic; blue; yellow; monoxide; soot; water vapour; less

d i Hydrocarbon fuel + oxygen ⟶ carbon dioxide + water

ii Carbon dioxide; water

iii Carbon dioxide turns limewater milky/white copper sulphate turns blue with water

(Any 1 = 2 marks)

Page 146 Energy

1 a Heat; light; sound; electrical *(Any order)*

b Exothermic; endothermic; exothermic; exothermic

2 a i Oxygen

ii Ethanol + oxygen ⟶ carbon dioxide + water

iii Ethanol and oxygen

b i

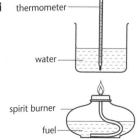

ii The mass of fuel; increase in temperature; mass of water

iii The same mass of fuel; same increase in temperature; same mass of water *(Any 1)*

P1 Energy for the home

Page 148 Heating houses

1 a Degrees Celsius; energy; joules

b Energy flows from warm to cooler body; temperature of warmer body falls

2 a 8 minutes

b Iron is a different material

c Specific heat capacity

3 a It changes state from solid to liquid

b It changes state from liquid to gas

c Melting ice; boiling water *(Any 1)*

d Specific latent heat

Page 149 Keeping homes warm

1 a Air is a good insulator/a poor conductor

b Cavity wall insulation; drawing curtains; sealing gaps; shiny foil behind radiators; carpets/underlay *(Any 3)*

c 120 4 40 = 3 years

d Shorter payback time

e Only 32% of energy input is useful; as energy output

f Energy is lost up the chimney

Page 150 How insulation works

1 Trapped; insulator

2 *(F in bottom left-hand corner of room = 1 mark)*

3 a Particles in solid close together; gap between glass filled with gas/vacuum; particles in gas far apart/no particles in vacuum; more difficult to transfer energy than in solid *(Any 3)*

b i Air in foam is good insulator; reduces energy transfer by conduction; air is trapped; unable to move; reduces energy transfer by convection *(Any 4)*

ii Energy from room reflected back into room in winter; energy from Sun reflected back outside in summer

Page 151 Cooking with waves

1 a Infrared; absorb; spectrum; water

b Microwave radiation is more penetrating than infrared; microwave ovens cook by conduction and convection *(Any 1)*

2 a Some evidence of heat energy being transferred to the body; young people more likely to be affected

b Microwaves need line of sight; no obstructions in space

c Amplified; retransmitted back to Earth

Page 152 Infrared signals

1 a True; false; true

b Digital

c

2 a

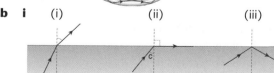

b i (i)   (ii)   (iii)

ii (See diagram)

Page 153 Wireless signals

1 a Can be used anywhere/portable
b Reflected
c The radio station is broadcasting on the same frequency; the radio waves travel further because of weather conditions
d Atmosphere; frequency

Page 154 Light

1 a Radio; microwave; infrared; ultraviolet; X-rays; gamma ray
(Any 3)
b (See diagram)

2 a (See diagram)   **b** (See diagram)

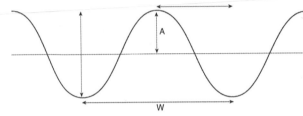

c Number of complete waves passing a point each second
3 a Semaphore; smoke signals; runner   (Any 1)
b Need to represent letters as electric signal

Page 155 Stable Earth

1 a Seismometer
b Fault; shock
c

description	P wave	S wave
pressure wave	✓	
transverse wave		✓
longitudinal wave	✓	
travels through solid	✓	✓
travels through liquid	✓	

2 a Climate change
b Carbon dioxide
c Reflects radiation back down to Earth
d i Sunburn; skin cancer   (Any 1)
ii Can stay in sun 30 times longer without burning

B2 Understanding our environment

Page 157 Ecology in our school grounds

1 a Artificial; community; habitat
b i Too cold/no food
ii Difficult to reach so difficult to explore
2 a Pooter is a small container with tubes attached; suck up insects through tube
b Six legs; coloured wings
3 $\frac{20 \times 10}{5} = 40$ voles in the wood

Page 158 Grouping organisms

1 a i Birds
ii Beak; feathers
b i Spider
ii No backbone

c

	food	shape	movement
animals	eat food	compact	move around

2 a Organisms that inter-breed; produce fertile offspring
b i Bobcat; ocelot   (Both = 1 mark)
ii First part of Latin name the same

Page 159 The food factory

1 a Carbon dioxide; water
b

product of photosynthesis	use in the plant
cellulose	cell wall
protein	growth/repair
oil	storage

c Starch is insoluble
2 a Grows slower
b Carbon dioxide; temperature
3 a Respiration
b Need the energy it provides to live

Page 160 Compete or die

1 a Space; shelter; water   (Any 2)
b i Grey squirrels out-compete red
ii Increase in numbers
2 a Badger/shrew
b i Decrease
ii More caterpillars; so more get eaten
c i Organism that feeds off another living organism
ii Mutualism

Page 161 Adapt to fit

1 a

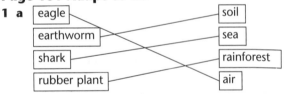

(3 correct = ; 1 or 2 correct = 1 mark)

b

adaptation	why it helps the camel survive
no fat on body, except in hump	whole body not insulated
hair-lined nostrils	stop sand getting into nose
higher body temperatures do not harm camel	higher body temperature reduces need to sweat

c Eyes at front of head
d i Layer of fat; for insulation; small ears; reduce heat loss; fur on soles; insulate feet
(Any 3 = 1 mark each)
ii Adapted to different habitats; cannot compete with brown bear in warmer habitat

Page 162 Survival of the fittest

1 a Evolution; rocks; deeper
b (B) C D A
(C before D =1; D before A =1; A at end =1 mark)
c Not all organisms become fossilised or some may not have been found yet
2 a When animals better adapted survive and pass on adaptation
b More resistant bacteria survive; pass on resistance

Page 163 Population out of control?

1 a i Gas/coal/oil _(Any 1)_

   ii Sulphur dioxide

 b Climate change/greenhouse effect; melting ice caps rise in sea level _(Any 2 = 1 mark each)_

 c i CFCs

   ii More ultra violet rays get through

2 a

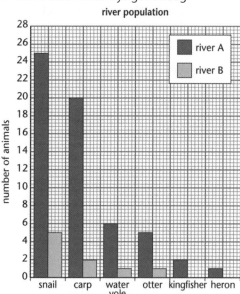

(5 bars correct = 3 marks; 3 or 4 = 2 marks; 2 correct = 1 mark)

 b Fewer numbers of each species; fewer different species

 c Increase

3 Indicator species

Page 164 Sustainability

1 a Extinct

 b Loss of habitat; hunted; other animals out-competed it; disease; habitat polluted _(Any 2 = 1 mark each)_

 c Osprey

 d i Protect the panda

   ii Captive breeding program/prevent hunting to extinction

2 a i Too cold

   ii Not enough food

 b For: provide food/jobs; against: whales could become extinct

3 a i Coal

   ii Ensure enough fish left to reproduce and maintain population

C2 Rocks and metals

Page 166 Paints and pigments

1 a To decorate surfaces; to protect surfaces

 b i Pigment; binding medium; solvent

   ii The tiny particles of pigment powder are spread through the oil; a mixture of solid dispersed in a liquid is called a colloid

 c Made of tiny droplets of one liquid in water which is called an emulsion; when emulsion paint has been painted onto a surface as a thin layer; the water evaporates leaving the binding medium and pigment behind; as it dries it joins together to make a continuous film _(Any 2)_

2 a i It changes colour

   ii It changes back to the original colour

 b Phosphorescent

 c Many people find that anything over 60 °C is too hot to hold so it can be used to paint cups; used to paint kettles; to act as a warning

3 a The juice of coloured berries

 b They give a brighter colour; it does not fade as much as a natural dye

 c Over the last 150 years chemists have been making man-made (synthetic) dyes; these give brighter colour and do not fade as much as a natural dye; give a wider range of colours

Page 167 Construction materials

1 a Granite; marble; limestone
    (Or any reasonable material from rock)

 b Aluminium; iron (steel) _(Or any reasonable metal)_

 c Limestone; marble; granite.

 d

building material	brick	cement	glass	iron	aluminium
raw material	clay	limestone and clay	sand	iron ore	aluminium

2 a Quarries and mines take up land-space; quarrying means an increase in noise, traffic and dust; landscapes are destroyed and have to be reconstructed

3 a Limestone; marble _(Accept chalk)_

 b Thermally decomposes

 c Cement, sand, and gravel are mixed with water and left to set

 d It is much stronger than normal concrete

 e Steel rods are put inside it; the concrete is poured around steel rods and left to set; it is therefore made of two materials

 f Calcium carbonate ⟶ calcium oxide + carbon dioxide _(Each compound = 1 mark)_

Page 168 Does the Earth move?

1 a

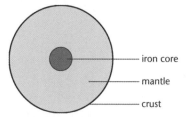

 b Molten rock

 c Tectonic plates; earthquakes; volcanoes

 d Less dense

 e Continental; oceanic

2 a i Igneous

   ii Lava

   iii Runny lava is fairly safe, thick lava can be given out violently and catastrophically

   iv Volcanic soil is very fertile

 b If the magma is less dense than the crust

 c

small crystals	large crystals
cool rapidly	cool slowly
basalt	granite

Page 169 Metals and alloys

1 a Compound; element; carbon

b It is cheaper to recycle copper than extract new copper from the ground; recycling also saves the energy needed to crush rock and to operate smelters and electrolysis cells

c It must first be analysed to find out how much of each element is present

d It has to be electrolysed again before it can be used

2 a Impure copper which dissolves into the electrolyte

b It is 'plated' with new copper

3 a It is a mixture of a metal element with another element

b
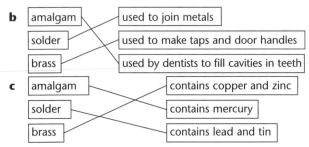

amalgam — used by dentists to fill cavities in teeth
solder — used to join metals
brass — used to make taps and door handles

c

amalgam — contains mercury
solder — contains lead and tin
brass — contains copper and zinc

d Pure copper conducts electricity so well

Page 170 Cars for scrap

1 a Oxygen; water

b Salt accelerates rusting which means that car bodies rust quicker

c It has a protective layer of aluminium oxide which does not flake off the surface

d It flakes off

2 a
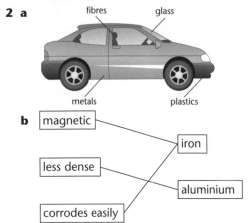

fibres, glass, metals, plastics

b

magnetic — iron
less dense — aluminium
corrodes easily — iron

c Iron; carbon

i Stronger; harder; does not rust as easily as pure iron *(Any 2)*

ii Advantages: the mass of a car body made of aluminium will be less than the same car body made from steel; the car body made of aluminium will corrode less; disadvantage: the car body of the same car will be more expensive made from aluminium

d The car body is cut into smaller pieces and an electromagnet is used to attract iron or steel

3 a More recycling of metals means that less metal ore needs to be mined; recycling of iron and aluminium saves money and energy compared to making iron from their ores; less crude oil is used to make plastics; less non-biodegradeable waste from plastics is dumped; recycling batteries reduces the dumping of toxic materials into the environment *(Any 3)*

Page 171 Clean air

1 a Oxygen; nitrogen; carbon dioxide *(Any order)*

b
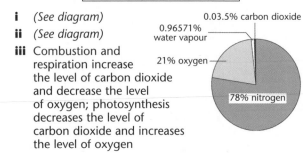

increases the level of carbon dioxide and decreases the level of oxygen — combustion, respiration

decreases the level of carbon dioxide and increases the level of oxygen — photosynthesis

c i *(See diagram)*

ii *(See diagram)*

iii Combustion and respiration increase the level of carbon dioxide and decrease the level of oxygen; photosynthesis decreases the level of carbon dioxide and increases the level of oxygen

0.03.5% carbon dioxide
0.96571% water vapour
21% oxygen
78% nitrogen

2 a In volcanoes

b These organisms could remove carbon dioxide from the atmosphere and add oxygen; eventually the level of oxygen reached what it is today

3 a

pollutant	carbon monoxide	oxides of nitrogen	sulphur dioxide
environmental problem	*a poisonous gas*	*photochemical smog and acid rain*	*acid rain that kills plants and aquatic life, erodes stonework and corrodes metals*
origin of pollutant	*incomplete combustion of petrol or diesel in car engine*	*formed in the internal combustion engine*	*formed when sulphur impurities in fossil fuels burn*

b It changes carbon monoxide into carbon dioxide and oxides of nitrogen into nitrogen.

Page 172 Faster or slower (1)

1 a i 33 seconds

ii No more gas is made or the reactants have run out

iii 33 cm^3

2 If the concentration/ temperature/ pressure/surface area is increased then the rate of reaction increases

3 a i *(See graph)*

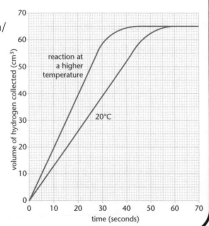

reaction at a higher temperature

20°C

volume of hydrogen collected (cm^3)

time (seconds)

ii (If gradient A is the reaction at 20 °C; gradient B is the reaction at a higher temperature) Gradient B, the higher temperature, has the steeper gradient

iii As the temperature increases the particles move faster; the reacting particles have more kinetic energy and so the number of collisions increases and the number of successful collisions increases

Page 173 Faster or slower (2)

1 a A reaction that takes place very quickly

b Burning hydrogen; custard powder; TNT/dynamite explosion *(Any 2)*

c Carbon dioxide; water vapour

2 a Powdered reactant will react faster as the surface area increases there are more collisions between reacting particles

b Carbon dioxide is given off

c **i** 25–27 seconds **ii** *(See graph)*

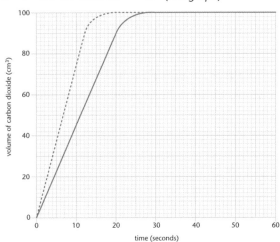

iii As there is less reactant there are fewer frequent collisions between particles

3 a A chemical that speeds up (changes the rate of) a reaction but remains unchanged at the end of the reaction

b Only small amounts of it are needed; it remains unchanged at the end of the reaction

P2 Living for the future

Page 175 Collecting energy from the Sun

1 Light for photosynthesis; heat for warmth

2 a Light

b Robust/not much maintenance; no fuel/no power cables; no pollution/no contribution to climate change; renewable energy source *(Any 4)*

c Less electricity produced

3 a **i** Black absorbs more energy

ii Convection

b Walls and floors radiate energy back into room

Page 176 Generating electricity

1 a Ammeter needle moves to left

b Stronger magnet; more turns on coil; turn coil faster *(Any 2)*

2 Magnetic field turns inside coil of wire

3 a Turbine turns generator

b Wires become warm and lose energy to surroundings

4 a Change size of AC voltage

b More energy would be lost as heat from transmission wires

Page 177 Fuels for power

1 a Straw; wood

b **i** Substance that burns; releases energy as heat

ii Atoms of uranium split

2 a Radioactive nuclear waste produced

b Nuclear; DNA; mutate; cancer

3 a Power = voltage x current
= 12 x 2
= 24 W

b Cost = power x time x cost per kWh
= 2.5 x 0.5 x 12
= 15p

Page 178 Nuclear radiations

1 a Geiger counter

b Radon gas; rocks and soil; cosmic rays; food and drink *(Any 2)*

2 False; true; true; false

3 Safe distance; do not handle directly; shield; use for minimum time; do not point at his body *(Any 3)*

4 a Kills living cells/bacteria

b **i** Tracer

ii Penetrating

c Wall is thinner

Page 179 Our magnetic field

1 a *(N at bottom of magnet = 1 mark)*

b Magnetic field is similar to a bar magnet

2 Navigation/GPS; spying; communication; mapping; weaponry *(Any 2)*

3 a Communication signals disrupted

b Charged particles

4 The presence of the Moon

Page 180 Exploring our Solar System

1 a

object		how object may be seen
artificial satellite		object cannot be seen at all
black hole		
comet		object seen because it produces its own light
meteor		
moon		object seen because it reflects light
star		

b **i** *(See diagram)*

ii *(See diagram)*

2 a Sending radio signals

b Always gravitational forces acting however small

c Avoid being blinded by Sun

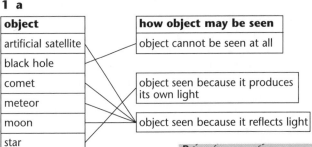

Page 181 Threats to Earth

1 a It got colder; there were lots of fires; tsunamis flooded large areas

b Mars; Jupiter

c Rocks left over when the Solar System formed

2 a

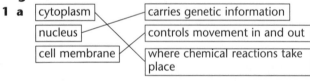

b When it is near the Sun

c Solar winds blow dust

3 a Near–Earth–objects/comets or asteroids whose orbits pass close to the orbit of Earth

b Increased accuracy of predicting if a collision may occur

Page 182 The Big Bang

1 a A single point

b Helium; hydrogen; protons

c Those furthest away

2 a Cloud of gas and dust

b i Red giant; core contracts; outer changes colour from yellow to red expands; planetary nebula thrown out; core becomes white dwarf; cools to become black dwarf *(Any 4)*

ii Red supergiant; core contracts; outer expands; core becomes neutron star; explosion/supernova; neutron star becomes black hole; supernova remnants become new stars *(Any 4)*

B3 Living and growing

Page 184 Molecules of life

1 a

cytoplasm	carries genetic information
nucleus	controls movement in and out
cell membrane	where chemical reactions take place

(3 correct = 2; 1 or 2 correct = 1 mark)

b Mitochondria

2 a Nucleus; gene; protein

b James; pattern is identical

3 a Biological catalyst; that speeds up reactions in body

b As temperature increases the rate increases; until 40 °C when it falls

c 40–42 °C *(Any temperature in this range)*

Page 185 Diffusion

1 a i Carbon dioxide

ii Move out of small intestine into blood then into body cells *(Any 2)*

b Movement of a substance from a region of high concentration to low concentration

c Carbon dioxide; waste

d Alveoli

2 a Evaporation

b Higher concentration outside diffuses through stomata lower concentration inside maintained by photosynthesis

Page 186 Keep it moving

1 a *(See picture)*

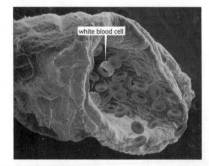

white blood cell

b

white blood cell	transports oxygen
red blood cell	helps clot blood
platelet	defends against disease

c i Disc-shaped: large surface area takes up oxygen quicker; no nucleus: more space to carry more oxygen

ii Haemoglobin

2 a Pump blood around the body

b i *(Left side top chamber, atrium = 1 mark)*

ii *(Left side between ventricle and atrium = 1 mark)*

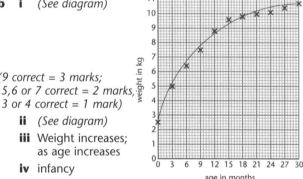

c Needs to pump blood further; at higher pressure

d Rejection; waiting for donor; need for anti-rejection drugs *(Any 2 = 1 mark each)*

3 Arteries transport blood away from heart; capillaries allow the exchange of materials with tissue; veins transport blood back to heart

Page 187 Divide and rule

1 a Grow; replace worn out cells; repair damaged tissue *(Any 2 = 1 mark each)*

b Mitosis

c Limits size organism can grow to; no cell differentiation; unable to form complex tissue e.g. nerves *(Any 2 = 1 mark each)*

2 a i So it can swim

ii Larger cytoplasm

b Contains enzymes; to break down egg membrane

c Meiosis

d Only contain one of each pair of chromosomes/contain half the number of chromosomes found in body cells

Page 188 Growing up

1 a i Cell wall; vacuole *(Either order = 1 mark each)*

ii Chloroplast

b i Cell differentiation

ii Stem cells

2 a B E A D (C)
(B before E =1; E before A =1; A before D =1 mark)

b i *(See diagram)*

(9 correct = 3 marks; 5,6 or 7 correct = 2 marks; 3 or 4 correct = 1 mark)

ii *(See diagram)*

iii Weight increases; as age increases

iv infancy

Page 189 Controlling plant growth

1 a Flowering; growth of shoots; growth of roots *(Any 2 = 1 mark each)*

b i Slows down growth

ii Stimulates root growth

iii Speeds up growth too much; so they die

iv Narrow leaves; they do not absorb as much weedkiller

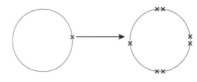
2 a i Up

  ii Root grows down

  b i Geotropism

  ii Because it grows in the same direction as gravity

Page 190 New genes for old

1 a A; B

  b Select characteristics; cross-breed; select the best offspring; breed these offspring over many generations *(Any 3 = 1 mark each)*

2 Radiation; chemicals (chemical example such as cigarette tar); occur spontaneously

3 a Find the gene for beta-carotene in carrots; remove gene; put gene into rice

  b Advantage: produces organisms with new characteristics; disadvantage: may have harmful effects

Page 191 More of the same

1 a Genetically identical copy   **b** Twins

  c Sperm collected from bull; cows artificially inseminated; embryo collected; embryo cloned; embryo implanted in surrogate cow
      (Any 3 = 1 mark each)

  d i Pig organs used for transplants instead of humans; reduces need to wait for donors to die

  ii Breeding pigs just to kill them; may not want an animal's organ; religious reasons *(Any 1 = 1 mark)*

2 a D B (A) C   *(D before B =1; B before C =1 mark)*

  b Advantage: characteristics all the same/mass produce plants quickly; disadvantage: susceptible to new disease/changes in the environment/lack variation

3 a Grow shoots from eyes; on tuber

C3 the periodic table
Page 193 What are atoms like?

1 a i *(See diagram)*

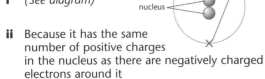

  ii Because it has the same number of positive charges in the nucleus as there are negatively charged electrons around it

  b Protons; neutrons   *(Both 1 mark)*

  c

	relative charge	relative mass
electron	−1	0.0005 (zero)
proton	+1	1
neutron	0	1

  d The number of protons in an atom

  e The total number of protons and neutrons in an atom

2 a Phosphorus

  b 20

  c A substance that cannot be broken down chemically

  d There are just over 100 elements in the periodic table

  e A substance that contains at least two elements that are chemically joined together

  f Isotopes are elements that have the same atomic number but different mass numbers

Page 194 Ionic bonding

1 a

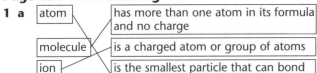

atom — has more than one atom in its formula and no charge

molecule — is a charged atom or group of atoms

ion — is the smallest particle that can bond with another particle

b

atom	ion	molecule
O	Na^+	H_2
H	Cl^-	NaOH
Mg	SO_4^{2-}	$MgSO_4$

2 a i An atom has extra electrons in its outer shell and needs to lose them to be stable

  b *(See diagram)*

  c i Positive

  ii Sodium/ lithium/ potassium

  d i Gaining

  ii Fluorine/chlorine/bromine/iodine

  e Positive; negative; lattice

3 a Have a high melting point; dissolve in water; do not conduct electricity when solid

  b Sodium chloride solution; molten (melted) magnesium oxide; molten sodium chloride

Page 195 Covalent bonding

1 a i Three   **ii** Two

2 a Covalent bonding

  b A molecule of water is made up of three atoms, two hydrogen and one oxygen; oxygen has six electrons in its outer shell; it needs two more electrons to be complete; hydrogen atoms each have one electron in their only shell; the oxygen outer shell is shared with each of the hydrogen electrons; each of the hydrogen atoms has a share of two more electrons making the shell full

  c Because they are covalently bonded; there are no free electrons

3 a i Group 1   **ii** Sodium; potassium

  b Sodium; silicon; sulphur

  c The group number is the same as the number of electrons in the outer shell; it has 1 electron in the outer shell

  d 7

  e i 2

  ii It is in the second row down because the first two electrons are in the first shell and the next 7 electrons are in the second shell; fluorine electrons occupy two shells so it is in the second period

Page 196 The group 1 elements

1 a They react with air and water

  b i Their density is less than the density of water

  ii Hydrogen

  c Sodium + water ⟶ sodium hydroxide + hydrogen

  d Potassium, sodium, lithium

  e

	melting point in °C	boiling point in °C
$_3$Li	179	1317
$_{11}$Na	98	892
$_{19}$K	64	774

  f They each have one electron in their outer shell so they react in a similar way

2 a

red — potassium

yellow — lithium

lilac — sodium

  b They moistened a flame test wire with dilute hydrochloric acid; they dipped the flame test wire into the sample of solid chemical; they held the flame test wire in a blue Bunsen burner flame

Page 197 The group 7 elements

1 a i Chlorine is used to sterilise water

ii Iodine is used to sterilise wounds

b A preservative; a flavouring; in the manufacture of chlorine *(Any 2)*

2 a

chlorine	green gas
iodine	grey solid

b They all have seven electrons in their outer shell

c

Reactivity ↑

$_9$F
$_{17}$Cl
$_{35}$Br
$_{53}$I

d Potassium + iodine ⟶ potassium iodide

3 a i Chlorine displaces the bromide ions which become bromine solution which is red-brown; a displacement reaction occurs

ii This is because chlorine is more reactive than bromine; bromine does not displace the chloride ions

b i Bromine + potassium iodide ⟶ potassium bromide + iodine

ii $Br_2 + 2KI \longrightarrow 2KBr + I_2$

Page 198 Electrolysis

1 Electrolysis; electrolyte; anode; cathode; anode; cathode; negative; positive

2 a The electrolyte is a dilute solution of sulphuric acid; two electrodes are connected to a dc source of electric current, between 6 V and 12 V, and placed into the electrolyte; the electrode connected to the negative terminal is the cathode; the electrode connected to the positive terminal is the anode; when the current is switched on bubbles of gas appear at both electrodes; water splits into two ions: H+ is the positive ion and OH⁻ is the negative ion; H+ is attracted to the negative cathode and discharged as hydrogen gas, H_2; OH⁻ is attracted to the positive anode and discharged as oxygen gas, O_2

b Because the formula of the compound breaking up is H_2O

3 a i Lighted splint burns with a 'pop' in hydrogen

ii A glowing splint relights in oxygen

4 a The ore of aluminium oxide is bauxite; aluminium oxide is melted; aluminium is formed at the graphite cathode; oxygen is formed at the graphite anode; the anodes are gradually worn away by oxidation; this forms carbon dioxide; the process requires a high electrical energy input *(Any 4)*

b Aluminium oxide ⟶ aluminium + oxygen

Page 199 Transition elements

1 a Conduct heat; are shiny; conduct electricity; are sonorous (ring when struck); are malleable; are ductile

b i Copper compounds are blue

ii Iron(II) compounds are pale green

iii Iron(III) compounds are orange/brown.

c i Iron is used in the Haber process to make ammonia

ii Nickel is a transition metal; because it is in the transition metal block

2 a A precipitation reaction

3 a Thermal decomposition

b copper carbonate ⟶ copper oxide + carbon dioxide

4 a

ion	colour
Cu^{2+}	form a blue gelatinous solid
Fe^{2+}	form a grey/green gelatinous solid
Fe^{3+}	form an orange gelatinous solid

Page 200 Metal structure and properties

1 a i C **ii** B **iii** C

b A **c** Lustrous; malleable

d It has high thermal conductivity and is malleable; it is also resistant to attack by oxygen or acids

2 a

b The particles are close together; in a regular arrangement

3 a Very low temperatures

b Materials that conduct electricity with little or no resistance

c Loss-free power transmission; super-fast electronic circuits; powerful electromagnets

P3 forces for transport

Page 202 Speed

1 a i Eve

ii Eve covered the same distance as Melissa but in a shorter time

b i Distance travelled; time taken

ii Distance: meter rule/tape; time: stop clock; light gates with accurate timer; data logger

c Distance = 8 x 1.5
= 12 m

Time = 0.5 s
Speed = distance travelled in 1 s = 12 x 2
= 24 m/s

d i Average speed = $\dfrac{distance}{time}$

$= \dfrac{390}{3}$

= 130 km/h

ii Car cannot maintain the same speed throughout

iii Yes; if average speed is 130 km/h the car must have gone faster (and slower) than this at times

2 a A to B; E to F **b** 80 s **c** 80 m **d** D to E

Page 203 Changing speed

1 a i Increases steadily from rest; reaching a speed of 10 m/s after 30 s; then travels at a constant speed of 10 m/s

ii

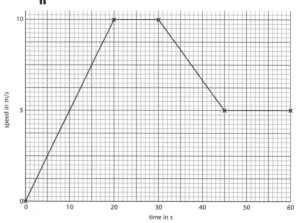

iii Area under graph

b i

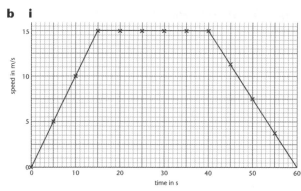

ii Yes; 50 km/h = 50 000 m/h

$$= \frac{50\ 000}{3600}\ \text{m/s}$$

$$= 13.9\ \text{m/s}$$

2 Acceleration = $\dfrac{\text{change in speed}}{\text{time}}$

$$= \frac{(40 - 10)}{6}$$

$$= 5\ \text{m/s}^2$$

Page 204 Forces and motion

1 Accelerate

   b i Increase

     ii Greater acceleration

   c Smaller acceleration

2 a $a = \dfrac{(v - u)}{t}$ **b** F = ma

$$= \frac{(40 - 0)}{20}$$ = 500 x 2

$$= 2\ \text{m/s}^2$$ = 1000 N

   c Resistive forces ignored

3 a Distance travelled by car between applying the brakes and the car stopping

   b Distance travelled by car between seeing the need to brake and applying the brakes (time for brain to react)

   c Stopping distance = thinking distance + braking distance

   d Increase; thinking/reaction time unchanged; but she will travel a greater distance in that time at a higher speed

   e Tired; under influence of alcohol/other drugs; distracted/lacking concentration   *(Any 2)*

Page 205 Work and power

1 a More   **b** Less   **c** None

   d The food that she eats

   e WD = force x distance

       = 80 x 2

       = 160 J

2 a Same

   b Chris is more powerful than Abi

   c 60 x 10 = 600 N

   d WD = force x distance

       = 600 x 3

       = 1800 J

   e Chris' power = $\dfrac{\text{WD}}{\text{time taken}}$

$$= \frac{1800}{8}$$

$$= 225\ \text{W}$$

   f Abi's power = $\dfrac{1800}{12}$

$$= 150\ \text{W}$$

3 a A

   b C

   c Fuel pollutes the environment; car exhaust gases are harmful; carbon dioxide is a major source of greenhouse gases; carbon dioxide contributes to climate change   *(Any 3)*

Page 206 Energy on the move

1 a Energy of an object that is moving

   b B; C

2 a i 1.6 litre diesel

     ii Diesel

     iii Higher mpg than both petrol cars

   b i Fewer road junctions; speed changes; gear changes

     ii $\dfrac{96}{24} = 4$

     iii Less

     iv Land Rover has a bigger engine capacity

3 a Recharging requires electricity from power stations which cause pollution

   b i Advantage: energy from Sun so causes no pollution; do not have batteries that need recharging; do not use electricity from power stations   *(Any 1)*

     ii Sun does not always shine; does not have a constant energy source   *(Any 1)*

Page 207 Crumple zones

1 a i Crumple zones

     ii Air bag

     iii Seat belt

   b

safety feature	how it works
seatbelt	designed to stretch a little so that some of a person's KE is converted to elastic energy
crumple zones	absorb some of the car's KE by changing shape (crumpling) on impact
air bag	absorbs some of a person's KE by squashing up around them

   c i Directly improve the safety of a car

     ii Indirectly improve the safety of a car

   d i ABS brakes; traction control; safety cage   *(Any 2)*

     ii Electric windows; cruise control; paddle shift controls; adjustable seating   *(Any 2)*

   e i To be effective they need to be kept in good working order

     ii Car crash may have damaged some of the safety features

     iii In case the belt fabric has been overstretched

   f i Anti-lock braking system

     ii Driver gets maximum braking force without skidding; can still steer car

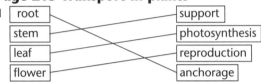

Page 208 Falling safely

1 a Gravity pulls them towards the Earth

b Increases

c Golf ball heavier than ping pong ball; so air resistance has a bigger effect on ping pong ball

d Golf ball

e i 10 m/s2

ii *(See diagram)*

iii Weight greater than air resistance

iv The faster she falls the more air molecules she displaces each second; so the greater the air resistance force; net/resultant force is less so acceleration is less

v Terminal speed

vi Balanced; equal in size but opposite in direction

2 a To reduce drag; air resistance force acting on them; slowing them down

b Crouch over handlebars; wear tight-fitting clothes; wear shaped helmet with no sharp edges and sleek shape; lubricate bicycle; have bicycle with no sharp edges and sleek shape *(Any 2)*

Page 209 The energy of theme rides

1 GPE; GPE; KE; GPE

2 a A: GPE; B: GPE + KE, C: EPE (elastic potential energy)

b Some energy is converted into thermal energy and sound

3 a B

b Increases

c C

d GPE to KE

e Energy is transferred to other forms: sound/thermal energy; due to friction

f Make B higher so it gains greater GPE; GPE lost = KE gained + energy transferred due to friction; its maximum KE will be greater; more KE means higher speed *(Any 3)*

B4 It's a green world

Page 211 Who planted that there?

1 a *(See diagram)*

b Chloroplast

2 a i From soil; through root hairs; up stem *(Any 2 = 1 mark)*

ii Through pores (stomata)

b Thin so gases or light do not have far to travel; chlorophyll to absorb light; network veins for support/ transport; stomata for gas exchange *(Any 3 = 1 mark)*

c Diffusion

3 a i *(See diagram)*

ii *(See diagram)*

iii *(See diagram)*

b *(See diagram)*

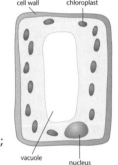

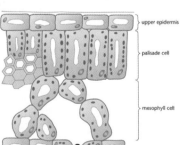

Page 212 Water, water everywhere

1 Not enough water; so no support

2 a Higher concentration water inside potato; water moved out

b Take on water; and burst (lysis)

3 a C D B (A) *(C before D =1; D before B =1 mark)*

b i Photosynthesis; cooling; support *(Any 2 = 1 mark)*

ii Waxy cuticle; small number of stomata on upper surface or more stomata on lower surface

Page 213 Transport in plants

1

root	support
stem	photosynthesis
leaf	reproduction
flower	anchorage

(4 correct = 3; 3 correct = 2; 1 or 2 correct = 1 mark)

2 a A = phloem; B = xylem

b Transport water or minerals; from root to leaves; support plant *(Any 2 = 1 mark each)*

3 a Light intensity

b Any value below 7.4 g

c Lowers rate

Page 214 Plants need minerals too

1 a i Help plant growth

ii Potassium; magnesium

b i 3%

ii 0.6 kg

2 a

mineral	why the mineral is needed
phosphate	respiration or growth
potassium	respiration or photosynthesis
magnesium	photosynthesis

b i Poor root growth; discoloured leaves

ii Poor flower or fruit growth; discoloured leaves

iii Yellow leaves

Page 215 Energy flow

1 a i Oak leaves

ii Makes own food

b i Caterpillar/shrew/fox

ii Eat food

c Sun

2 a Numbers of organisms; at each stage of food chain

b

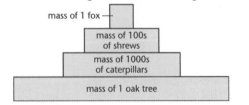

c Heat from respiration; egestion of waste; movement *(Any 1)*

3 a Photosynthesis

b Alcohol

4 Yeast is used to ferment the sugar; to produce alcohol; alcohol is mixed with petrol *(Any 2 = 1 mark each)*

Page 216 Farming

1 a

herbicide	fungus
insecticide	insect
fungicide	weed

(3 correct = 2; 1 or 2 correct = 1 mark)

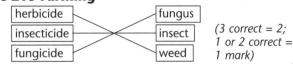

b Free range hens

c DDT gets into plankton; passed along food chain; does not breakdown; builds up to toxic levels in seals *(Any 3 = 1 mark each)*

d By hydroponics; roots grow in water containing correct nutrients

2 a Farmer who does not use manufactured chemicals

b Use of animals' manure or compost; nitrogen fixing crops; weeding; growing seeds at different times *(Any 2 = 1 mark each)*

c i Biological control

ii No predators so population keeps increasing

Page 217 Decay

1 a i 6.2 – 5.8 = 0.4

ii Carbon dioxide

iii Water/correct temperature

iv Microorganisms had been killed

b i Detritivores

ii Breaks up remains; increasing surface area

2 a Freeze; make jam; dry *(Any 2 = 1 mark each)*

b Freezing: kills or slows growth of bacteria; jam: kills bacteria or fungi by removing water; dry: bacteria and fungi need water to grow *(Any 2 = 1 mark each)*

Page 218 Recycling

1 Decay; nitrogen; recycled

2 a i: burning ii: respiration iii: photosynthesis

b Photosynthesis

c Carry out respiration; when they break down the dead plant and animal material

3 a To make proteins for growth

b Break down dead plants and animals; turning nitrogen compounds into nitrates

c Unreactive

C4 Chemical economics
Page 220 Acids and bases

1 a i Neutralisation

ii The manufacture of fertilisers; cleaning metals; car battery acids *(Any 2)*

b i A base when it dissolves in water

ii Acid; water

c Copper carbonate + sulphuric acid $\longrightarrow$ copper sulphate + water + carbon dioxide

d The salt formed is sodium nitrate

2 a i Strong acid

ii Strong alkali

b Increases from a low number to 7 on neutralisation; then from 7 to a higher number if excess alkali is added

c The pH at the start is high; colour is purple
The pH falls as the acid neutralises the alkali; colour changes to blue; when neutral, the pH = 7; colour is green

Page 221 Reacting masses

1 a i 56

ii 23 + 16 + 1 = 40

iii 40 + 12 + (16 × 3) = 100

b 40 + 2 (16 + 1) = 40 + (2 × 17) = 74

c i The reaction has given off a gas

ii Oxygen from the air has probably reacted with the chemical

d In filtration: small amounts stay on the filter paper; in evaporation: some chemicals spit out into the room; in transferring liquids: tiny amounts of liquid stick to the sides of the beaker because more than one reaction might be taking place so the reactants are being used up in a different reaction *(Any 2)*

2 a i 28   **ii** 42

iii $\dfrac{\text{Actual yield}}{\text{Percentage yield}}$ × 100

iv $\dfrac{28 \times 100}{42}$ = 66%

Page 222 Fertilisers and crop yield

1 a Minerals through its roots

b Nitrogen (N); phosphorus (P); potassium (K)

c Fertilisers

d To increase their crop yields

e They are dissolved in water so they can be absorbed by plants through their roots

f $(NH_4)_2SO_4$
$Mr = 2(14 + 4) + 32 + (16 \times 4)$
$= 132$

2 a C D B A

b A: acid is added from a burette to an alkali; B: the crystals are filtered off; C: alkali is measured and put into a flask; D: water is evaporated off to leave crystals

c Water

d i Phosphoric acid

ii Ammonium hydroxide

iii Phosphoric acid + ammonium hydroxide $\longrightarrow$ ammonium phosphate + water

Page 223 The Haber process

1 a Ammonia   **b** The air

c Reversible reaction

2 Nitrogen is obtained from the air; hydrogen comes from natural gas; the gases are passed over an iron catalyst under high pressure; an optimum temperature of 450 °C is chosen; there is a recycling system for unreacted nitrogen and hydrogen

3 a The cost of building the plant; people's wages; the cost of the raw materials; nitrogen and hydrogen and the energy costs; how quickly the new substance can be made (cost of a catalyst) *(Any 3)*

b

factor	explanation
cost of building the plant	The bigger the plant the longer it takes to repay so putting up cost of fertiliser
people's wages	Constant cost added to cost of fertiliser
cost of the raw materials	Constant cost added to cost of fertiliser
energy costs	The higher the pressure used the more energy needed as a cost added to cost of fertilser
how quickly the new substance can be made	The quicker it can be made the less the cost of energy and people's wages needed

(Any 3)

c 400 atmospheres   **d** Increases   **e** Decreases

ANSWERS

Page 224 Detergents

1 a

active detergent → to do the cleaning

water softener → to soften hard water

bleaches → to remove coloured stains

optical brighteners → to give a whiter than white appearance

enzymes → to remove food stains at low temperatures

b Organic acid + alkali ⟶ detergent (salt) + water

c It dissolves grease stains; it dissolves in water at the same time

d i It is better to wash clothes at 40 °C instead of at high temperatures because washing machines have to heat up a lot of water; this needs energy; so the lower the temperature of the water the less energy is used and less greenhouse gases are released into the atmosphere

ii As many dyes are easily damaged by high temperatures; it also means that many more fabrics can be machine washed as their structure would be damaged at higher temperatures

2 Solvents; solute; solution; soluble; insoluble

3 a Dry-cleaned

b It does not mean that no liquids are used, just that the liquid solvent is not water

Page 225 Batch or continuous?

1 a i Speciality chemicals, such as medicines and pharmaceutical drugs, are often made on demand in a batch process

ii Bulk chemicals such as ammonia

b Need to be made for a smaller demand; sterile conditions required so need to re-clean, need to change type of drug produced *(Any 1)*

c If a chemical is needed in large amounts it is usually made by a continuous process which can be more highly automated

2 a Extracted from plants

b Chemicals are held in the plant cells; plant cells have tough walls, so to extract the compound the plant is crushed to break the cell walls; then the chemical must be dissolved. This only works if a suitable solvent is used; the solvent dissolves lots of different compounds, so the desired compound is then separated from the others; this can be done by chromatography *(Any 4)*

3 a Research and testing; labour costs; energy costs; raw materials; development time *(Any 3)*

b

strict safety laws → They may be rare and costly

research and development → They take years to develop

raw materials → The medicines are made by a batch process so less automation can be used.

labour intensive → People need to be feel a benefit without too many side effects

Page 226 Nanochemistry

1 a

	buckminster fullerene	graphite	diamond
appearance	black and opaque	black solid	lustrous and colourless
solubility	*deep red solution in petrol*	*insoluble in water*	*insoluble in water*
electrical conductivity	conducts electricity	conducts electricity	*does not conduct electricity*
uses	semiconductors in electrical circuits	electrodes/pencil lead/lubricant	cutting tools/jewellery
reasons for use	*can join together to make nanotubes*	conduct electricity/ high melting point/ slippery and black/ slippery	very hard/lustrous and colourless

b

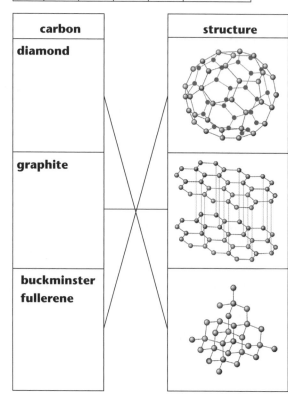

carbon	structure
diamond	
graphite	
buckminster fullerene	

2 a Deep red

b i Very strong; conduct electricity

ii Semiconductors in electrical circuits; industrial catalysts; reinforcement of graphite in tennis rackets

Page 227 How pure is our water?

1 a Lakes; rivers; aquifers; reservoirs.

b A cheap raw material; a coolant; a valuable solvent

c Dissolved salts and minerals; pollutants; insoluble materials; microbes (killed by chlorination)

d Nitrate residues; lead compounds; pesticide residues

e Clean water saves more lives than medicines

2 Sedimentation → filtration → chlorination

Sedimentation: larger bits drop to the bottom; filtration: sand is used to filter out finer particles; chlorination: kills microbes

3 a

chlorides	white precipitate
iodides	yellow precipitate

b Add two drops of barium chloride solution

c Lead nitrate + potassium chloride ⟶ lead chloride + potassium nitrate

P4 Radiation for life

Page 229 Sparks!

1 a Negative

b i Acetate/perspex

ii It will pick up the pieces of paper

c Copper is an electrical conductor so charges will not stay on it

2 a So that charge cannot pass through her

b So that she does not get an electric shock

c i Sally becomes charged

ii All her hairs gain the same charge; like charges repel so the hairs move away from each other

3 a The car becomes charged due to friction with the air on the journey; you are not charged so charge flows through you when you touch the car door

b Lightning may strike the tree as it is the tallest object around

c Cling film becomes charged due to friction as it is unrolled (as electrons are transferred from one part of the film to another, areas acquire opposite charges, so attract)

d Nylon is an electrical insulator; Priya becomes charged by friction as she walks

e Bare wire is highly charged; when Tom touches it charge flows through him to Earth (giving a serious electric shock)

Page 230 Uses of electrostatics

1 a To re-start a heart

b Makes the heart contract

c Place paddles firmly on chest; no clothes/hairs

d It only passes for a very short time

2 a Even coverage; less paint wasted; paint covers awkward places *(Any 1)*

b Paint droplets all have the same charge; like charges repel

c To attract the paint droplets to the frames; as opposite charges attract

3 a To remove harmful particles that pollute the atmosphere

b Fossil fuel power stations

c Positive

Page 231 Safe electricals

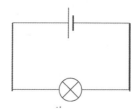

1 a i Circuit incomplete

ii *(Complete circuit = 1 mark)*

b i Varying brightness

ii Ammeter in series; voltmeter in parallel with lamp

iii 24 ohms

2 a Live; neutral; earthed; power station

b Battery is dc, mains is ac; battery is lower voltage than mains

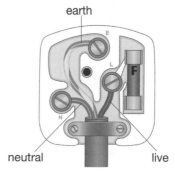

earth

neutral   live

3 a *(Live: on right (to fuse); neutral: on left; earth: at top)*

b Live

c i *(See diagram)*

ii Breaks circuit if a fault occurs

d i Earth

ii It is connected to the metal case of an appliance to prevent it becoming charged if touched by a live wire; it provides a low resistance path to the ground

e 13 A

Page 232 Ultrasound

1 a Vibrations are in same direction as the wave

b The number of vibrations in a second

c i Vibrations set up pressure wave in air – compressions (higher pressure) and rarefactions (lower pressure); make eardrum vibrate

ii Frequency increases

iii Sound of a higher frequency than humans can hear

2 a To check the condition of the foetus

b 1 000 000 Hz (or 1 MHz)

c Measure speed of blood flow; clean teeth/old buildings/jeweller; break down stones in the body *(Any 2)*

d Pulse; tissues; reflected; echoes; image; gel; probe; skin; ultrasound/pulse; reflected; skin

e i Very rapid ultrasound vibrations break the stones down into small pieces that are excreted from the body in the normal way

ii It needs to be powerful enough/carry enough energy; to break up the stones

Page 233 Treatment

1 a Diagnosis: finding out what is wrong with a patient; therapy: treatment

b Similarity: both electromagnetic radiation (of very short wavelength); difference: gamma rays emitted from the nucleus of an atom, X-rays are not (produced in an X-ray machine)

c Both very penetrating/can pass into the body to treat internal organs

d Alpha particles cannot penetrate skin; beta particles would be stopped by a small thickness of tissue and by bone

2 a It damages and destroys cancerous cells

b Destroying cancerous cells by exposing the affected area of the body to large doses of radiation

c To make sure all the cancerous cells are removed (by surgery) or destroyed (by radiotherapy)

d To sterilise equipment

3 a A tiny amount of a radioisotope introduced into the body

b To investigate a problem without surgery

c Occasionally beta but usually gamma radiation

d Thyroid

e X-rays are produced in an X-ray tube; gamma rays can be emitted inside the body and their progress monitored

Page 234 What is radioactivity?

1 a $\dfrac{\text{Average number of nuclei that decay every second}}{\text{rate of decay}}$

b i Geiger-Muller tube

ii Ratemeter

c The decay of one nucleus

d i Activity $= \dfrac{\text{number of nuclei that decay}}{\text{time taken in s}}$

$= \dfrac{750}{30}$

$= 25$ Bq

ii Decrease

iii Radioactive decay is a random process; all experimental results should be repeated if possible

2 a

type of radiation	charge (+, – or 0)	what it is	particle or wave
alpha	+	helium nucleus	particle
beta	–	electron	particle
gamma	0	electromagnetic radiation	wave

b Gamma; alpha; alpha; gamma; beta

Page 235 Uses of radioisotopes

1 a Ionising radiation that is always present in the environment

b Radioactive substances present in rocks (especially granite) and soil; cosmic rays from space

2 Detect leaks in underground pipes; monitor the uptake of fertilisers in plants; check for a blockage in a patient's blood vessel; track the dispersal of waste material; track the route of underground pipes *(Any 3)*

3 a It is highly ionising/short range in air

b Alpha particles ionise atoms in the air; + and – ions move towards – and + plates respectively; this creates a tiny current which is detected; if present smoke particles attach themselves to the ions neutralising them; current falls setting off alarm

4 a Very little change in count rate over 200 year period

b Seeds; animal bone

c Rocks never contained living matter

Page 236 Fission

1 a

b Source of energy; water; steam; steam; turbine; generator

2 a i Uranium

ii The splitting of a large nucleus such as uranium with the release of energy

b i Chain reaction

ii Chain reaction controlled in nuclear power station, but is out of control in a nuclear bomb

3 a i Put the materials in a nuclear reactor

ii To produce artificial radioisotopes; in hospitals to diagnose/treat patients; in industry as tracers to detect leaks *(Any 1)*

b i An uncharged particle found in the nucleus of an atom

ii Uncharged; so can penetrate deep inside nucleus easily; producing unstable isotope

4 a Embedded in glass discs and buried in the sea/incinerated under strict controls (very low waste only) *(Any 1)*

b Reprocessed